STUDIES IN ECONOMICS AND BUSINESS ADMINSTRATION

Published under the Direction of the

GRADUATE SCHOOL OF BUSINESS ADMINISTRATION

THE UNIVERSITY OF NORTH CAROLINA

AT CHAPEL HILL

VOLUME 5

STUDIES IN ECONOMICS AND BUSINESS ADMINSTRATION

THE MARKET FOR COLLEGE TEACHERS

*An Economic Analysis
of Career Patterns
Among Southeastern
Social Scientists*

THE MARKET FOR

The University of
North Carolina Press · Chapel Hill

An Economic Analysis
of Career Patterns
Among Southeastern
Social Scientists

COLLEGE TEACHERS

by David G. Brown

To my wife

PREFACE

Clichés about how and why college teachers find and choose jobs are common to all campuses; for example, "jobs are never found by listing one's availability in the journals" and "professors don't care about money." This book examines the validity of the clichés: an attempt is made to determine if the common beliefs about professors and their jobs are fact or fiction. Going beyond a mere description of behavior, an attempt is made to explain why the market is structured as it is and why professors behave the way they do.

For reasons that are explained in some detail in the first chapter, I have become convinced that we must increase our understanding of professional labor markets in general and professorial labor markets in particular. Human and financial limitations demanded that my analysis be limited to only one segment of one of the professional labor markets, college professors in Southeastern universities. Although the propositions derived will not necessarily apply to different markets, I hope that some of the ideas presented here may stimulate further thought and further research about other professional labor markets.

Educational administrators should profit from a study of this book, but I have written primarily for labor economists. Academic labor markets are described for what they are, not what they should be. My intent has been to describe and analyze behavior, not to suggest means of altering it. This is an academic study of the labor markets in which academicians locate jobs.

Many persons have contributed to the development of this study. My first debt is to the 150 professors who must remain anonymous, who willingly gave an hour or more of their time to be interviewed. For helpful comments and criticisms on the first draft I am indebted to Professor Jerry L. L. Miller of the University of Arizona, Professor Juanita Kreps of Duke University, and Professor Donald Reeb of The University of North Carolina at Chapel Hill. In addition, my colleagues at Carolina, Professor William Pfouts and Dean Maurice Lee, contributed constructive suggestions. Chapter VII profited from the comments of Dean Howard Schaller of the University of Indiana, Dean James Morris of the University of South Carolina, Professor Edison Bowers of Ohio State University, and Professor Fritz Machlup of Princeton University which were addressed toward a paper that I presented to the Southern Economics Association in 1962.

Special thanks are due my wife who conducted many of the interviews and contributed her editorial comments to the entire first draft.

Finally, I should like to express my appreciation to the University Research Council and the Business Foundation, both of The University of North Carolina at Chapel Hill, for the financial assistance that made this study possible. To Mrs. W. W. Humphrey and Miss Faye McLaurin, I am grateful for excellent typing and secretarial assistance. For assistance in preparing the manuscript for the printer and in indexing, I am indebted to Miss Nancy Earle.

TABLE OF CONTENTS

TABLES

THE MARKET FOR COLLEGE TEACHERS

*An Economic Analysis
of Career Patterns
Among Southeastern
Social Scientists*

I

INTRODUCTION

The Problem

In an economy which allows individual workers and employers freedom of choice, the labor market is vital to the distribution of labor. For it is at the point where buyers and sellers come together that the allocation of a limited resource, manpower, is determined. At the labor market, employers bid competitively for the scarce manpower services. At the labor market, potential employees proffer their services and decide to whom they shall be made available. When employer and employee return from the market, the allocation of labor has been determined. The concept of the labor market is, therefore, central to economics.

This is a labor market study, a study of the markets in which professorial teaching and research services are supplied and demanded. In these markets, college faculty are the primary suppliers of their own services; deans and department chairmen are the representatives of an institutional demand which is in turn derived from the demand for college educations and the advancement of knowledge. The primary purpose of the analysis contained herein is the same as that of labor market studies of blue collar workers: to wit, to increase our understanding of how and why workers move among jobs so that ultimately we may do a better job of allocating scarce manpower. More specifically, the purpose is to develop an understanding of the economic and institutional factors bearing upon the distribution of one of the most scarce species of professional manpower, college professors, and, on the basis of this knowledge, to suggest measures to improve the utilization of manpower.

Specifically, answers to the following questions are attempted:

1) *What are the channels of communication in academic labor markets?* How do college teachers learn about vacant jobs? How do employers locate available candidates? What is the relative importance of employment agencies, tips from friends and former graduate instructors, want ads in newspapers and professional journals, unannounced letters to possible employers, and chance? Do factors such as years of experience, field of specialization, prestige of educating and of hiring institution, extent of education, geographic location, sex, race, or age influence which channels of communication are used?

2) *What are the characteristics of the supply of college professors?* Which professors may be regarded as "supply" to the market? How mobile are professors? What are the factors that influence a professor-in-training to accept a job before he actually completes that training? Why do professors choose certain jobs? What roles do friends, climate, work load, physical research facilities, rank, and administrations play in the job switch and job choice decisions? How responsive is supply to wage differentials? How do the factors that cause professors to leave one job differ from those that attract them to another? How do the factors that attract professors to first jobs differ from the factors that draw them to second and third jobs?

3) *What is the nature of the demand for college faculty?* Who is responsible for making hiring decisions? How flexible are the hiring specifications regarding years of experience, extent of education, field of specialization, quality of training, ability and interest in teaching versus research, and so forth? In short, what is the marginal rate of substitution between various types of professors? Do universities have general hiring policies and, if so, what are these policies? What is the relative importance

of quality demands and cost constraints in the formulation of hiring policy? Is the demand for college professors price elastic?

4) *What are the sources of imperfection in labor markets?* Do professors and employers act as economically rational men? How much do professors know about their new jobs, and employers about their new faculty, at the time of contract signing? To what extent are prospective professors actually able to visit their new campus before signing a contract? Is the balkanization of academic labor markets by geography, doctrine, experience, or size of school a source of imperfection? How related are the imperfections in professorial labor markets to those in the labor markets for blue collar workers? To what extent does collusion impede competition?

5) *Do the observed imperfections cause a misallocation of teaching manpower?* If so, what can be done to improve academic labor markets?

Note that emphasis is placed upon the problems of allocating optimally a fixed supply of manpower. The methods of altering the level of scarce resource (e.g., by attracting more young people to teaching careers), though interesting and vital, are covered only tangentially.

Significance of the Problem

The answers to these questions should be interesting not only to economists but also to college administrators, government officials, businessmen, and professors themselves. For the economist, this study may serve as a prototype of a professional labor market. Although the percentage of the U.S. labor force employed in "professional, technical, and kindred" jobs has almost doubled in the last fifteen years and now stands around 12 per cent, and although the labor market concept is central to distribution theory, very little is known about behavior in the labor markets through which professional workers pass. Study has been focused upon blue collar labor markets. Undoubtedly there are many similarities between the labor markets for professional and production workers, but there are also many differences. For instance, as a rule, professional jobs require more training, demand greater responsibility, attract more alert people, require talents that are less easily rated, and pay better wages. It therefore behooves economists, among others, who are responsible for developing methods for optimizing the distribution of a given labor force, to learn more about professional labor markets. Only by knowing the forces acting upon the labor markets as we know them today is it possible to know how to alter the markets so that they may be better tomorrow. If economic theory is to be used meaningfully in describing professional labor markets in general and academic labor markets in particular, the markets must be defined, the general shapes of the demand and supply curves must be noted, the relevance of the normal assumptions (e.g., perfect knowledge and the economic rationality of man) must be studied, and the sources of market imperfections must be identified.

If we can learn enough about professional markets to understand how much and in what ways they differ from non-professional markets, it may be possible to relate the extensive researching and theorizing about the non-professional markets to operational decision-making in the relatively unknown markets for professionals.

Among the various professional labor markets that might be studied, the markets for college professors are especially crucial. The large cohorts of postwar babies that are already overcrowding our institutions of higher learning require large quantities of college teaching services. Manpower capable of providing these services is in relatively short supply and must be economized whenever possible. Those government officials and citizens that are concerned with making the most of what we have available should benefit greatly by fuller knowledge of the market behavior of college teachers. At the micro-level, college administrators who are now facing the increased necessity of attracting new personnel and retaining their present staffs will do a better job if they understand the markets where they are hiring. Other hirers of highly trained personnel capable of teaching and researching at a university or college, such as businessmen and government officials, face the same problems and stand to reap the same benefits. And finally, college professors, the sellers of teaching and research services, can be expected to increase the rationality of their behavior if they know more about academic labor markets. Hopefully, the professor who learns of new techniques of finding out about vacant jobs and of new methods of investigating the desirability of jobs will be able to find a more satisfactory job. In all, a better understanding of academic labor markets should enhance understanding of already, and increasingly, important professional labor markets, develop skills in allocating an already and increasingly scarce resource, and increase the satisfaction of both the sellers and buyers of teaching and research services.

Methodology

The study of academic labor markets cuts across at least three more or less distinct areas of literature—education administration, social organization and social psychology, and labor economics. At first it seemed that meaningful answers to the questions cited above might be determined simply by synthesizing and analyzing the information on academic labor markets already available from these diverse sources, by connecting the lines of communication between the various disciplines. But after an extensive examination of the literature in each field, it became obvious that the data that had been collected were not all subject to analysis from a labor market perspective and that new data were needed.

Thus detailed accounts of recent labor market experiences were collected from 103 "new" faculty members and 50 department chairmen at 18 of the largest Southeastern schools. All accounts were gathered by personal interview. All interviews followed closely structured questionnaires, with the interviewer reading the question and recording the interviewee's answer during the interview. As a rule, the interviews lasted about one hour, though a few extended to two and three. Two interview guides were used, one for the department chairmen and one for new faculty.[1]

One of the most serious problems in surveys of this type is that of stimulating interviewees to relate their true actions and feelings rather than those that they think the interviewer wants to hear. This problem could have been especially acute among a sample of professors, a group who are generally more capable of reasoning abstractly and ascribing motives to the actions of other persons. In order to minimize this type of bias, each interview was centered around a specific change of job. New faculty were asked to reconstruct, step by step, their relatively recent movement to their present job: why they were looking for a job in the first place, how they sought to learn about possible vacancies, what they knew about their present job and other jobs at the time they accepted an offer, why they accepted one offer and rejected others (if any), and so forth. Department chairmen were asked to describe in detail one of their most recent appointments: why did they need to hire a new man, how did they go about locating names of persons who might be qualified to fill the vacancy, how many candidates did they consider seriously, where were these candidates from, how did they evaluate these candidates and why did they choose X rather than Y or Z, what guidelines were used to determine the salary to be offered, how many candidates turned them down and why, and so forth.

Generalities and conjecture were avoided whenever possible. New faculty were not asked "what would you do if . . . ?" but rather "what did you do when . . . ?" Department chairmen were not asked "what is your general policy concerning . . . ?" but rather "what did you do when . . . ?" By asking professors to think in terms of specific events in the recent past, the tendency to answer the questions in terms of "what he wishes he had done" or "what he thinks he should have done" was minimized. Most questions were open-ended, allowing elaboration.

Both participation and co-operation were a researcher's dream. Over 98 per cent of the persons asked agreed to give interviews:

1. Copies of these guides are included in Appendixes A and B.

only two professors refused.[2] Co-operation was equally excellent. Professors talked freely and extensively. Many seemed to appreciate the opportunity to share their observations and experiences in an area that is generally avoided in conversations among colleagues. Fears that professors would be reluctant to answer questions of a personal nature addressed to them by a fellow professor were entirely unfounded. The problem of the interviewee's talking too much and infringing upon another's appointment was far greater than that of his talking too little.

The decision to use personal interviews with prearranged interview hours, instead of mail questionnaires, was probably the major reason for the good response. Personal interviews also allowed us to pursue especially touchy personal matters in greater depth. Personal interviewing permitted more, and more pertinent, questioning. Also, by interviewing, many extremely insightful digressions and side-comments were gathered that would otherwise have been lost. The personal interviews had many advantages.

However, the use of interviews combined with time and money constraints necessitated the restriction of the size and the nature of the sample of professors interviewed and thereby limited the generality of our conclusions. Rather than developing case histories on all types of professors, in all regions of the country and at all types of institutions of higher learning, this study includes only social scientists currently teaching at one of eighteen of the larger colleges or universities in the Southeast.

Sample

Our sample of universities was chosen according to several criteria: geographic location, size, and type of school. In spite of the acknowledged fact that the labor markets for professors are national, we sampled only in the Southeast in order to minimize the time and money costs of travel between schools. Since we

2. Though they were willing, eleven persons contacted could not be interviewed because they were away from campus either temporarily or permanently on the day we visited for interviews.

desired to interview two recently appointed faculty members
(not including the department chairman) in each of three departments, it was necessary that (a) the school have clearly defined
departments of economics, sociology, and history and (b) each of
these departments have at least three members. More than three
members was desirable in order to allow some selectivity by date
of appointment. Only larger schools met these criteria; therefore, interviews were conducted only at schools with student
bodies of twelve hundred or larger.

To insure geographic dispersion of schools within the Southeast, in each state the largest publicly supported school stressing
liberal arts was designated for interviewing; there were nine in
all. To balance nine publicly supported schools, nine privately
supported Southeastern liberal arts schools were chosen as follows. First, private schools with enrollments below twelve
hundred were eliminated from consideration.[3] Among those remaining, schools without at least three faculty members in clearly
defined departments of sociology, history, and economics were
eliminated. Many otherwise "qualified" schools could not be
included in our sample because of our inability to distinguish the
faculty of economics from business administration, even after
intensive examinations of the school catalogues. After the second
cut, nine schools in seven states remained, including four
"denominational schools" with enrollments under twenty-five
hundred and five schools that were no longer highly dependent
upon their religious founders. The sample of eighteen thus included the larger and, in most cases, better known educational
institutions in the Southeast, an admittedly unrepresentative
sample.

Whenever feasible, nine full-time faculty members were interviewed at each university—three economists, three sociologists,
and three historians. The choice of disciplines was motivated by
the desire to sample attitudes of persons with training in disciplines where the scarcity of trained personnel differs and by the
belief that social scientists would be most sympathetic to survey

3. American Council on Education, *American Universities and Colleges* (8th
ed.; Washington, D.C.: American Council on Education, 1960).

research and therefore willing to participate. A conscious decision was made to restrict the interviews to no more than three relatively homogeneous groups so that meaningful intergroup comparisons could be made in spite of the relatively small total number of interviews.

Three of the nine interviews on each campus were with department chairmen, one in each department.[4] The remaining six interviews were selected from faculty rosters in annual catalogues according to date of appointment, rank, and education. The primary criterion was recentness of appointment. Since many of the most recently published annual catalogues were already out of date, doctrinal listings of recent appointments in the *American Sociological Review,* the *Southern Economic Journal,* and the *Mississippi Valley Historical Record* were a great help in determining the most recently appointed. As for rank, a conscious effort was made to interview faculty at all ranks, though the assistant professor group is considerably larger than the others due to the greater mobility at this level. As for education, Ph.D.'s teaching at an institution other than the one where they received their degree were preferred. No one was interviewed who had been appointed before 1952; most had been appointed in 1961 or 1962. When the catalogue indicated that fewer than two persons had been appointed since 1952 in one or more of the pertinent departments, persons who had been appointed too late to make the most recent catalogue were contacted. In the few cases where there actually were fewer than two new faculty members since 1952, the interview was omitted. Three sociologists, two economists, and one historian were omitted in the end.

Limitations

The study was restricted for practical reasons to economists, historians, and sociologists. Natural scientists and professors in the humanities were not interviewed. Although it would have

4. In four instances department chairmen did not exist or were away from campus at the time of the interview. Thus there were only fifty department chairmen interviews, not fifty-four.

been meaningful to talk with persons who had left college teaching for jobs in government or business and to graduate students who had decided to delay the beginning of their career employment for one more year, only persons currently teaching were sampled. The labor markets experienced by almost all of the interviewees were ones of excess demand; no attempt was made to locate individuals who had passed through markets characterized by excess supply. Part-time professors were not included. Because of the sample of schools, the professors had more years of "better" education than the average college teacher. Only the relatively large schools were sampled. In spite of the fact that Southeastern schools have some unique recruitment problems, no schools outside the Southeast were included in the sample.

The sample was not random; therefore, we cannot validly generalize. The market behavior noted in this study is unique to time and place. Although there are certainly many similarities between the sub-academic labor markets under study and other markets, there are also many differences. For instance, we would expect that the channels through which persons pass to find jobs at some of the very small colleges and the criteria that these small college professors stress in job selection would differ from those noted by our interviewees. It is not our intention to offer broad generalizations that apply to all academic labor markets. Depth not breadth is sought, and thereby generality must be sacrificed. This is *a* labor market study, not *the* labor market study.

Plan of Analysis

This study is more than a recording of newly gathered data. Although the interviews are prerequisite, the main effort is directed toward an analysis of the response. The results from other studies of both academic and other labor markets including those by Caplow and McGee, Stecklein and Lathrop, Stecklein and Eckert, Miller, Anantaraman, and Wilson, among others, are cited for comparison and contrast. Observed behavior is contrasted to the theoretical ideal. Where they seem in order, policy recommendations are set forth. Specifically, the analysis begins, in Chapter II, by setting the scene for the data interpretation: the changes in excess demand for college professors are traced. In Chapter III the nature of the demand is examined in detail. The sources of supply of college teaching and research services are explored in Chapter IV. In Chapter V the concept of a labor market for college professors is developed. In Chapters VI and VII, respectively, the processes by which employers and employees make decisions in the academic labor market are examined. The entire analysis is drawn together in Chapter VIII.

II

THE GENERAL SCARCITY
OF PROFESSORS

In recent years academic labor markets have favored sellers. Jobs have outnumbered professors. Ever since the early 1950's, when large cohorts of World War II veterans who had pursued graduate studies under the G.I. Bill flooded the market, college teachers have been scarce. Numerically, the opportunities in college teaching have been expanding more rapidly than the pools of persons qualified to take advantage of them. Schools and universities have been experiencing difficulty in filling all their positions with even minimally qualified personnel. Newly qualified college teachers have found many jobs to choose among. Although not all types of professors have been equally scarce (e.g., scientists have been in shorter supply than humanitarians), most of the markets for college teachers have been tight.

Because we might expect employers and candidates to perform differently in a seller's market than in a buyer's, for the purpose of our study, it is important to develop a clear understanding of whether or not the markets that we propose to study favor the buyer or the seller. Even within the same discipline, job changers in a seller's market, such as the 1957-62 period, might well move for very different reasons than job changers in a buyer's market. Similarly, differences in the methods of and reasons for job changes of classics professors, a group in relatively excess supply, and engineers might be explained by tightness of markets rather than more basic differences in the types of professors. Conclusions concerning the distribution of a given group of academicians (say, historians between 1957 and 1962) among alternative schools cannot be accurately interpreted without some knowledge of the juxtaposition of the overall forces of demand and supply; the conclusions are unique to a given level of excess demand.

We need to do more than assert that the market favored sellers. For this reason the present chapter, which is concerned with identifying the over-all adequacy of the supply of college professors-in-general and of various types of college professors, is a necessary digression.

Professors Needed

The demand for college professors is derived from desires for college educations: more college students require proportionally more professors. Like most service industries, there are very few economies of scale in education. A reduction in the ratio of faculty to students is generally believed to result in a deterioration in the quality of education, just as a reduction in the ratio of clerks to customers almost certainly leads to poorer service in a department store.

Since the end of World War II, the opportunities for persons trained as college professors have been soaring. Between 1946 and 1962, the number of degree credit students seeking college educations has more than doubled, from just over two million to over four million.[1] Enrollments in graduate level curricula, where the demands for qualified faculty are the greatest, have more than tripled.

Although some of the increased college enrollment is attributable to the simple fact that there are now more people of college

1. U.S. Department of Health Education and Welfare, *Opening (Fall) Enrollment in Higher Education, 1960: Analytic Report* (OE-54007-60, Circular 652; Washington: Government Printing Office, 1962), pp. 12, 13; Garland G. Parker, "Statistics of Attendance in American Universities and Colleges, 1962-63," *School and Society* (January 12, 1963), p. 21.

age than there were in 1946, the increased importance of a college education is the primary factor. Each year the ratio of "degree candidates enrolled in colleges" to "population 18-21 years old" rises. A positive decision to attend college is being made by higher and higher percentages of our young people. College is becoming a necessary prerequisite for employment. The last twenty-five years have produced unprecedented advances in science and technology that have transformed our economy from agrarian to industrial, our work force from blue to white collar. The dynamics of the U.S. economy have both destroyed and created jobs. The jobs destroyed typically required little skill, some dexterity, much muscle, and low frequency mental powers; the jobs created require educated manpower. The old employer demands for "warm bodies" have changed to "warm bodies who know calculus."

The new jobs must be filled by men with high school or college educations, qualifications rarely possessed by the displaced workers. Between 1950 and 1962, for instance, in white collar occupations, employment increased by about 40 per cent. At the same time, employment in blue collar occupations *decreased* slightly. Employment in professional and technical jobs, which normally requires some college training, increased over 80 per cent. In June, 1962, unemployment among blue collar workers was twice as high as among white collar workers in general and three times as high as among professional and technical workers. With differential employment opportunities such as these, it is not at all surprising to learn that more and more young people are choosing to attend college.[2]

Increased desire to attend college as stimulated by the greater earning power and employability of the college man is not the only reason why college enrollments have risen. Higher family incomes, rising from an average of $3,720 in 1947 to $6,120 in 1961, are releasing young adults from the responsibility of earning food and shelter for their parents and brothers and sisters; father's

2. For more of the same, see Selma J. Mushkin (ed.), *Economics of Higher Education* ("Office of Education Bulletin, No. 5"; Washington, D.C.: Government Printing Office, 1962), Part I, pp. 3-60.

income suffices to keep the family going and thereby frees his son to continue in school. At the same time, increases in scholarship aid to the talented but needy, from $20 million in 1940 and $63 million in 1950 to $130 million in 1958, are enabling many more young people to continue their educations into colleges.[3] Also reducing the financial burdens of college educations is the increased availability of loans to college students.

Better high school counseling and guidance has fostered a desire to continue into college. Since Sputnik, even mass communication media have been continually stressing the importance of higher education. In sum, an increased awareness of the opportunities for those with a college education, economic prosperity and the development of scholarships and loans, and sheer population growth, all of these factors have combined to cause a doubling in college enrollments in just over fifteen years. In 1962, as compared to 1946, roughly twice as many professors were needed to teach the twice as many students.

The actual need for additional professors was even greater than double. Although teaching is the primary, it is not the sole function of college professors. A full statement of the demand for college professors must account for the needs for their skills not only as teachers but also as administrators and as academic researchers.

Consider first the demand for professorial administrators. Since a majority of professors spend less than 5 per cent of their time performing administrative services[4] and precise estimates of changes in the demand are difficult to obtain, the following statement should suffice: the increase in demand for professors' administrative services is probably less than proportional to increases in enrollment due to certain economies of scale and the trend toward shifting administrative activities to specialists hired only for that purpose.

Increased demands for professors as administrators have been shadowed by the increased demands for professors as teachers

3. *Statistical Abstract,* 1962, p. 132.
4. John E. Stecklein, *How to Measure Faculty Work Load* (Washington: American Council on Education, 1961), pp. 28-29.

and as researchers. The research function within the university has expanded even more rapidly than enrollments. In 1940 expenditures for organized research in institutions of higher education were only $28.1 million, but by 1961 expenditures had risen fiftyfold to $1,500 million. At the same time that universities are hiring more and more faculty-qualified persons to spend full time on research projects, they are reducing the teaching loads of others to free them for work on the projects. The overall effect is to stimulate the demand for additional persons qualified to teach at the college level. Research within the universities has been a definite cause of the excessive demands for professorial skills, especially in the applied and scientific fields.

Professors Available

What the exact supply of professors to meet these new demands for researchers, teachers, and administrators has been is not immediately apparent; for college professors are not required to certify their qualifications (like elementary and high school teachers) and many persons who could receive "certification" choose not to teach. Many professors are not qualified, and many qualified are not professors.

In attempting a quantitative measure of supply a common error is to equate supply and quantity hired; for example, to infer from the fact that 283,080 professors are hired in 1959-60 that supply is 283,080.[5] It should be obvious that 283,080 is not "supply." In the first place, to the economist supply connotes an entire supply schedule, with the quantities supplied differing according to the salaries offered; the 283,080 quantity supplied is unique to the 1959-60 salary level. Secondly, the fact that 283,080 persons were actually hired does not preclude the possibility that there were additional thousands of equally qualified applicants who were not hired because they were not needed. The 283,080 is neither supply nor quantity supplied; it is number hired.

5. See, for example, Dael Wolfle, *America's Resources of Specialized Talent* (New York: Harper and Brothers, 1954), p. 124.

Using changes in this number hired statistic as a measure of quantity supplied *over time* is extremely deceptive, for the hiring standard is likely to change. Labor supply is likely to be defined differently in each year. To illustrate, assume that the labor supply in terms of the number of Ph.D.'s, number of M.A.'s, number of experienced teachers, and so forth was the same in two consecutive years, but that the demand for professors was much greater in year $n + 1$ than in year n. Since the demand was relatively low in n, the hiring standards would be high: only experienced Ph.D.'s need to be hired. In $n + 1$, a sharp increase in demand required colleges and universities to "redefine" supply by lowering their hiring standards. Many persons were hired as college teachers before completing their Ph.D.'s and without previous teaching experiences. Many more persons were hired in $n + 1$ than in n. If supply (or quantity supplied) is defined as the number of persons hired, the supply of professorial labor has increased between the two years. But, by the "quality-constant" definition of supply at the outset of this example, supply was assumed the same in n and $n + 1$. Supply of the same quality has in fact remained constant. It is not supply itself, but rather the definition of supply, that has changed.

An economically meaningful discussion of supply must rely upon a supply measure that is not subject to large variations in quality. For, even at one point in time, the supply of college professors increases as the requirements are reduced, for example, from "Ph.D. with experience" to "M.A. without experience." If quality is not held constant from one year to the next, it is impossible to distinguish a change in supply of a given quality from a change in supply resulting from a change in the quality requirements.

In Table 1 an effort is made to indicate what the supply of college professors would be if the "quality" of the work force remained stable at the 1947-48 level. Used as a rough measure of quality is the ratio of college professors with Ph.D.'s to all college professors. Although this quantitative measure of quality is not without fault, it is a conspicuous and easily obtained measure

Table 1

Estimation of Quality-Constant Supply of
College Teachers, 1947-48 to 1961-62

Academic Year	College Teachers Continuing From Previous Year[a]	Persons Who Are Teaching With A Ph.D. for the First Time[b]	Persons Without Ph.D.'s Who May Be Hired Without Reducing the Ratio of Ph.D.'s to All College Teachers[c]	Number of College Teachers Available[d]
1947-48				175,111
48-49	166,355	1771	2146	170,272
49-50	161,758	2442	2959	167,159
1950-51	158,801	2945	3569	165,315
51-52	157,049	3229	3913	164,191
52-53	155,981	3381	4097	163,459
1953-54	155,286	3692	4474	163,452
54-55	155,279	3994	4840	164,113
55-56	155,907	3925	4757	164,589
1956-57	156,360	3953	4790	165,103
57-58	156,848	3888	4712	165,448
58-59	157,176	3902	4729	165,807
1959-60	157,517	4155	5035	166,707
60-61	158,372	4364	5289	168,025
61-62	159,624	4695	5690	170,009

[a] Based on the assumption the 5 per cent of the teachers in year n do not continue to year $n + 1$. Computed at .95 times the number of teachers available in the previous year.

[b] Based on assumption that 44.4 per cent of the Ph.D.'s granted in academic year n will enter teaching in year $n + 1$. Between 1956 and 1958, 44.4 per cent of the Ph.D.'s did in fact enter college teaching. Computed as .444 times the number of Ph.D.'s granted in year $n - 1$.

[c] Based on assumption that the ratio of "college teachers with Ph.D.'s" to "all college teachers" remains at the 1947-48 level, .4521. Computed as column 2 times 1.2119. For an explanation of the .4521, see footnote 7 of this chapter.

[d] Computed as sum of columns 1, 2, and 3.

Source: Per cent of New Ph.D.'s Entering Teaching: National Education Association, *Teacher Supply and Demand in Universities, Colleges, and Junior Colleges, 1957-58 and 1958-59* ("Higher Education Series, Research Report 1959-R10"; Washington, 1959), pp. 81 and 83.

Per cent of College Teachers with Ph.D.'s: Computed from Walter Crosby Eels, "Highest Earned Degrees of Faculty Members in Institutions of Higher Education in the United States, 1954-55," *College and University* (Fall, 1958), pp. 5-38.

Number of New Ph.D.'s: U.S. Office of Education, *Earned Degrees Conferred, 1959-60: Bachelor's and Higher Degrees* ("OE-54013-60, Circular 687"; Washington: Government Printing Office, 1960), p. 2; U.S. Office of Education, *Summary Report on Bachelor's and Higher Degrees Conferred During the Year 1960-61* ("OE-54010-61"; Washington: Government Printing Office, 1962).

Total Instructional Staff of All Universities, Colleges and Junior Colleges in 1947-48: U.S. Office of Education, *Bienniel Survey of Education in the United States: Statistics of Higher Education* (Washington: Government Printing Office, 1962), p. 34.

which is generally accepted as an indication of quality. As one expert has expressed, ". . . abundant evidence supports the generalization that preparation for college teaching is appraised in terms of degrees earned more often than in terms of teaching experience and teaching qualifications."[6] As a rule, professors with the Ph.D. are considered to be better teachers than those without, though many exceptions exist, especially in certain fields such as creative writing and journalism. Similarly, colleges with a relatively higher percentage of Ph.D.'s are considered to be better schools, and any decline in the ratio of "college professors with Ph.D.'s" to "all college professors" is viewed as a deterioration in the quality of education.

To compute the "quality-constant supply," it is assumed that 45 per cent of all college teachers in 1947-48 had Ph.D's.[7] The

6. Robert E. Iffert, "The College Teacher Shortage," in *Quality of College Teaching and Staff*, ed. Roy J. Deferrari (Washington: The Catholic University of American Press, 1961), p. 155.

7. The actual ratio of Ph.D. college teachers to all college teachers in 1947-48 was not available. The 45 per cent estimate was obtained in the following manner. First, it was assumed that Ph.D.'s enter the labor force in the year following the receipt of their terminal degree, that 44.4 per cent of all Ph.D. recipients enter college teaching, and that 5 per cent of the stock of college teachers in year n does not continue to year $n + 1$. These assumptions are detailed in the explanation of Table 1. Second, the number of Ph.D. teachers was computed for the only year for which sufficient data exist, 1954-55. According to Eels, 34 per cent of all college teachers in 1954-55 held Ph.D. degrees. Interpolating from Office of Education data, there were 218,083 college teachers in 1954-55. Thus, there were 74,148 college teachers with Ph.D. degrees in 1954-55. Third, using the 1954-55 statistic as a starting point, the number of Ph.D. teachers in the previous academic year (i.e., 1953-54) was obtained by subtracting the Ph.D.'s who taught in 1954-55 but not in 1953-54. The number of persons who taught only in the latter year (3,994) was taken from column 2 of Table 1. Since a 5 per cent attrition rate was assumed, the number of persons who taught only in the former year could be estimated as .05 of all Ph.D. professors who taught in 1953-54. Thus,

$$\text{Number of Ph.D. Teachers in 1953-54} = 74,148 - 3,994 + .05 \left(\text{Number of Ph.D. Teachers in 1953-54} \right)$$

A more general version of the same formula is—

$$P_{n-1} = P_n - N_n + .05\, P_{n-1} = \frac{P_n - N_n}{.95}$$

where P_n represents the number of Ph.D.'s teaching in year n and N_n represents the number of Ph.D.'s teaching for the first time in year n. Fourth, the above formula was applied until P_{n-7}, the number of Ph.D.'s teaching in 1947-48, was obtained. Fifth, P_{n-7} (i.e., 79,169) was divided by the number of college teachers in 1947-48 (i.e., 175,111) to obtain .4521 or roughly 45 per cent. See Table 1 for sources.

question is, "if this percentage were maintained, how many college teachers would there have been in [say] 1959-60?" In answering the question, the net changes in the numbers of professors between consecutive years were computed and summed. For example, the net change in professors between 1947-48 and 1948-49 was obtained in the following manner:

1) In 1947-48 there were 175,111 college teachers. Five per cent of this stock of 1947-48 professors, or 8,756, was subtracted from the stock on the assumption that illness, death, or retirement had prevented them from continuing to teach in 1948-49. The remainder is 166,355.

2) Forty-four and four-tenths per cent of the Ph.D.'s granted in 1947-48, or 1,771, was added to the stock on the assumptions that all persons receiving Ph.D.'s in 1947-48 had been available for some type of employment in 1948-49 and that 44.4 per cent of those available for some employment had entered teaching.

3) 1.2119 times the persons added in step two were added; for this many new non-Ph.D. teachers could have been hired without violating the quality standard that 45 per cent of all teachers had to be Ph.D.'s.

Carrying these calculations forward to 1959-60, these data, built upon special but not unrealistic assumptions, indicate that the quality-constant supply of teachers had decreased to 166,707 or by nearly 5 per cent.[8]

The Scarcity of Professors

While quality-constant supply decreased 5 per cent, enrollments rose 44 per cent.

Between 1947-48 and 1959-60, enrollments rose by slightly over one million students to 3,364,000. If only 13.35 students were to be assigned to each faculty member, as in 1947-48, 251,994 college teachers were needed (see column one in Table 2). If

8. Since the average real salaries of professors increased during the period, the quality-constant quantity supplied (at the same salary level) probably decreased by even more than the amount indicated; for it seems reasonable to assume that fewer persons would have pursued college teaching careers if salaries had not risen.

Table 2

Excess Demand for Professors
1947-48 to 1961-62

Year	(1) Teachers Needed[a]	(2) Teachers Available[b]	(3) Absolute Teacher Shortage[c]	(4) Absolute Change in Shortage[d]
1947-48	175,111[e]	175,111	0	0
48-49	179,990	170,272	9,718	9,718
49-50	183,099	167,159	15,940	6,222
1950-51	170,846	165,315	5,531	−10,409
51-52	157,415	164,191	−6,776	−12,307
52-53	159,833	163,459	−3,626	3,150
1953-54	167,084	163,452	3,632	7,258
54-55	183,233	164,113	19,120	15,488
55-56	198,686	164,589	34,097	14,977
1956-57	218,545	165,103	53,442	19,345
57-58	227,436	165,448	61,988	8,546
58-59	241,598	165,807	75,791	13,803
1959-60	251,994	166,707	85,287	9,496
60-61	267,359	168,025	99,334	14,047
61-62	288,087	170,009	118,078	18,744

[a] Based on the assumption that the student-faculty ratio remains constant at the 1947-48 level, 13.3528. Computed by dividing student enrollment by 13.3528.

[b] Based on the assumptions that the ratio of college teachers with Ph.D.'s to all college teachers remains at .4521, the 1947-48 level, and that 44.4 per cent of the persons receiving new Ph.D.'s enter college teaching. Taken from Table 1 of this chapter.

[c] Column 1 minus column 2.

[d] Change in column 3.

[e] This figure has been rounded.

Source: Enrollment data from U.S. Office of Education, *Opening (Fall) Enrollment in Higher Education, 1960: Analytic Report* ("OE-54007-60, Circular 652"; Washington: Government Printing Office, 1962), pp. 12, 13; Garland G. Parker, "Statistics of Attendance in American Universities and Colleges, 1962-63," *School and Society* (January 12, 1963), p. 21. Other data from Table 1.

a 13.35 student-faculty ratio were to have been maintained, 76,883 professors would have to have been added to the faculties of American colleges and universities. This 76,883 was the requirement for "net additions" to present faculty. Since death, retirement, illness, and other circumstances would have prevented many of the Ph.D.'s who were teaching in 1947-48 from teaching in 1959-60, the actual number of persons that would have had to have been hired in order to effect the desired expansion greatly exceeded 76,883. If 5 per cent attrition between academic years is assumed, another 119,430 new professors would have been needed as replacements. In all, nearly 196,313 new professors would have been needed between 1947-48 and 1959-60 in order to maintain the 1947-48 ratio of students to faculty.

During the period approximately 112,000 persons received Ph.D.'s and, among these, approximately 44.4 per cent, or 50,000, chose careers in college teaching. The 50,000 additional Ph.D.'s would have allowed colleges to take on about 61,000 non-Ph.D.'s without eroding the mixture of Ph.D.'s to non-Ph.D.'s, since the quality of the professorial labor force is maintained as long as 45 per cent of the professors are Ph.D.'s. The total quality-constant supply of new teachers available was the sum of the Ph.D.'s and non-Ph.D.'s, or 111,000. Subtracting the professors available (111,000) from professors needed (196,313), we find that, if the quality of teachers in general (reflected by the percentage of all professors holding Ph.D.'s) and the quality of teaching in general (reflected by the student-faculty ratio) were not to deteriorate, 85,313 more college teachers or slightly over 38,570 more college teachers with Ph.D.'s would have been needed by 1959-60. To recruit these additional Ph.D.'s to college teaching, a much greater number (approximately 86,872) of new Ph.D.'s would have had to be granted, for only 44.4 per cent of the trained Ph.D.'s would have actually chosen to teach. Presently we are training slightly over 13,000 Ph.D.'s per year. At this rate, it would take over six years to train the Ph.D.'s needed to overcome the deficiency. The actual period needed would, of course, be considerably longer, for during the six years new demands would be created by expanding enrollments and by depletions in the existing stock of professors due to retirement, illness, and death.

At least since 1952, if not since World War II, the demand for college professors has far outstripped supply. The desired number of *qualified* candidates has simply not been available.

Faced with inadequate supply of the desired quality and recognizing that Ph.D.'s could not be produced overnight, college administrators had to make a choice: either the quality of teaching or the quality of the teaching staff had to be sacrificed to cover the classes. Either the same number of professors could serve more students, which would result in a rise in the student-faculty ratio; or college teaching staffs could be augmented by non-Ph.D.'s, which would result in a deterioration of the ratio of Ph.D.'s to all college professors. The only other choice was to deny admission to the larger numbers of students. Additional Ph.D.-qualified candidates were not to be had.

Colleges chose to dilute the Ph.D.-non-Ph.D. mix,[9] for too large classes are more obvious than too few Ph.D.'s. Moreover, the teaching superiority of Ph.D.'s is not clearly established, so that administrators could console alumni and themselves with the rationalization that "the near-Ph.D.'s" are sometimes better teachers.

A comparison of the numbers of professors that would have been hired if "quality" had not been compromised, and the number of teachers actually hired is most revealing in this regard. In the academic year 1959-60, the most recent year for which these data are available, the instructional staffs in American colleges, universities, and junior colleges numbered 285,080.[10] For the same years, by Table 1, it has been calculated that if 45 per cent of the college teachers were to have their Ph.D.'s, only 166,707 teachers would have been available. By 1959-60, the colleges had compromised "constant-quality" to the extent of hiring 116,373 non-Ph.D.'s above and beyond those allowed under the "45 per cent standard." The "45 per cent standard" was sacrificed. On the other hand, the ratio of students to faculty not only did not rise; it fell. Only 85,313 additional non-Ph.D.'s needed to be hired to preserve the student-faculty ratio at 13.35.

9. Resisting the general trend, a small group of financially powerful and prestigious universities actually increased the proportions of Ph.D.'s on their faculties during the period. As a result, the undesirable consequences of the quality scarcity were emphasized in the less wealthy liberal arts colleges and junior colleges.

10. U.S. Department of Health, Education and Welfare, Office of Education, *Summary Report, Faculty and Other Professional Staff in Institutions of Higher Education, 1959-60* ("OE-53014"; Washington: Government Printing Office, 1961).

The hiring of 21,886 additional non-Ph.D.'s allowed the student-faculty ratio to be reduced to 11.89.[11]

Only by understanding the deterioration in the "quality" of college faculty is it possible to understand the lament of inadequate supply so often heard in the past decade. It would appear that since the student-faculty ratio has declined, the supply of faculty has been increasing more than the demand. But such is not the case. The increases in the number of faculty hired have been achieved by hiring less adequately prepared faculty, by deterioration in the quality rather than by an inordinate increase in its supply.

The labor market for Ph.D.-qualified professors has been a seller's, not a buyer's, market in which colleges have been competing among themselves for the too-few Ph.D.'s. In the postwar period, the labor market for college professors has been occasioned by excess demand, in spite of appearances to the contrary. The jobs have not gone vacant, but college administrators have gone begging for more qualified applicants.

The concern of college administrators about the quality of available professors is reflected in a great number of statements made under varied circumstances. In 1960, Columbia University's Institute of Higher Education asked 503 college presidents, "Have you had difficulty in the past several years in obtaining properly qualified teachers?" Approximately 75 per cent acknowledged that they had had difficulties and that they anticipated even more difficulties in the future.[12] Speaking to a group of educators gathered in Washington, J. Fletcher Wellemeyer, Jr., a well-known consultant in education and manpower, stated: "Nearly every institution of higher learning has already been having difficulties in hiring new teachers with adequate training and

11. This impressive reduction in the student-faculty ratio must be qualified. Much of the reduction has resulted from hiring more faculty members to work solely upon research, not smaller classes. Also, the practice of using graduate students in beginning courses has probably become more popular during the period studied.

12. Earl J. McGrath, *The Quantity and Quality of College Teaching* (New York: Institute of Higher Education, Bureau of Publication, Teachers' College, Columbia University, 1961), p. 5.

ability." To prove his point, Wellemeyer cited National Education Association statistics that show that the percentage of new
teachers who were hired with a Ph.D. degree declined from 31.4
per cent in 1953-54 to 20.8 per cent in 1958-59.[13]

Four years earlier at another Washington meeting which was
sponsored by the American Council on Education and the Ford
Foundation, J. Paul Leonard, president of San Francisco State
College, opened his remarks with: "The problem of [faculty]
shortages is one that confronts most of us."[14] The discussion that
followed, involving a virtual "Who's Who in American Education," emphasized and re-emphasized the existing and future
crises in staffing American colleges and universities.

In 1957-58 and 1958-59, the 914 institutions responding to the
National Education Association questionnaire reported that 1,276
existing full-time teaching jobs could not be filled because properly
qualified candidates were not available.[15] There is now, has been
at least in the recent past, and will be in the foreseeable future
a shortage of qualified college teachers.

Variations in Scarcity

Up to this point, the discussion has centered on a very broadly
defined labor market, the market for college professors-in-general
during the postwar years. Though it is conceptually possible to
envision a single broadly conceived labor market, the conception
has little operational meaning; for the products exchanged within
the market are quite heterogeneous and far from completely substitutable. The services of a specialist in Elizabethan poetry are
not substitutable for the services of an urban planner.

In practice, colleges do not seek professors-in-general; nor

13. J. Fletcher Wellemeyer, Jr., "Sources of New Teachers, Full- and Part-
Time," in *Quality of College Teaching and Staff*, ed. Roy J. Deferrari (Washington: The Catholic University of America Press, 1961), p. 179.

14. J. Paul Leonard, "Recruiting Talent for College Teaching," in *Expanding
Resources for College Teaching*, ed. Charles G. Dobbins ("American Council on
Education Studies Series I, Number 60"; Washington: American Council on
Education, 1956), p. 7.

15. National Education Association, *Teacher Supply and Demand in Universities, Colleges, and Junior Colleges, 1957-58 and 1958-59* ("Higher Education
Series, Research Report 1959-R10"; Washington, 1959), p. 19.

does the aspiring professor look for a job teaching anything. The requirements on both the demand and the supply sides of the labor market are far more specific. The college is typically looking for a man with an ability to teach one or several rather specialized subjects, the extent of specialization required increasing with the size of the school. Whether it is a very small school looking for a "social scientist," a larger school seeking an "historian," a still larger school hunting a "European historian," or a very large university searching for a "German historian specializing in wars of the 19th Century"—in any case the hirers' demands are more specific than professors-in-general.

Academic labor markets are not so broadly conceived. The labor market for professors-in-general does not exist. There is no single market. *The* academic labor market, as discussed in the previous section, is really the summation of many balkanized labor markets, differing in time, place, and the types of labor services exchanged. The labor markets of 1962 differ from those of 1959, the markets for college professors on the East Coast differ from those on the West Coast and in the Southeast, and the markets for specialists in economics differ from the markets for historians. Each group (distinguished by time, place, and skills) selling closely substitutable labor services defines a separate labor market. It is absurd to believe that an excess supply of American historians will compensate for an excess demand for mathematics professors. Similarly, though the isolation of markets by geography and by time is not as complete as by doctrine, professors offering their services in 1963 are not comparable to professors available in 1949 and professors with a passion for living on the West Coast cannot be regarded as supply for vacant positions in the Southeast. To be meaningful, a statement of market conditions in academic labor markets must be applied to a specific market.

Variations Over Time

Although the period 1947-48 through 1959-60 was generally one of excess demand, the prospects for professors-in-general were quite different depending on the year of the job hunts. Assuming, as before, that the quality of teaching and teachers remained constant throughout the period, Table 2 shows the excess demands for professors in each year since 1947-48. From the professors' point of view, the market, generally characterized by excess demand, was relatively weak in the early 1950's and unusually strong in the middle 1950's. The Korean War was undoubtedly the cause. Between the fall term 1950-51 and the fall term 1953-54 total student enrollment (and therefore demand for professors) dropped slightly while the production of Ph.D.'s, uninterrupted by the partial war, continued to rise. The need for teachers declined while the supply increased. As many of our interviewees related, teaching jobs were hard to find during this period. But the job scarcity was not to last long, for in 1954-55 two factors combined to cause a dramatic change in the market. Young people just turning eighteen were joined by others who would have gone to college in earlier years if they had not gone to war instead. The result: more than a 35 per cent jump in enrollment in three years. This rise in demand occurred about four years after the initial drop in enrollments, a time when the drop in undergraduate enrollment was first affecting the number of graduate degrees granted. Since an undergraduate degree is typically prerequisite to entrance into graduate school and eventual receipt of a Ph.D., enrollments in graduate schools lag enrollments in undergraduate schools and Ph.D.'s lag Bachelor degrees granted. Just as the undergraduate enrollment declined between 1950-51 and 1953-54, the number of Ph.D.'s granted per year declined between 1953-54 and 1956-57. As shown by column four of Table 2, the resulting changes in the shortage of college professors were enormous.

The rate of increase in the teacher shortage declined after the postwar effects were dissipated; nevertheless, the absolute teacher shortage has continued to increase and is now quite large. Although the data do not allow any rigorous statement of secular trend, there are signs that the annual deficits of new teachers needed but not trained are getting larger. In 1961-62, the increase in the teacher shortage was the largest of the entire period, excepting the unusual post-Korean War year of 1956-57. Whatever the future may hold, there is no doubt that the period during which most of our interviewees were changing jobs, between 1955-56 and 1962-63, was a period of high and increasing excess demand for professors-in-general.

Variations By Region

In the Southeast, the professor shortage was not as critical, for in this region, graduate school enrollments (supply) were expanding more rapidly and undergraduate enrollments (demand) less rapidly than in the rest of the nation. Many graduate departments were founded and many others enlarged so that between 1950-51 and 1959-60 the Southeastern annual output of Ph.D. candidates rose by 131 per cent, compared to the non-South increase of 20 per cent.

Since recipients of Ph.D.'s from Southeastern universities tend to accept jobs in other Southeastern schools,[16] the high regional growth rate in Ph.D.'s granted undoubtedly resulted in a more than proportional (to the rest of the nation) increase in the supply of Ph.D.'s available to Southeastern schools. At the same time that regional inbreeding among a significantly larger number of Ph.D.'s granted was augmenting supply, the Southeast was blessed with a less than average increase in total college enrollments during the 1950's, as shown by Table 3.

The result: in sharp contrast to the rest of the nation where the increases in college enrollments were more than twice as great as the increase in number of Ph.D.'s granted, in the Southeast exactly the opposite was the case. The supply of new Ph.D.'s increased twice as rapidly as the number of college students seeking degrees. The excess demand for qualified professors was not as great in the South as in the other parts of the nation.

16. A recent study indicates that 68 per cent of the Ph.D. recipients in eight southern universities accepted their first job in another southern university. Jerry L. L. Miller, *An Exploratory Study of Factors Influencing the Choice of an Initial Job by Ph.D. Students* (Atlanta, 1962), p. 37.

Table 3

Percentage Change in Number of
Ph.D.'s Granted and Total Enrollments Between
1950-51 and 1959-60, by Southeast and Non-Southeast

Region	Change in Number of Ph.D.'s Granted	Change in Degree-Credit Enrollment
Southeast*	131%	61%
Non-Southeast	28%	72%

* "Southeast" includes Virginia, North Carolina, Tennessee, Mississippi, Alabama, Louisiana, Georgia, Florida, South Carolina.
Source: Computed from data available in *Statistical Abstract, 1962*, p. 134, *Statistical Abstract, 1961*, p. 126, *Statistical Abstract, 1952*, p. 125, and Federal Security Agency, U.S. Office of Education, *Earned Degrees Conferred by Higher Educational Institutions, 1950-51* ("Circular 333"; Washington: Government Printing Office, 1952), p. 9.

This differential in excess demand can, however, be over-stressed, and against this danger we must guard. Although many professors are regionally oriented, the market for college professors is a national one. Even after the recent expansion in Ph.D. programs, the South demands more Ph.D.'s than it supplies. In 1959-60, nearly 12 per cent of American college students were enrolled in Southeastern schools. The same schools granted only 7.3 per cent of the nation's Ph.D.'s. Southern schools must still enter the national market for many of their Ph.D.'s and are, therefore, affected by conditions in this nationwide market.[17] If, as during the greater part of the 1950's, the national demand for college professors exceeds the supply, the Southern schools must adjust their recruiting policies accordingly, and professors recruited by Southern schools should take advantage of their bargaining position.

Moreover, the Southern demand has not expanded as slowly as the raw statistics on enrollment might imply. For several reasons, the demand for Ph.D. qualified college professors in the South has been increasing more rapidly than the demand for college professors-in-general. First, the South is awakening to the in-

17. The major southern universities are more active participants in the national market than the smaller colleges in the South.

adequacies of its education system and desires to upgrade the quality of higher education. Significant improvements are demanding qualified, Ph.D.-trained, personnel. Starting with a much lower than average ratio of Ph.D. to total faculty members, the South is demanding, not as effectively as it might hope, large numbers of Ph.D.'s simply to raise the quality of the work force to the non-South standards. Secondly, as more and more graduate schools are opened and expanded in the South, non-Ph.D.'s cannot be tolerated. Graduate courses require Ph.D. qualified teachers. As long as the South was not educating graduate students, it could get away with maintaining very few Ph.D.'s relative to total faculty. But now that the South is upgrading its degree, it must also upgrade the quality of its faculty.

In spite of these qualifications, it is probably accurate to state that the professor shortage was slightly less severe in the Southeast than in the nation as a whole.

Variations By Discipline

Regardless of the area of the country, qualitative evidence suggests that the shortage of economists and sociologists was greater than the shortage of historians during the period studied. In our interviews, history department chairmen complained less about the unavailability of good appointees than either the sociologists or the economists. Many history departments found that they could attract new Ph.D.'s at the instructor rank and at a salary that was consistent with the rest of the salary structure. Economics and sociology departments had to offer assistant professorships to all Ph.D.'s and, in many instances, had to pay inordinately high salaries in order to compete favorably with other schools. The hirers of economists and sociologists felt a tightness in their markets that was not evident in the replies of historians.

Admittedly, these qualitative findings are at best speculative. To assess accurately the balance of demand and supply in the various doctrinal labor markets, it would be necessary to develop quality-constant supply and demand functions similar to those presented for all professors earlier in the chapter. Unfortunately, the data needed for such computations are not available.

Summary

With small variations by time, place, and doctrine, the period during which our interviewees changed jobs was one of faculty shortage. For candidates moving through this market, the major problems centered around the selection of the best among several job offers rather than the location of any job. It must be kept in mind that the conclusions that we reach concerning the structure of academic labor markets in these times of excess demand might not apply to markets during times when there are more professors than jobs.

III

THE DEMAND FOR FACULTY

Each individual university or college seeking new faculty, and each potential college professor seeking a new job, has unique demands and unique sources of supply. Each college operates in its own sub-labor market with its own supply and demand. To the hiring institution and the job-seeking individual, the general market conditions are important only insofar as they affect the quantity and quality of options available within their relevant sub-markets. A small college in North Carolina finds little comfort in the knowledge of a general glut of Ph.D. specialists in American History if unable to attract the bright, young Ph.D. that it needs. Likewise, the young econometrician is more frustrated than aided by the knowledge of an excess demand for his skills, when unable to identify specific demanders. The balance between the forces of demand and supply must be examined in light of specifics. An extreme example of how a specific hiring situation may be isolated from general market conditions is offered by the double coincidence of wants reported by a Florida school. Late in the year, this school recognized a need for a "business economist with wide experience." At the same time, a "business economist with wide experience" was told by his doctor that to preserve his health he must leave industry and return to teaching, preferably in a warm climate. Realizing the scarcity of business economists, especially business economists with wide experience available in August to teach in September, the school had little hope of finding a man. Recognizing that teaching jobs in Southern business schools are hard to find, especially in August, the patient had little hope of carrying out doctor's orders for at least a year. When economist and school learned of each other and negotiated a contract, both were left with the feeling that the market was not as tight as they had envisioned. For them it was not. Specific conditions dominated the general.

In order better to understand behavior in specific labor markets, the next chapters concentrate upon the maneuvering of hiring schools and job hunting professors in actual hiring situations. The forces of demand and supply within the sub-labor markets faced by an individual university and an individual job hunter are examined in detail. Most of the comments are based upon the responses in our interviews with recently appointed faculty and department chairmen, though in some cases the experience of previous researchers must be relied upon.

Institutions of higher learning provide a wide variety of services, each directly or indirectly associated with the production, preservation, and dissemination of knowledge. Whether the service provided is the instruction of degree credit students in regularly scheduled classes, the teaching of special students in evening classes, special institutes, or lecture series, or the discovery of new principles or new applications of existing knowledge through research, the production of the service requires personnel, primarily faculty. College professors are the production workers of the universities.

The precise nature of the demand of a given university in a particular situation depends upon the demand from which the demand for the professor is derived. If there is an increase in enrollment in the first survey course, the school can hire a young, inexperienced, "near-Ph.D." without serious consequences. But if the need is to replace a retiring department chairman who was the primary mentor of graduate students, a man of experience and repute is required. And if the man is to take charge of a sponsored research project, classroom ability can be of less concern to the hiring officials. Depending on the circumstances, a university's demand for a professor may be instruction, research, or administration oriented; rigid or flexible in regard to age, teaching and research specialties, reputation, experience, rank, salary-demanded; urgent or postponable; administration-initiated or department-initiated; or replacement or expansion caused. Demands differ greatly. Out of this diversity certain generalizations can, however, be derived and it is to this task that we now turn.

Hiring at the Bottom

Regardless of the unperformed service that requires additional staffing, the predominant practice in institutions of higher learning is *hiring in at the bottom and promoting from within.*[1] When death or retirement leaves a position at the top of the occupational hierarchy, it is typical for everyone to "move up a notch" and for the new man to be added at the bottom.

Actual practice in this matter appears to vary some by size of department and the wealth of the university involved. In very large departments, the loss of a specialist in Oriental history can be anticipated by nurturing and maintaining a younger and less well-known Oriental historian in reserve. When the top specialist leaves, the second man can take command and a new reserve man can be hired at the assistant professor rank. Similarly, in very small departments, where the specialties of senior professors are not crucial, if an Oriental historian who is also chairman of the department retires, the void may be filled by hiring a junior man to cover the courses in Oriental history and promoting a previously employed senior professor to the chairmanship.

It would be wrong to imply that these departments never hire at the senior level. Departments offering instruction at the graduate level for the first time, such as many of the Southeastern

1. Universities do not have a monopoly on the practice of promotion from within. In fact, universities probably practice within promotions less than most other employers. For a similar observation see Logan Wilson, *The Academic Man: A Study in the Sociology of a Profession* (New York: Oxford University Press, 1942), p. 53.

sociology departments, often must fill previously unimportant positions by raiding other schools for senior faculty. Occasionally the large departments misplan or have their plans disrupted by a backup man who becomes impatient with his blockage problem and decides to accept an offer from another school where he can be the head man without waiting. Very small departments may be unable to carry more than one man of the caliber of a department chairman or may be unable to recruit successfully at the lower ranks. One of the chairmen in a small department at one of the less prestigious state universities always hires Ph.D.'s at the associate level because he cannot attract them at a lower rank and salary. But these are the exceptions rather than the rule.

Only the "middle-sized" department, the department large enough to offer graduate courses but too small to maintain a "stand in" in each field, must regularly resort to direct replacement of senior professors.[2] As one middle-sized department chairman put it: "With graduate students knocking at our door, we can't afford to wait for assistant professors to ripen." And even these schools seek a man at the associate level instead of at the full professor level.[3]

The case for the "hire low and promote" policy is both extensive and convincing. Money is the mainstay of the rationale. Junior faculty cost less. "Financial limitations demand that most hiring be at the bottom" was the statement of one department chairman at a poverty-stricken, church-supported school. "No money," "money," "Can't afford senior professors" answered others to the question, "Why do you do most of your hiring at the assistant professor level?" To schools pressed financially, the rank distribution of faculty is extremely important. Since junior faculty members expect smaller salaries and larger teaching

2. These middle-sized institutions, therefore, are usually top-heavy with a disportionately large number of full and associate professors relative to assistants.

3. There is one large exception to this general rule, the distinguished research professorship. In developing institutions, especially throughout the South, a prestige symbol is the high-paying research chair that draws faculty from the major graduate schools of the North. In this case, the price paid per se increases value.

loads, their cost per hour of instruction is considerably lower. Large financial economies can be achieved by maintaining a high ratio of assistant professors and instructors to total faculty.

To encourage hiring at the lower ranks, all college administrators sometimes specify to the department chairman a maximum amount of money that a new man may be paid. This maximum is often so low that a man who is already established with non-vested interests in fringe benefits plans, and who is faced with the prospect of additional moving costs,[4] cannot afford to consider the offer. Only the young, assistant-professor material emerging from graduate school without a large family can be expected to apply.

At the junior faculty ranks, the poor schools can be, and are, far more competitive than at the higher ranks. By underpaying their senior faculty members who have developed non-monetary allegiances to the school and community that keep them from leaving even though the salary increases are no longer as frequent nor as large as might be expected at other schools, many schools have channeled their limited funds into relatively high salaries at the lower ranks. In essence these schools are offering high starting salaries instead of regular and significant salary increases. Instead of hiring associate professors at low salaries, they are hiring assistant professors at salaries that are competitive. Although the schools hope that the new young professors will develop non-monetary allegiances before they become dissatisfied with salary advancement, they realize, with full recognition of the moneysaving consequences, that the assistant professors may outgrow their positions and salaries and choose to move on. Of course, allowing the salaries of senior professors to fall below competitive levels virtually precludes hiring at the senior ranks. To quote the department chairmen: "We can get better men at the assistant professor level since our salaries can be more competitive," "Our wage scale is less competitive at the associate and full ranks," "We can't compete on any other

_____

4. The graduate student has moving costs, but they are not "additional." No matter what job he accepts, he must move. This contrasts to the situation of a man who may stay where established.

[than assistant] rank," "We can beat salaries only at the assistant level," and "Our top salaries aren't competitive."

At the lower ranks, the less wealthy schools have a comparative, competitive advantage in some of the non-salary aspects of teaching jobs. The assistant professor, destined to spend several years teaching large sections of elementary courses with only an occasional nibble at an upperclassman if he accepts a position at one of the major graduate schools of the North or West, is often lured to the South by the prospect of immediate graduate teaching. To the senior professor, graduate teaching is no bonus, but to the younger man the typical Southern university is able to offer something that more prestigious schools cannot. Here the young man is offered an opportunity to develop a field, to grow and flourish with the department. The personal satisfaction gained through such an experience is rich reward to the individual.

The hiring institution also benefits: a new field is added.

The younger the man is when hired, the more years of productive service he has ahead. "We get more mileage from a young man," one department chairman said. A man hired at twenty-five has many more years of teaching left in him than a man hired at fifty-five. Many scholars are most productive in their early years. In any case, a young man "on the make" is nice to have around and may well spark an entire department. Also, a man that becomes devoted to the school early in his career is less likely to leave.

Hiring in at the bottom also circumvents internal morale and incentive problems. To combine several quotes from the chairmen interviews: "hierarchy is important," for "tradition" dictates that it is "most appropriate" to "start a new man at the bottom." Bringing a man "in at the top" is welcomed no more by college professors than other groups of workers, for it upsets the hierarchy and frustrates the hopes and ambitions of present employees. If room is left at the top and present faculty members are constantly moving toward this top, they will work more effectively than if all their time is spent griping about the new man from "nowhere." Department chairmen can use promotion in rank as an effective goad to better teaching and more research only as long as their staffs have faith in the system and positions remain open at the top. Even though most universities do not have fixed tables of organization,[5] there is a general belief that the number of senior positions in a given department is approximately fixed and that if an "outsider" is promoted to one of these positions, the promotion of an "insider" will be at best delayed. Many department chairmen have concluded that the internal frictions fostered by the hiring of a senior professor are not commensurate with the gains. Nearly half of the chairmen interviewed complained of already "top heavy" departments with far too few young and developing scholars. Especially in history departments, where many freshmen survey classes must be covered, the greatest manpower needs are for younger men who are not immersed in a specialty. The solution is not more generals but more privates.

Initial appointments at the junior faculty level also simplify the task of evaluation. Although, at the time of hiring, less can be known about a prospective instructor or assistant professor than a senior man who has published widely and taught in several institutions, in the long run what is known about a man at the time of hiring is far less important than the state of knowledge at the time the decision is made to give a man tenure. In the case of a senior faculty member, the decisions to hire and to give tenure are usually made simultaneously. In contrast, before a man hired at a junior rank is tenured, the deliberating committee will, through on-campus observation, know far more than it could have hoped to know about any professor at the time of hiring. Risk is minimized by hiring at the bottom. Even though the chances of hiring a totally unacceptable professor for one year are increased, the mistake may be corrected if the original appointment is made without tenure.

Finally, for the department chairmen, mostly from smaller departments, who have definite preconceptions about how a man

5. Only one, a state university, openly specified an exact relationship between junior and senior faculty members; it is fifty-fifty.

should teach, how he should conduct his personal affairs, how he should allocate his time among teaching, administration, and research, there is an additional advantage of hiring junior faculty. The only men able to meet particularized tastes of these chairmen are neophytes who are willing to act upon the advice of their department chairman. Realizing that it is easier to train than to retrain, these chairmen hire inexperienced personnel.

Thus, there are many diverse reasons for the general policy of hiring low and promoting from within. It is not surprising that most universities follow the policy.

Flexibility

Let us now turn to the second of the generalizations concerning the demand side of the professorial labor market: *there is typically a great deal of latitude in regard to subject area orientation, extent of formal training, teaching experience, and exact year of availability of the candidates considered, but very little flexibility on price.* Faced with a choice, university administrators will typically hire a "mediocre but sufficient" candidate who is willing to teach for an amount within a budget rather than pay more for the type of professor desired and needed, or do without altogether. The study suggests that at most Southern universities the greatest concerns are for faculty costs and numbers, not quality.

If a university finds that it is unable to attract the new professors that it needs, it has recourse to three courses of action. First, the school may make the jobs more attractive by raising the salaries offered, decreasing the teaching loads, subsidizing housing, and the like. This is the solution suggested by traditional economic theory which posits that the supply curve to an individual employer is upward sloping, such that if the compensation (be it monetary or non-monetary) is increased, more candidates will be attracted. The operational feasibility of this course of action is strongly dependent upon how much a job must be changed in order to attract the desired candidate or, in more technical jargon, the "net advantage" elasticity of the supply curve. And the elasticity of supply is, in turn, dependent upon worker preferences. Since worker preferences are not examined in detail until Chapter VII, a complete and intelligent evaluation must wait. Suffice it to suggest at this point that college professors do not appear to be responsive to small differences in "net advantage" and that, consequently, the costs of attracting additionally needed staff by this method can be very high.

Second, a school may overcome its faculty shortage by increased expenditures of time and money on recruiting. A department chairman may write more letters to lesser friends around the country, circulate more widely at conventions and professional meetings, telephone more of the major graduate schools, canvass the candidates trained in other countries, place advertisements in professional journals, make contact with placement offices, list the vacancy with commercial employment agencies specializing in teacher placement, respond to the many letters received from job seekers, or engage in an extensive campus interviewing campaign of the type frequently pursued by business. This course of action also has its shortcomings which will become fully evident only after a discussion of the means by which colleges and professors tend to meet.

There is still another solution to faculty shortage. College professors are hetergeneous: a wide spectrum of quality exists, ranging from the major author situated at a prestigious major university to the new baccalaureate. Though the spectrum is not quite so broad, the price demanded and availability of these prospective candidates also vary in rough proportion to their quality. A school seeking a new Ph.D. from a major university with a speciality in Latin American History may, after several months of fruitless searching, decide upon a new Ph.D. from a not-so-major graduate school, or a new Ph.D. with only a secondary interest and ability in Latin American History, or a near Ph.D., or an M.A. with some teaching experience. Quality standards can be compromised. Instead of buying better ammunition, or shooting more times, a school may increase the number of times it hits the "bull's eye" by redefining the "bull's eye" to include a larger area. Candidates that would be rejected in a buyers' market are given a second and third look. Although most administrators are understandably reluctant to admit to it, there are a number of signs that indicate that this third course of action is the one most frequently pursued.

Most professor hunts commence without a clear and explicit formulation of the final objective. Department chairmen typically set out to market with only a vague notion of what they are shopping for, much like a Christmas gift shopper without a list. Rather than establishing an "ideal candidate" and seeing how close they can come, the procedure is to see what is available and take the best. Hiring decisions are made on relative, rather than absolute, criteria. Throughout his interviews with department chairmen, this author was left with the distinct impression that the entire concept of a "before search ideal" is foreign to the hirers of professors. There is almost always some flexibility in the hiring standard.

Often this flexibility is reflected in a willingness to accept a large number of "specialty areas." Rather than seeking a Latin American historian, the department chairman will look for a specialist in one of several areas including the Latin American field. Department chairmen insisted on one particular specialty in less than one-fourth of the hirings studied, and in most of these instances preferences regarding secondary and tertiary interests and abilities were not clearly formulated. In small departments, so few fields are covered that a man trained in almost any field is acceptable as long as he is willing to teach some courses not currently covered. If the new man's interests are in an area where no courses are offered, a common practice is to delete previously offered courses in which the current faculty has no interest and replace them with courses that the new faculty member prefers teaching. Since it is difficult to determine exactly what curriculum is best, beyond certain basic courses, the actual offerings of a department are often determined by faculty interests and abilities. Similarly, in large departments, the areas of competence of an incoming faculty member, especially at the junior ranks, are not vital; for course assignments can be shifted among pre-viously employed departmental faculty to allow the new man to teach at least some of the courses that interest him most. Many large departments have not decided whether it is better to staff at least one man in all areas for breadth or to achieve depth by concentrating several men in a few areas. This indefiniteness in development plans means that the departments more or less stumble forward, taking a "good man" whenever available re-gardless of field of interest.[6]

The same controversy over what kind of department is the best kind and what kind of training produces the best teachers also causes hirers of professors to be flexible regarding the extent of education and the amount of classroom teaching experience of the man hired. The Ph.D. is rarely regarded as a fixed require-ment, even within the disciplines where tradition holds it up as a measure of quality and achievement. By the time a man becomes eligible for a senior faculty appointment, the Ph.D. is not as good an indicator of ability as his record of publications and the opinions of his colleagues. At the junior faculty level, only the very best schools in the South regard a Ph.D. as "a must" when seeking a man, and even in these schools "near Ph.D.'s" are often hired.[7] Evidently, in this regard, the South is typical of the nation, for according to the recent studies of the National Educa-tion Association only about 25 per cent of the new teachers hired have earned doctorates.[8]

The requirement of classroom teaching experience is the most

6. Rapidly developing departments of sociology stand out as exceptions to this general rule. Many sociology chairmen have clear and definite long-range goals.

7. In special circumstances, however, the requirement for a Ph.D. remains quite rigid. Some schools do not allow non-Ph.D.'s to teach on the graduate level in areas where a Ph.D. is normally achieved. Other schools, saddled with many non-Ph.D.'s in tenure positions, must constantly remain aware of the Ph.D. to total faculty ratio required by accreditation authorities. The accreditation standards of the American Association of Collegiate Schools of Business, for example, often demand that only economists with Ph.D.'s be hired since economics is one of the areas within a business school faculty where the Ph.D. requirement is most easily met.

8. National Education Association, *Teacher Supply and Demand in Univer-sities, Colleges, and Junior Colleges, 1957-58 and 1958-59*, p. 11. The statistic cited excludes junior colleges.

flexible of all, with a substantial majority of the interviewed chairmen answering "not important at all" to the question, "How crucial was teaching experience [in this particular hiring situation]?" Whether this flexible attitude toward experience stems from the research orientation of the departments consulted as is suggested by the fact that sociologists (who tend to emphasize research more than either economists or historians) were significantly more willing to assess experience as unimportant, or from the inability to attract otherwise qualified and experienced teachers, as is suggested by the greater concern of "high quality" departments for experience, is not immediately apparent. It seems likely that different types of schools for different reasons regard teaching experience as less important than other qualities in a new professor.

Though schools are generally flexible in their demands for teaching experience, earned degrees, and areas of specialization, it is important to note that there is a point beyond which universities are unwilling to stretch their standards, the point at which the long-run costs outweigh the short-run benefits derived from an expeditious hire. If there is a great lethargy about ousting mediocre professors, even those without tenure, the long-run consequences of compromising hiring standards can be quite serious. For if the man hired is obviously underqualified, he will never get a more attractive offer from anyone else. In instances where qualified men cannot be found, positions are either left open or some type of temporary arrangement that avoids the long-run costs is effected.

A frequently used method of maintaining the cost constraint, covering classes, and minimizing the long-run consequences of appointing an underqualified professor is the one-year or one-semester appointment. At the outset, both parties explicitly recognize that the appointment is definitely temporary and that neither is making any commitment beyond the term of the appointment. Graduate students in need of money to continue their studies, older professors bored with retirement, and optimists hoping that the one-year appointment may develop into a permanent one often seek such appointments. In over one-fourth of the fifty hiring situations discussed in detail with the department chairmen, a temporary appointment had been made prior to the appointment of a "permanent" person.

Other methods used to delay the hiring of permanent faculty in year n to year $n + 1$ include the denial of requested leaves of absence, delay of retirement, and "stretch out." "Stretch out," a term placed by labor unions upon the management practice of requiring more work for the same pay, is at least as common as the temporary appointment. Unable to locate sufficient, qualified faculty, universities often eliminate the classes that would have been taught if the faculty could have been found and redistribute the students among the remaining classes. The result is large student loads, though the number of hours taught by the present staff remains the same. In many cases there is also a reshuffling of responsibility for particular courses. In spite of the frequency of its use, department chairmen definitely regard the "stretch out" as a temporary expedient that can, if used too frequently, result in the deterioration of faculty morale and the quality of instruction. A school may squeeze by with larger classes than desired at the elementary level for the first year but will usually make a temporary appointment to cover the classes if its search for "permanent" faculty is fruitless two years running. In total, these delaying tactics allow a school to extend its search for qualified permanent faculty over several years. This is, in fact, a fourth element of flexibility to faculty demand.

For the policy of maintaining the four types of flexibility described above as opposed to a policy of flexibility in salaries, there are several sound rationales. First, understaffing and overpaying are far more conspicuous signs of an inability to recruit than is the hiring of underqualified staff. Quality judgments are hard to make, requiring both a knowledge of the teachers' subject matter and the time to observe and analyze. On the other hand, canceling courses, increasing the average enrollments in classes, and failing to balance the budget are quickly noted as evidence of deterioration and may be expected, at best, to alarm the Board of Trustees, or, far worse, to initiate a mass exodus of present faculty. The public relations image of a school faced with a faculty shortage can be better maintained by hiring an under-qualified staff.

The separation of responsibility for quality judgments on the one hand and quantity-cost judgments on the other also encourages flexibility in the hiring standard. It is much easier for all-college administrators, whose primary concern must be covering classes without incurring financial deficits, to remain steadfast in their decisions to hire new men at no more than $7,000, when they do not have primary responsibility for actually locating someone who is willing to come at the specified price and when they do not fully realize how poor the quality of the service they can buy at their price actually is. A department chairman, saddled with impossible constraints, is likely to allow the only factor which he has any control over to give way to the realities of the marketplace. Afraid to reveal his own inadequacies as a recruiter, the department chairman is then likely to justify the quality of his find to his superior. The all-college administrator is left with the impression that his rigidly set constraints caused the recruiter to work harder and locate the perfect man, when in fact the recruiter was required to compromise quality.

Third, downward flexibility of the hiring standard is a way of raising the quality-constant rate of pay without requiring pay increases for present faculty. If new faculty, equal in quality to the present faculty, are hired at a rate of pay comparable to the pay of present faculty, justice is preserved. But today's market is such that justice must be a minor concern of university administrators facing faculty shortages. Today the payment of premium salaries to attract new faculty is so common that "old faculty members," as one chairman related, "have learned to expect and tolerate the differential." There are, however, limits to the tolerability of incomparable pay scales for new and old faculty. "Invidious" comparisons will be made. When the more established members of the faculty learn that men of comparable abilities and considerably less experience are being paid salaries higher than or equal to their own, discontent with administrative policy is bound to grow and faculty morale will almost certainly deteriorate. Although non-vested interests in fringe benefit plans, non-monetary loyalties to the present job, and the unavailability of suitable alternatives will probably prevent the loss of these senior men, the quality of their teaching may be consciously allowed to deteriorate. How frequent is this attitude which the author has heard expressed by senior faculty? "If they want to pay me half what I'm worth, then I'll give them half of my time and spend the rest consulting, textbook writing, and earning 'outside' income in other ways!"

Given these undesirable consequences of paying too high premiums to attract new faculty of comparable quality (which may be added to the fact that higher salaries cost more), schools have understandably seized upon the second alternative of paying comparable salaries to less than comparable recruits. A standard pay scale is applied to all. The best professors are underpaid and the poorest overpaid, in terms of opportunity cost. For example, instead of raising the entire range of salaries offered to new assistant professors, a school may pay a recent M.A.-recipient the top salary in the range, a pay rate previously reserved for those with Ph.D.'s. The senior faculty remains comparatively satisfied, for new faculty are being paid at "comparable" rates. As before, the incomparability of quality is less obvious than incomparabilities measured by dollar and cents differentials. Constrained by financial limitations from achieving "real justice," schools achieve "apparent justice" by offering comparable salaries to professors who are not comparable.

To summarize, when a school is unable to attract the type of men it would like to hire at the terms it feels it can afford to offer, either the desires or the terms must be compromised if classes are to be covered. Faculty attitudes, budgetary restrictions, and the "net advantage" inelasticity of supply speak against the use of higher salaries as a solution. Because of the rigidities in the labor market and the costliness of recruiting, additional recruiting efforts are not a solution either. The only feasible alternative is flexibility in the hiring standard.

Replacement Versus Expansion

Consider now the third generalization which relates to the relative characteristics of the two aspects of faculty demand, replacement and expansion: *replacement demand is usually more specific, less postponable, and less anticipatable than expansion demand.*

The need for new faculty arises for two reasons: a desire to replace persons who have resigned,[9] retired,[10] or moved to administrative positions (such as a deanship), and a desire to expand the total size of the faculty because of increased enrollments or administrative recognition that the department should offer courses in a new area. A rough indication of the relative importance of expansion and replacement demand can be gained by studying faculty rosters in two consecutive years. By counting the total number of names on a school's faculty roster in 1961-62 and subtracting this figure from the 1962-63 roster total, the number of net additions to the faculty (or expansion demand) can be obtained. In order to determine the additional number of hirings that had to be made to sustain the faculty roster at its 1961-62 total (i.e., replacement demand), one can count the names that appear on the 1961-62 roster that do not appear on the 1962-63 roster. For the eight schools within our sample of Southeastern schools for which faculty rosters for these two years were readily available, such counts were taken. The eight schools combined had expanded their faculty 323, from 5,945 to 6,268, between the years. In order to achieve this expansion they had to hire a total of 1,186, for 863 were needed simply to fill positions

9. The reasons why professors quit are examined in detail in Chapter VII.

10. The flexibility of retirement policies is an important factor in understanding the nature of demand for university faculty. A comprehensive, though slightly dated, statement of prevailing practices is given by the National Education Association in "Instructional Staff Practices and Policies in Degree-Granting Institutions, 1953-54," *Research Bulletin,* Vol. 32, No. 4 (December, 1954), p. 179 and Appendix.

that had been vacated. If these figures are typical, they indicate that for every professor that is hired as a net addition to the faculty, three others are hired simply to account for attrition. Most demand is replacement demand.[11]

The relative size of expansion versus replacement is important because of the different natures of the two demands. In the first place, replacement demand is less postponable than expansion demand. The intra-faculty frictions created by failure to replace tend to be greater than those growing out of failure to expand. Being human, professors are less likely to complain about the absence of a reduction in class size (that would result if the faculty were expanded) than an increase in class size (that would result if a replacement could not be found). An undesirable *status quo* is more acceptable than an undesirable change from *status quo*. Because of this tolerance for the *status quo*, expansion demand can remain unmet until the desired man is located. It is not at all unusual for a department to delay the actual addition of a new man for three or four years after the original authorization.

The student surplus is likely to be not only less acceptable but also greater if a replacement appointment is not made than if an expansion appointment goes neglected. Like their professors, students also have a preference for the *status quo* and tend to demand the types of teaching services provided previously. A course offered in year n and not in $n + 1$ will be missed by many more students than a course not offered in either year. Just as larger classes will be noted, the absence of smaller ones will not.

Also, since most departments attempt to maintain a fairly stable student-faculty ratio, net additions to the faculty are often sought prior to the year they are absolutely needed. When the ratio of students to faculty starts to rise above normal, the department takes on another member which, in the short run, causes the student-faculty ratio to drop below normal. In time

11. The ratio of replacement to expansion demand varied a great deal among the schools studied. At one extreme, a large private school experienced a slight net loss in faculty between the years even though 129 new professors were hired. At the other, a large state school met its attrition needs by hiring 254 and went on to expand the faculty by 130.

further expansion in enrollments then brings the ratio back to normal. When first hired, the new faculty member is in a sense hired half time to cover past expansion and half time to take care of enrollment expansion anticipated in the future. At the time of hiring, it would not be necessary to hire a "whole" faculty member to bring the student-faculty ratio back to normal. In contrast, when hiring to replace a man who has left, a "whole" faculty member is needed to replace the "whole" faculty member who left. In the latter case, demand is less postponable.

There is a second imporant difference between replacement and expansion demand. Replacement demand cannot be as readily anticipated and as completely planned for as expansion demand. Some unpredictable expansions in departmental enrollments do occur, but they are relatively rare. An administration usually has several years to contemplate exactly when a new man should be hired to take care of expanded enrollments. In sharp contrast, resignations are difficult to predict. In order to protect his own relationship with his present employer, a man who is planning to resign usually has another offer quite firmly in mind before tendering his resignation. Resignations are usually presented about March 15.[12] By this time many of the Ph.D.-degree-receiving graduate students have already signed a contract. Especially the better schools usually sign new men early in the spring semester. Only two months are left, by the generally accepted standards set by the American Association of University Professors, before raiding the faculties of other schools is considered unethical. Although some hiring occurs as late as early September, the cream is drained off the market by April 15. Replacement hiring, therefore, requires that a recruiter move fast and remain flexible in his hiring standards.

The Mechanics

Although the procedures vary widely depending upon whether the demand is for replacement or expansion, for an assistant or a

---

12. March 15 is the median figure in the resignations discussed with department chairmen. The range was from June of the previous year to June of the same year.

full professor, for a position at a large public school or a small private one, and so forth, a fourth generalization can be drawn concerning the *mechanics of the determination of faculty demand.* Although much of the process was hinted at earlier and will be referred to in subsequent analysis, it is desirable that these bits and pieces be consolidated in a succinct, chronological description of the actual process.

The decision whether to replace or expand the staff of any given department within the university is typically that of the academic dean, who is responsible for allocating a fixed sum of money set aside for "all faculty salaries" by the president or board of trustees. The dean may divide his salary fund among departments and individuals as he sees fit. Department chairmen and sometimes other senior faculty members informally, and sometimes formally, submit a statement of needs. They may argue, for instance, that the average class size has, in the past two years, increased by seven students and that, therefore, the addition of a new faculty member in their department is necessary to restore the previous, desirable student-faculty ratio or, in another vein, that a new man is needed to offer a new set of courses in a developing area within the discipline. Having made their cases, the department chairmen continue to lobby on the behalf of their disciplines. Though most deans do their best to reduce it to a minimum, politicking is bound to play a part in the final decision of which departments will be allowed to expand, which remain the same, and which will be asked to contract. The unobstreperous department chairman that simply sends a written memorandum in reply to the dean's request for a statement of staff needs is much less likely to have his need filled than the department chairman who continually reminds the dean of his perhaps less pressing need.[13]

13. The success of politicking stems from the inherent difficulty of the dean's decision. Phrased in economic terms, the dean faces the task of using a fixed amount of money to distribute labor among various departments so as to maximize the quality and quantity of services rendered. He can regard the amount of capital and land as given. In an ideal decision-making setting, both inputs and outputs are known and homogeneous. The decision maker knows exactly how much additional "output" will be produced by another homogeneous unit of

Once the decision has been made about the allocation of salary funds among departments, the department chairmen are usually vested with the responsibility of locating and selecting new faculty. Our limited evidence indicates that the degree of freedom allowed to department chairmen in hiring is directly

---

labor and what that output is worth. He also knows the exact cost of the additional unit of labor. To distribute his fixed resources optimally, the idealized decision maker allocates dollars to the user where they will produce the greatest output. The optimal allocation is achieved when the return from the last unit of labor hired into each department is the same; for example, when the ratio of the value of the marginal product contributed by the last professor hired into the economics department to the additional costs incurred because of the hiring of the last economist is equal to the comparable ratios for the history, the sociology, and other departments. If an equilibrium situation is achieved, the school cannot increase the total quantity and quality of service rendered by changing the distribution of faculty among departments. More would be lost by reducing staff in one department than would be gained by adding staff in another.

In actual practice the dean's decision cannot be so rational. How is he to measure output? Comparing the worth of two assistant professors in history and a full professor in art, especially if the dean comes from a chemistry background, is an extremely subjective and necessarily speculative process. How is he to qualify inputs? What is the output worth? For example, is he to equate three hours of classroom teaching of Western civilization to twenty students to three hours of twenty students in an advanced laboratory course? How much do particular professors cost? If the dean asks the professors themselves, they are likely, in self-interest, to overstate the amount of compensation required to attract them to or keep them at his school. On the other hand, the dean has little more to rely upon and he does not want to risk losing a man because of too low pay if it can be helped. How will a high salary granted to professor A affect A's productivity, and the productivity of B and C as well? However desirable, the answers to these questions and myriads of others like them cannot be given in quantitative terms. Labor inputs are neither homogeneous nor precisely measurable; product outputs are diverse, immeasurable, and non-comparable; and the functional relationships between inputs and outputs are the most nebulous of all.

Though marginal productivity reasoning is an accurate abstraction of what the decision-making process should be, if all could be known, and should be held up by university administrators as a goal toward which to strive, in the hour of decision the dean must push the theory into the background and base his decision on criteria that are theoretically less justifiable but far more practical and expedient. Apparent, as contrasted to real, need is one of these criteria. Persistent department chairmen, willing to voice their case when the chance arises, often win the sympathies of the dean. Another criterion is tradition. Assuming that the decision made in the past to staff a given department with a given number of faculty was a valid one, deans are usually far more willing to honor requests for replacement than for expansion demand. Deans should not be condemned for these acts of expediency. Most deans are doing the best possible job but the job of a dean is impossible. The tools with which they must work are too imperfect to expect a perfect product to result.

related to the size of the hiring school. This observation is strengthened by Stecklein and Lathrop's observation concerning the University of Minnesota that "the individual departments and colleges are allowed almost complete freedom in their faculty employment procedures."[14] In most of the schools surveyed in the present study, department chairmen had similar freedoms.

A department chairman is usually given a maximum amount of money (often not specified precisely) and asked to recruit a man who will meet the need that he has previously outlined to the dean in his justification. Keeping in mind the nature of the need, the extent of his financial constraints, and the general market conditions, the chairman, often aided by members of his department, determines the type of professor to be recruited. Since a detailed description of the actual recruitment process is included in Chapter V, suffice it to say at this point that the chairman is sent on the hunt with a gun of known and limited power and must decide for himself what type of game he will be able to bring home.

A Caveat

The observations noted in this chapter are based upon the comments of department chairmen, not deans. There is no guarantee that the attitudes of deans are accurately reflected by department chairmen. In fact, the possible discrepancies of opinions must be raised as a major caveat when interpreting all of the comments previously made in this chapter on the nature of faculty demand: the generalizations stated have been derived from the comments of department chairmen who, in many instances, are not the real employers. Department chairmen must play the dual role of union representative, fighting with the dean for high pay, and employer representative, placating the too high pay requests demanded by staff. As a member of the department,

14. John E. Stecklein and Robert I. Lathrop, *Faculty Attraction and Retention: Factors Affecting Faculty Mobility at the University of Minnesota* (Bureau of Institutional Research; Minneapolis: University of Minnesota, 1960), p. 3. See also Theodore Caplow and Reece J. McGee, *The Academic Marketplace* (New York: Basic Books, Inc., 1958), p. 199.

the department chairman's personal interests and loyalties lie as frequently with his "inferiors" as with his "superior." Caplow and McGee state that the department chairmen are the men in the middle and suffer from the "Swivel Effect."[15] Department chairmen must be only incidentally concerned with university problems as a whole, for they have been delegated primary responsibility for administering to one specific subsection of the entire faculty. The attitudes of deans and department chairmen are very likely to differ on some of the matters discussed above.

Summary

With the realization that the generalizations have been derived from the comments of department chairmen, not deans, let us summarize our observations about the demand for faculty.

1. Because of the effects of the policy upon the budget and faculty morale, institutions of higher learning do most of their hiring at the instructor and assistant professor ranks. The senior positions are filled through promotion from within.

2. Because of the effects of the policy upon the budget and faculty morale, institutions of higher learning are more willing to compromise their original hopes concerning the characteristics of the man they might hire than their original statements of salary maxima.

3. Because of the actions and expectations of students and faculty, the demand created by the need to refill a recently vacated position is more specific, less postponable, and less anticipatable than the demand created by the need to fill a newly created position.

4. Because of the deans' many duties, they typically decide only the distribution of financial resources among various departments and allow department chairmen to select individual faculty members.

15. Caplow and McGee, *The Academic Marketplace*, p. 199.

IV

THE SUPPLY OF FACULTY

Potential professors can be found almost anywhere. The professors we interviewed had been recruited from a number of unlikely places. Changes of the party in power on the state level and the elimination of a federal agency caused economists to seek jobs. Other economists had been working as a consultant to the Ford Foundation, a research analyst for a California bank, a salesman for an oil company, an economic analyst for an automobile concern, an economist with the Canadian government, a consultant with a private research agency, a director of research for a chamber of commerce, and a stockroom boy in Gimbel's Department Store. The economics department of a large state university recruited a conservation expert with a degree in forestry who was no longer needed by the botany department of the same university. Several historians and anthropologists were museum curators. A publisher's representative, a librarian, a retired university president, a retired professor of history from a midwestern institution, an editor of an historical journal, a high school teacher, a C.I.A. employee, and a graduate student in mathematics were included among the "immediately previous" occupations of other historians interviewed. Sociologists were recruited from the staffs of mental hospitals, welfare agencies, private and university-affiliated research organizations, and museums.

Recruits came from schools of all sizes and kinds, in all major regions of the country and some foreign countries: several prep schools, a number of junior colleges, a couple of teachers' colleges, an agricultural school, a polytechnical institute, several extension divisions, a U.S. army training school, many small colleges, and a large number of major universities.

For the purposes of exposition and analysis, with the exception of the unemployed, all sources of potential professors can be placed into one of three categories: graduate students, current professors, and persons who are currently working but not as professors. The characteristics of the supply from these three sources will be discussed in the following sections. What source a particular university taps depends primarily upon its need and ability to meet the need. For example, a school does not seek among graduate students for a man with an established reputation. A school struggling against bankruptcy does not normally seek new professors among the new Ph.D.'s emerging from the major graduate schools, for the students' asking prices are beyond the school's ability to pay.

Graduate Students as a Source of Supply

Graduate students are a primary source of supply as shown by Table 1.

Table 1

Previous "Job" of Interviewees, by Type*

Type	Number
Graduate student	42
Teaching at another school	43
With business	7
With government	8
Other	3
TOTAL	103

* In his study of 707 economists, Marshall found a very similar distribution. If Marshall's sample were 103, his distribution would have been 50, 40, 9, 4, 0. Howard D. Marshall, "The Labor Market for Economists," *The Review of Economics and Statistics*, XLV, 3 (August, 1963), 330.

Source: Individual Interviews

Many department chairmen prefer to draw upon this source. Although graduate students are inexperienced and unknown in the class-room situation, difficult to evaluate regarding future prestige value and research interests, and prone to move on to another school after only a few years of service, they are also willing to work for less pay, to accept a position at the bottom of the departmental hierarchy, and to receive constructive criticism. Graduate students are recently trained and knowledgeable about the latest developments in their fields. Because graduate students have recently been in close contact with some of the better known men in the field, the hiring department is usually able to locate a trusted and respected recommender.

At any time, the exact size of the pool of graduate students available for hire is difficult to determine. Many students desire to continue their studies and are, therefore, not in the market. Many other students are available for hire only if the job offered is very attractive. For the graduate student, the decision to seek a job is a marginal one. Weighing the marginal benefits of remaining for another year of graduate study against the marginal benefits of accepting employment in lieu of graduate study, each student must every year decide upon the intelligence of making himself available for hire. Because this decision must be made when the hiring is taking place (i.e., January through May), a student must make a commitment often without the knowledge of how close he will be to his degree at the time he must put aside his graduate studies to accept teaching responsibilities and without the knowledge of the specific jobs that would be available if he were to seek them. In spite of the difficult nature of the decision, the fact that six of every seven of our interviewees who had come to their present jobs directly from graduate school were seeking jobs before jobs were seeking them indicates that the decision is not procrastinated.[1] From the view-

1. It is interesting to note that a significantly higher proportion of economists had not started looking for jobs at the time an eager employer sought them out. The earlier scheduling of the regional and national conventions in economics may explain the differential behavior. In both sociology and history, either a regional or a national association convention is held during the spring, whereas in economics both the regional and national conventions are held in late fall and winter. See also footnote 3 below.

point of a hiring department, the problem is determining which graduate students have made what decisions.

Other things equal, students nearer the completion of Ph.D. work are more likely to have decided to enter the market. As a student nears his degree, the net benefits of staying tend to diminish while the net benefits of leaving tend to increase. Compared to a beginning graduate student, the third or fourth year student is more likely to have accepted the financial responsibility of a family, exhausted former savings, depleted sources of financial aid, and accumulated all of the personal and financial debts that he feels he can bear. The older student is less likely to sacrifice permanently his chances of receiving a terminal degree by leaving before the degree is completed. The older student has often completed his course work and his residency requirement. Moreover, as a student approaches his Ph.D. degree, the opportunity costs of remaining in graduate school rise. Graduate students who are farther along are, as a rule, more qualified and, therefore, offered better jobs. Whereas the best job offer available to a beginning graduate student might be from a junior college at four thousand dollars, the near Ph.D. may be offered eight thousand dollars by a well-known university. Our interviews with department chairmen indicate that even the high quality schools regard near Ph.D.'s and Ph.D.'s as substitutable.

Although financial capacity is related to "nearness to the Ph.D.," it should be listed as a second factor influencing the availability of graduate students for hire. Regardless of their progress toward the degree, students who cannot locate financial support from previous savings, well-to-do parents, working wives, fellowship and scholarship aid, income from outside jobs including assistantships, grants-in-aid, or loans must seek permanent employment. Statistics collected by the National Science Foundation, which show that 27 per cent of the economists, 26 per cent of the sociologists, and only 21 per cent of the historians are on financial aid, suggest that graduate students in history may be forced to seek jobs because of the lack of financial ability to continue more often than either economists or sociologists.[2] Real-

2. U.S. National Science Foundation, *Graduate Student Enrollment and Sup-*

izing that their limited scholarship funds must be used in the competitive battle for first-year graduate students, the chairmen of departments of history may be forced to push fledglings into the employment market in order to make way for the new crop of students.

Closely related to need is a third factor, the attitude of the graduate school and the particular department within the school concerning financial support and the advisability of a full-time teaching experience prior to the Ph.D. In some graduate programs all students are advised to seek a full-time teaching position prior to receiving the Ph.D., whereas in other programs the importance of proceeding to the Ph.D. without interruption is emphasized. Undoubtedly, the actions or inactions of students' graduate schools influence their decisions concerning availability.

The changes in market conditions also influence the supply of graduate student services available. Each year the graduate student must decide if this is *the year* to seek a job. If he decides not to enter the market in year n, then he must consider $n + 1$, and perhaps $n + 2$. If he expects the excess demand in year n to be greater than $n + 1$, he is more likely to seek a job in the earlier year. If he expects the excess demand to increase with time, the graduate student is less reluctant to pass by a good job offer, for he feels that equally good ones will be available in the following years. In some of the very narrowly defined markets where the future needs can be predicted with considerable accuracy (such as Indian historians capable of graduate teaching), dynamic estimation of future markets is undoubtedly a quite important determinant of supply. Though rare, our interviews uncovered several instances where thesis advisers were preparing a certain graduate student for a specific position that could be expected to be open several years hence.

Differences in change in market tightness, the attitudes of schools and individuals, financial need, and nearness to Ph.D. provide at least some clues to the factors affecting the receptiveness of a large group of potential professors to the proposals of

port in *American Universities and Colleges, 1954* (Washington: Government Printing Office, 1957).

faculty recruiters. Unfortunately, the recruiters' contacts with particular graduate schools are so sporadic, and the turnover of department chairmen is so high, that a full understanding of the subtle factors affecting availability of graduate students at any one school and especially at a spectrum of schools is rarely achieved.[3]

Faculty at Other Schools as a Source of Supply

If the graduate schools are regarded as the primary source of professors, the faculties at roughly 2,000 other colleges and universities provide an equally significant secondary source. For many reasons it is rare for a professor to end his career at the same institution where he taught first. "Job shopping" is the norm during the earlier years of academic, as well as most other, careers.[4] It therefore behooves the college recruiter to peruse the faculty rosters of other schools. As shown by Table 1, persons willing to switch teaching jobs are a big source of professors for any individual school within the entire system, even though they do not augment total supply. Professor X teaching at University A is potential supply to all universities other than A.

3. In the above paragraph, the effect of changes in market conditions upon the supply schedule is discussed. This effect must be distinguished from the effect of market conditions upon quantity supplied. Statically tight market conditions result in higher salaries. The higher salaries mean that the opportunity costs of remaining in graduate school are higher. Thus, more students leave school to accept jobs; the quantity supplied is larger. By moving the market to higher price-quantity relationships on a given supply curve, tight market conditions influence the number of students available. The effect noted here is a static effect upon quantity supplied, whereas the effect noted in the text is a dynamic effect upon supply itself.

The effect noted here may partially explain why more economists than historians or sociologists are drawn into teaching before completing their degrees: the tighter market for economists means that employers must offer more attractive teaching positions. The better offers increase the opportunity costs of foregoing a year's income in order to continue school. In turn, the quantity of labor supplied increases.

4. Cf. Venkatraman Anantaraman, *Mobility of Professional Economists in the United States* (Madison, Wisconsin: Industrial Relations Section, University of Wisconsin, 1961), pp. 5 and 7. In his study of economists, Anantaraman notes that economists over age fifty-five had spent an average of 13.4 years at each job. If they had held their first job at age thirty, this means that during their lifetime they would have held, on the average, slightly more than three different jobs.

Currently employed professors may be seeking another job for one of two reasons: either they desire a job switch or their employers do. Accordingly, the impending termination may be either voluntary or involuntary. Judging the relative importance of involuntary separations on the basis of employee interviews is extremely hazardous, for few persons will admit to having been asked to leave and many have been handled so gently that they honestly do not regard the separation as involuntary, though their past employer does.

Our particular sample of individuals is especially unsuited to any judgment regarding the importance of voluntary and involuntary movement, for one would expect that persons who were involuntarily separated in the past would now be teaching at the smaller colleges and junior colleges not included in our sample. The best indication, though only partially reliable, of the extent of involuntary mobility in the colleges surveyed is offered by the interviews with department chairmen, who may have been inclined to underestimate the number of voluntary departures, when they were asked, "What percentage of the men have left the department in the last five years because you purposefully encouraged them not to stay or you out-and-out asked them to leave?" Only one-fourth of the chairmen could name any employer-initiated dismissal in their department, a strong indication that most mobility in academic labor markets is employee-initiated.

In most instances where professors were asked to leave, the case against them was explicit. In general, the reason for firing reflects the emphasis of the school. Denominational colleges release men for lecturing "on too high a plane," failing to "spend time preparing lectures," maintaining "poor informal relations with students," and neglecting to bring "classroom techniques up to par." High quality universities claim to dismiss junior faculty because of failure to publish. "Failure to finish thesis" was the cause of dismissal of faculty at all types of schools. Rarely are men asked to leave universities for lack of teaching ability, or colleges for lack of research ability.

Except in the "high quality" schools, the seven-year, non-tenure limit subscribed to by most schools with AAUP chapters sneaks by unnoticed and the school is left permanently with a less than adequate staff member. At the seventh year, the pain that would result from making a personal attack upon an individual teacher typically exceeds the discounted value of future pain. Procrastination beyond the point of no-return results. Only in instances when the incompetence is excessive or where the damage that could be wrought by a slightly less than competent person is great is firing worth the trouble.[5]

The amount of forced movement among teachers is relatively small and concentrated at the lower ranks in the better schools. Most of the experienced college teachers who are job hunting are doing so on their own initiative. They are voluntary job hunters. They have the option of keeping their old job but find it advantageous to investigate alternative employment.

Types of Job Seekers

Different persons have different reasons for investigating jobs other than the one once thought to be the best. According to why they find voluntary job seeking advantageous, professors can be classified into the following groups: spectators, confidence seekers, telegram wavers, heaven hunters, waiters, risers, victims of circumstance, victims of deceit, and wanderers.

1. *Spectators* are a very unreliable source of potential supply. Recruiters understandably resent them. The spectator has been forced to enter the labor market because he has a special prob-

5. Nevertheless, some professors are dismissed and provide a pool of potential hirees to the recruiting schools. Appreciating the magnitude of the incompetence required to cause men to be dismissed, department chairmen are extremely reluctant to hire them. None of the chairmen admitted to knowingly hiring a man fired from his previous job. If his previous employer's dissatisfaction becomes known, the incompetent must step down to schools that cannot afford to be particular. But, as shall again be emphasized in Chapter V, the firing department cannot be relied upon to tell the next employer the truth about the dismissal. As one department chairman put it, "Some [firing] department chairmen absolve themselves of all guilt for firing a man by perjuring a letter to the next employer glowing with highest recommendations [and] never hinting of a dismissal." The firing chairman feels a greater responsibility to the fired than to the profession.

lem. He wants to keep abreast of the market for his services but cannot. "One loses touch without keeping up with the market. There is virtue in keeping up with the market. If you don't you'll be exploited." Since labor is not homogeneous and jobs are extremely difficult to evaluate, a professor cannot get a true appraisal of his opportunities without proceeding relatively far into a job negotiating session. Before he can make more than a guess about a job, he must visit the school and know the specific compensation arrangements. He must simulate a sale to see the customer's reaction, never letting the buyer know the merchandise is not for sale.

2. *Confidence seekers* engage in the same type of fake activity but for a different reason. Rather than curiosity, the confidence seeker searches other jobs to assure himself that he is still wanted by others, still able to quit and go some place else, still not totally dependent upon his current employer.

3. *Telegram wavers* are legendary. Many universities, because of their need to economize scarce resources, pay their faculty as little as the traffic will bear. Since ignorance about alternative job opportunities is widespread and professors often become emotionally involved in the school and the community, many universities can get away with paying their faculty less than the faculty could earn teaching elsewhere.

In order to keep the university from taking advantage of him, an individual professor must convince his employer that he is both willing and able to move elsewhere on more attractive terms. Here is where the telegram is useful. The telegram is a job offer from another school. Once in hand the telegram is presented to the department chairman or dean with a threat, either explicit or implicit, to leave if the conditions of the current job are not improved. The professor's hope is that his threat will be met by an improvement of conditions on his present job, but he must be willing to leave if his bluff is called. To get such a telegram requires entry into the labor market and, again, false activity. In this case, the employee knows his own worth but must convince his employer.

4. *Heaven hunters* are always looking for the ideal job,

Caplow and McGee's "El Dorado." Relatively well satisfied with their present job, these professors are continually rumbling about moving so that if some fantastic job opportunity should arise they would be considered. They have little real hope of finding El Dorado but feel that the occasional letter and infrequent trip needed to maintain their availability is commensurate with the changes of success. Since El Dorado is rarely found, much of this activity proves to be false also.

5. The remaining types of job hunters are much more promising sources of potential supply to recruiting administrators. *Waiters*, for instance, are victims of the small size of most academic labor markets. In any given year, only a small percentage of the total jobs in a given field become vacant. In some years many jobs open; in others, only a few. If a graduate student faces a year in which only a few jobs have opened up and cannot extend his studies, the best available job may not be as good as he would have been offered in a better year. Yet, he must accept it and does. But this acceptance does not prevent him from re-entering the market a year later if things improve. The waiters are moving from a job which they originally accepted only to tide them over into another year and hopefully into a better market.

6. Another group of professors are seeking jobs because *changes in circumstances* have caused a once acceptable job to become unacceptable. For instance, the individual may outgrow the job. Usually the teaching positions held while completing dissertations are unacceptable once the degree is achieved. In some cases the inequity can be rectified by promotion and raises at the same school, but in many cases the problem is with the quality and type of school and thus requires a job switch. A similar problem arises when a young Ph.D. "comes of age" for promotion but there is no opening to which to move. Here the individual has grown experienced, but the need of the school has remained the same. This problem frequently requires junior faculty at the "high quality" schools to start hunting.

7. Or, the *job requirements* of a once acceptable position may *change* and make the job less desirable than before. One young

professor in our sample was drawn to a particular school to work half time on a special research project and teach half time. When the project was completed, even though he was asked to stay on as a full-time teacher, he decided to seek another similar half research—half teaching position. Similarly, the redistribution of courses resulting from a change in staff or a change in administration may alter the attractiveness of a given position.

8. Or, circumstances relating neither to individuals nor jobs may change in a way to make the present job less attractive relative to another job. One interviewee, for instance, had located at a home town university to be near his parents but felt free to leave after their death. Professors are often *victims of circumstance changes.*

9. Misinformation, deceit, and miscalculation at the time of hiring also cause re-entry into the labor market. *Miscalculators* have the correct facts at hand when hired, but interpret them incorrectly. They infer potentials in jobs that do not materialize. They fail to fathom the true significance of some seemingly minor feature of the job. For example, a prospect might think that he could live with a chairman reputed to be obnoxious only to conclude later that he was wrong. Since it is virtually impossible to evaluate fully any job without trying it for a while, many false moves are made that must later result in additional moves. In a discouragingly high number of cases (24 of our 103 interviewees felt that they were victimized), false moves were made because of *intentional deceit* on the part of the hirer. Interviewees mentioned being deceived about the usual rank at which Ph.D.'s are hired into the department, speed of promotion, salaries at the higher ranks, importance of economics within the business school, and the strength of the nepotism rule to mention only a few. It is no wonder that over half of the 24 were back on the market actively seeking another job at the time we interviewed them.

10. The *wanderers* were described by one department chairman as "ping-pong balls yearly bouncing from one school and onto the next with little inclination or ability to settle down." They have the wanderlust and cannot tolerate the idea of living in one location for the rest of their lives. An annual change of

environment is always desired: a year on the West Coast, one in the South, etc. Wanderers are always in the market.

It is obvious that the urgency of finding another job differs greatly among the various subgroups. At the one extreme are the wanderers and the deceived who will almost certainly change jobs; at the other, the specators and confidence seekers are primarily interested in information and shy away from outside offers.

The Mobility of College Faculty

Almost all college professors are "in the market" to some degree. One hundred and one of the one hundred and three individuals interviewed wanted their friends and acquaintances to contact them if they learned of a job that looked interesting. As shown by Table 2, 22 per cent, an amazingly high percentage of the interviewees, all of whom had moved relatively recently, were actively seeking alternative employment for September as early as the preceding October when we interviewed them.

Almost certainly others would have been actively seeking jobs were it not for the costs involved. Job hunting and evaluating is quite time consuming for all individuals. If a man is *always* hunting actively, his work is neglected, recommenders become wearied by the many requests for letters, present employers become suspicious and distrustful, and persons in a position to refer jobs become skeptical about the sincerity of the seeker. For these reasons 78 per cent of the currently employed professors were not seeking jobs in an active way. Even the inactive, however, never venture far from the fringes of the market and always keep their eyes and ears open to new opportunities. There are very few professors who would not change jobs if the new opportunity were made attractive enough.

The willingness of professors to change jobs should not be surprising. As a rule, the more educated tend to be more mobile.[6] Moreover, most of the work performed by college teachers is not

6. Cf. Lloyd G. Reynolds, *The Structure of Labor Markets* (New York: Harper and Brothers, 1951), p. 80.

tied to any particular college or university. The abilities applicable to one school are readily transferable to another. Tending to be oriented toward their disciplines more strongly than their schools, professors think of themselves first as economists, sociologists, or historians and second as members of the faculty of a particular institution. To borrow an analogy from trade unions, the orientation is craft, not industrial. Most professors work independently so that when they switch institutions neither the colleagues left behind nor those joined need to make major changes in their work habits.

Of course, by moving some professors have more to gain and less to lose than others. For example, consider two professors. Assume, for the moment, that the benefits to be gained from moving are comparable, that both are offered new jobs comparable to their present ones but paying a 50 per cent greater salary. Depending on the circumstances, the two men may reach different decisions as to acceptance of the offer. The costs of not staying and the actual moving expenses may differ greatly. For instance, one of the men might have children enrolled in local schools, nonvested interests in various fringe benefits such as a pension plan, a well-developed research center with several unfinished projects, a house full of furniture, a home that has to be sold at a loss, and lifetime friendships developed over the years at his present school. In sharp contrast, the other man might be young, single, renting, and unattached to his environs. To move, the former might require as many as three months away from productive work whereas the bachelor might lose only a couple days. Differentials in the time costs of moving were common among our interviewees.

Switching assumptions, regard the costs as comparable and consider the possible variations in benefits. The length of time that a professor will receive the differential must be considered. The discounted value of a 50 per cent higher salary paid annually for three years will not be as great as when the differential is received for more than three years. Accordingly, professors nearer retirement will receive less benefit from a given differential. Also to be considered is the size of the differential. A professor who has been receiving regular advances in pay and rank is probably being kept relatively competitive and cannot expect to be offered as large a differential as a professor who has, without cause, been denied advancement for several years. Similarly, professors in greater demand might well expect a larger differential. The greater the benefits and the lesser the cost, the more likely a given professor will be actively seeking another job, for the marginal benefits expected are more likely to exceed marginal anticipated costs.

Table 2

Characteristics of Interviewees Who Were
Actively Looking for Another Job at the Time of the Interview[1]

Groups	Percentage of Group Actively Seeking Another Job
All Interviewees (100)	22%
By Department:	
Economics (33)[2]	18%
Sociology (33)[2]	39%
History (34)[2]	6%
By Quality of School:	
High Quality (35)[3]	31%
Low Quality (30)[3]	10%
By Type of School:	
Public (53)[2]	30%
Private (47)[2]	14%
By Degree Status:	
With Ph.D. (79)[2]	24%
Without Ph.D. (20)[2]	15%
By Years Taught at Present School:	
1-3 Years (40)[3]	12%
4-6 Years (38)[3]	34%
7-9 Years (22)[3]	18%
By Academic Rank:	
Assistant Professors (44)[3]	23%
Associate Professors (35)[3]	31%
Full Professors (15)[3]	7%

1. The figures in parentheses refer to the total number of persons in the group. For example, seven of thirty-three economists or 18 per cent were actively seeking.

2. Hypothesis of independence rejected with 95 per cent confidence.

3. Hypothesis of independence could not be rejected with 95 per cent confidence.

Some indication as to whether or not the actual behavior of professors accords with our a priori expectations is offered by the data presented in Table 2, where subgroups of interviewees are formed according to their answers to the question, "Are you actively looking for another position at the present time?" In general, the affirmative respondents had been teaching sociology at a better than average public university for more than three but less than seven years, as an assistant or associate professor with Ph.D. degree.

Compared to historians, job seeking activity was three times as frequent among economists and six times as frequent among sociologists. It is likely that the benefits to be gained by a move and the psychic costs of not moving are both largest for sociologists. At the schools surveyed there were more vacant positions in the sociology department than in either history or economics, in spite of the fact that the sociology departments were generally the smallest when at full strength. Sociology, a discipline still uncertain about its future, has been experiencing growing pains. Descriptive, empirical, and theoretical sociologists all think that they are using the only approach that will allow the discipline to survive. Everyone is dissatisfied and anxious to get out before the collapse if his department is not developing along the lines he feels to be best. Because of these cleavages, dissension within sociology departments tends to run much higher than among the members of the more developed disciplines of history and economics.

The fact that some professors are profession or discipline oriented whereas others are committed to a particular institution to some extent explains the greater restlessness at the better known and often public schools. From the faculty at the smaller denominational schools one gains the impression of a commitment to the college, a strong personal involvement in the success of a particular college which cuts across departmental lines. They speak of "we the college" rather than "I" or "we the department" or "we historians." In contrast, at the large universities one senses almost total indifference to institutional environment. The university is incidental to the discipline; the professors are independent of institutional ties. Professors on the way up fear that non-disciplinary interests will interfere with professional development and therefore tend to dodge committee work and to avoid the sinking of roots. Rather than buying a house and planting a garden like their colleagues at the less prestigious schools, professors at high quality institutions are always seeking professional advancement and are constantly ready to change locations if required.

Advancement seeking is especially frequent among that group of professors, the assistant and associate, for whom there is a possibility of advancing in rank as well as other aspects of job compensation. At the full professor level, the desire to switch jobs is minimized. Because he has been on the fringes of the market long enough to realize his true salary-drawing power, he has often passed the peak of his productive career, he is likely to have had a longer time to develop an institutional commitment to his present school, he has grown older and less flexible, he has accumulated fringe benefits and friends, the full professor is less desirous of a job switch. Even if he desires to change jobs, the full professor often remains in place, for at the full professor level, even more than at lower ranks, the ethic is that the candidate should play the role of a "reluctant maiden" waiting for admirers to seek her out. The uncourted but unsatisfied full professor usually cannot afford to change to the type of job he can find on his own. Whether they are seeking telegrams to scare their present employers into promotions or honest changes of positions, associate and assistant professors are expected in the market where full professors are regarded with distrust and suspicion. The man that has hitched his career to a particular institution for many years is, unless he becomes quite prominent, destined to complete his career at the same school, and he usually knows it.

Even at the assistant and associate ranks, however, there are considerable differentials in job seeking activity. Here expectations deceive. It would seem that the professors most recently arrived on campus, who are typically young and marketable under the prevailing "at the bottom" hiring policy and who have not had the time to sink deep roots in the community and school, would be the most active job hunters. For these men there are no apparent restraints upon mobility. The median and modal length of assistant professors' contracts at the schools surveyed is only one year. Even at the schools where longer contracts are in use, the prevailing practice is to let a professor go before expiration of contract if he desires. Yet, as shown by Table 2, job seeking activity was nearly three times higher among professors who had been at one institution for four to six years than among those in the one- to three-year group. In contrast to unskilled and semiskilled labor markets, voluntary propensity to move was not concentrated among the last hired. A similar tendency to remain on a particular job for several years, was noted by Behrend in a study of grammar school teachers in Midlands, England, and is, we suspect, common to most groups of teachers.[7]

There are several reasons why teachers remain at a job for several years. Most prominent in the responses of interviewees were unsolicited comments regarding the undesirability of too much mobility such as "Too much movement looks bad" and "If I moved again next year people would start getting suspicious." Even though department chairmen, by their own expression, rarely discriminate against the man who has been moving if the moves represent advancements, the younger professors apparently have the unfounded fear that they will be somehow penalized if they do move too much. Second, because of the great variety and complexity of faculty duties, more than a year or two is required to learn what a job is really like, to learn the promotion policies, committee assignments, and research opportunities. Instead of moving quickly to another job, professors tend to "give it a try" for at least three years. Third, even after the decision to move has been made, there is likely to be a time lag between this decision and actual job seeking. Open season on professors ends May 15. If a professor has not decided to change jobs prior to that date, he is likely to wait until the opening of the next season

7. Hilde Behrend, "Normative Factors in the Supply of Labour," *Manchester School of Economic and Social Studies*, 23 (January, 1955), 62-76.

(around December 1) before actively initiating an intensive job hunt. The fact that from May to December a decision to change jobs cannot be implemented undoubtedly means that new jobs are sought slightly later than new jobs are desired, on the average. The relatively low interest in seeking other jobs during the first three years can also be explained by the pains of frequent relocation. Not until after the passage of at least three years is the unpleasantness of packing, house-hunting, learning a new set of institution procedures, and so forth sufficiently discounted to allow consideration of going through it all again. Finally, as pointed out above, one of the primary causes of availability is change in circumstances: either the person outgrows the job or vice versa. Within the first three years neither job nor professor is likely to change enough to warrant a job switch. After three years, however, when the individual starts thinking about promotions and the school about tenure, both the voluntary and involuntary reasons for switching jobs are maximized. It is only after three or more years that circumstances require the parties to reconsider their original commitments.[8]

For a variety of reasons many professors determine that a net gain can be made by switching jobs. It is this group that is a primary source of supply of new faculty for university administrators desiring to hire more than a graduate student.

Other Sources of Supply

Taken together present professors and graduate students are the dominant source of supply. The only other sources worth mentioning are government and business. Occasionally persons who have temporarily stepped out of the training-teaching milieu of the higher educational institutions to accept a job with either industry or government desire to return. For instance, our sample includes a state tax expert impatient with party politics, an industrial sociologist desirous of pursuing theory, and a gov-

8. Several department chairmen, recognizing that the man who expects a promotion that he does not get is very vulnerable to outside offers, conscientiously study the rosters of other schools with the intention of raiding.

Table 3

Percentage of 1958-59 Ph.D.'s Accepting Jobs
in College Teaching, Business, and Government, by Discipline

First Job After Ph.D. in:	Economics	Sociology	History
Teaching Institution	72.5%	79.0%	83.2%
Business or Industry	7.5	0.7	1.4
Government or Social Work	11.9	11.6	6.7
Other	8.1	8.7	8.1
TOTAL	100.0%	100.0%	100.0%

Source: National Education Association, *Teacher Supply and Demand in Universities, Colleges, and Junior Colleges, 1959-60 and 1960-61* ("Higher Education Series, Research Report 1961-R12"; Washington: National Education Association, 1961), pp. 84-85.

ernment archivist wearied by the impersonality of stacks and files. Each wanted to teach and to do the type of research the university setting affords.

The adequacy of this source of supply varies a great deal by discipline, depending upon the numbers employed outside teaching. An indication of these numbers is given by Table 3, which shows the percentage of new Ph.D.'s entering the various fields outside teaching: 28 per cent in economics, 21 per cent in sociology, and 17 per cent in history. Accordingly, the supply of persons who could be drawn from other-than-teaching positions appears to be the largest in economics.[9]

Within our sample, fifteen economists, but only one historian, came from non-academic positions. Economists evidently find it easier to move between government, industry, and university. Venkatraman Anantaraman, reporting upon his 1960 study of 280 economists randomly selected from the *American Men of Science*, states that 52 per cent of his respondents had held jobs in two or more of the three areas.[10] Although comparable statistics are not available for historians, a survey of 227 sociologists conducted by the Committee on the Profession of the Southern Sociological

9. These percentages would undoubtedly be higher in all fields if the populations also included persons with graduate training but without the Ph.D., for relatively higher percentages of these "partially" trained persons take jobs outside teaching.

10. Anantaraman, *Mobility of Professional Economists*, p. 6.

Society in the same year indicated that only 25 per cent had, at any time in their career, been employed professionally outside of the academic field.[11] The percentage of historians employed outside academics is almost certain to be less. The outside academic supply source of professors, small in all three disciplines is smallest in history.

Unavailable Supply

A great deal has already been said about the types of professors who are willing and able to accept a new job with a particular university. In order to understand more fully the nature of supply, let us concentrate upon the group of professors and potential professors who do not meet the "wanted and willing" requirements, the supply that is either unavailable or irrelevant to a particular demand.

To any one university desiring to fill a particular position, not all supply is relevant. For example, if there are one thousand economists seeking new teaching jobs, the supply of economists to any one hiring institution is less than one thousand for a variety of reasons.

The Nature of Demand

In the first place, the nature of the demand constrains the relevancy of the total supply. Particularized requirements regarding age, experience, reputation, training, and religious background may preclude the consideration of economists that could be hired by another school. Although demand is flexible, it is not infinitely elastic. The marginal rate of substitution of a man in economic development and a man in transportation is less than one because the two men are not capable of teaching the same courses. In departments such as history where a relatively high proportion of the staff is teaching underclassmen, the marginal rate of sub-

11. The Southern Sociological Society, "A Report on the Southern Sociologist," 1960, Table 6. (Mimeographed)

stitution among specialties is undoubtedly greater, but still less than one.

Similarly, the better schools will reject a large portion of the supply because of "quality": no Ph.D., Ph.D. from the wrong school, and so forth. To these schools low quality supply is not relevant.

Otherwise acceptable supply may be ruled out on the basis of race or religion. Several department chairmen recalled specific instances where qualified candidates could not be pursued because of race. In one instance, a Negro who had been interviewed by phone would have, by accident, been offered a job at a state school in the deep South if one of the recommenders had not inadvertently referred to the candidate's race. None of the schools interviewed had ever hired an American Negro professor, though some alleged that they would if a qualified candidate applied.[12]

Religious discrimination is less pronounced in the schools studied. All but two schools, both denominational, had members of all three major faiths currently on the faculty. The notable absence of persons of non-Western religious faiths appears to result more from lack of supply than discrimination. Although at all denominational schools surveyed there is some evidence that, other things equal, faculty members of the sponsoring denomination are preferred to others, the preference, especially within Protestantism, is generally a weak one. For almost all denominational and all public schools, persons of all faiths are relevant supply.

No attempt was made to measure the extent to which women are discriminated against, though a quick study of faculty rosters indicates that all schools surveyed had more than one woman on the faculty. Believing that failure in marriage reflects a basic fault

12. Persuading trained Negroes to teach at white universities in the South promises to be a large problem for integrationists. Not only the social costs but also the monetary opportunity costs are extremely high for the Negro. Denied equal education, especially in the South, qualified Negroes who desire to locate in the South are few and far between. At the same time, Southern all-Negro universities are, in their attempts to obtain equal though separate facilities, bidding up salaries to unrealistic levels in order to obtain the few willing and able Negro Ph.D.'s. The result: a Negro can often earn considerably more by teaching in a Negro school than in a white one.

of character to which college age students should not be exposed, two schools were reluctant to hire divorcees.

Inbreeding and Raiding

Anti-inbreeding and no raiding policies also limit the acceptability of available supply. Except under unusual circumstances, most schools do not hire their own graduate students directly out of graduate school. To quote the chairmen: "We have a general policy against hiring our own graduate students as permanent faculty," "I don't like to hire my graduate students," "We would not hire a man with all his experience [training] here," "We have the general feeling that one should not hire his own people until they have taught elsewhere. . . ." As the last phrase of the last quotation suggests, schools are not nearly so reluctant to hire their own Ph.D.'s after they have been broadened by teaching elsewhere. The inbreeding taboo extends to recent Ph.D.'s. Most schools feel that the best interests of both the individual and the school are served by requiring even the best students to familiarize themselves with at least one other institution. For the individual, the experience is broadening and confidence giving. If he is a successful teacher and scholar, the graduate school gains from the advertising of its product. After several years, however, both the advertising and broadening returns from teaching at another school diminish. The factors that originally spoke against teaching at the same school where the Ph.D. was received dissipate and thereby free both parties to consider a return. At this time, the advantages of inbreeding start to outweigh the disadvantages. The facts that a man already knows what is expected of him, that a man can be rated accurately even in regard to intangibles such as personality, and that a man can be recruited with minimal expense and effort[13] begin to override the disadvantageous factors noted above. Thus, only a school's very recent graduates are regarded as unavailable supply. Inbreeding taboos are not a major constraint upon supply.

13. Wilson, *The Academic Man*, p. 55.

More important are "no-raid pacts," either informal or formal. No school wants to lose a good professor, because the replacement of any professor is time consuming and the replacement of a good professor is very time consuming and sometimes impossible. Any recruiter that lures faculty from school A to B risks his harmonious relations with A and is open to spiteful counterattack. Where counterattacks are likely to be most successful and where the importance of harmonious relationships is the greatest, anti-pirating arrangements have evolved. About 25 per cent of the department chairmen interviewed stated a reluctance to hire away from kindred (usually geographically) institutions without prior permission. In most cases, the anti-pirating pacts are oral and bilateral, and apply to a department rather than the university or college as a whole. The agreements are typically at the level of department chairman though several multi-campus state systems have developed formal within-system anti-raiding agreements that apply to all departments.

Anti-pirating clauses are negotiated between departments of comparable stature and departments of conspicuously different stature. What is to be gained by two comparable departments is quickly apparent. By forcing both department chairmen to recruit elsewhere rather than simply horse-trade, the average quality of the two faculties will be increased and over-all turnover will be slightly lower. Though it is not certain, both departments stand to gain. In the case of incomparable departments, since almost all raiding would be initiated by the better department (poorer departments would be unable to attract anyone the better department desired to keep), all of the direct benefits from a no-raiding pact flow to the poorer department. The better department, however, often gains indirectly. By maintaining harmonious relationships with the smaller schools within a state university's area of influence, the smaller schools are encouraged to direct their better students toward the larger school's graduate program. And, if the smaller school is allowed to retain good faculty, the new graduate students are likely to have received better training than they would have if the star faculty member had been hired by the larger school. For the large state schools, the risks of arousing animosity and lowering the quality of the state's undergraduate educational offerings may outweigh the gains from raiding. Other non-raiding agreements stem from a desire to maintain personal friendships and (in one case where two brothers were both in positions to hire similar persons) family relations between department heads.

It is important to realize that the raiding pacts discussed here are the exception, not the rule. In special situations a limited number of bilateral no-raiding pacts can be profitably agreed upon, but in the vast majority of cases there is no particular reason for such a pact. Only in cases where the recruiter has a concern for the raided department or where there is a strong probability that the raided may harm the raider is there a basis for a "no-raid" agreement. This explains why the portion of total supply unavailable because of a "no-raiding pact" is relatively insignificant.

Recruiting Costs

Another factor causing supply to any one university to be less than supply to the market as a whole is the cost of the search. In a market as imperfect as the academic labor market, one school cannot be expected to know of everyone on the market. Determination of who is available is expensive. Although another school in the Northwest may know of the availability of a person (Professor A) currently teaching at a junior college in Seattle, the expenditures of time and effort that would normally be necessary if recruiters from a small Southeastern college were to learn of A are prohibitive. Even if the Southeastern college sensed that there was a Professor A somewhere who was better than the best man (Professor B) that a modest search could locate, A would have to be sufficiently better than B to at least offset the marginal cost of finding A. Since these costs are so high, and the knowable differentials in professors are comparatively small, even the most rational recruiters stop looking before identifying all supply.

There is a point beyond which the marginal costs of further searches are not offset by expected marginal gains. The supply that has not been located before this point is, in a sense, unavailable.

The most likely groups of unlocated candidates are those which are the hardest to locate. As we shall see in the next chapter, these are the professors who are the least in touch with the primary placement centers, the graduate schools. New Ph.D.'s are well advertised by their graduate departments. Writings advertise the whereabouts of productive full professors. It is the aspiring assistant and associate professors who have cut their ties and not yet become well known through their writings that are the most difficult for prospective employers to locate.[14] The most obscure of all are persons who have cut their ties with the academic world and want to return to teaching.

Preferences of Candidates

Even assuming that two schools "find" the same acceptable candidates (i.e., correct specialization, race, religion, school of origin, etc.), not all of the supply relevant to one school may be available to the other. To take an extreme example, when asked what the minimal characteristics were of a job that could draw him from his present one, one of our interviewees responded, "An offer from ABC University [his graduate school] with my present salary." El Dorado seekers like this individual are unavailable supply to all but ABC University. Labor supply has a will of its own. If a professor decides that he will teach only in a large metropolitan area, his presence on the labor market is irrelevant to all schools except to those so located. Should a professor decide that he must live in a warm climate and near the ocean, many colleges and universities are immediately ruled out. Whether for professional, economic, or emotional reasons, if a professor decides that he does not want to teach at a particular school at a realistic salary, he becomes part of the unavailable supply. The biases may be irrational and unfounded, yet they

14. *Ibid.*, p. 50.

limit relevant supply. Failure to respond to a feeler or an offer is tantamount to being not on the market from the viewpoint of an individual school.

Geographic Location

According to Southern observers, the fact that a university is located in the South cuts it off from a sizeable portion of available supply. To quote a history department chairman from one of the better departments, "This regional matter limits our recruiting; it narrows the range of prospective appointees. Many men refuse to consider jobs in the South. I have had more than a few sharp-tongued replies on this score, especially during the period when the schools were [involved in] the integration issue." Among the major graduate institutions of the North, there is a tendency to regard the entire South as educationally backward and to envision all southern universities, regardless of individual merit, in terms of the merit of the region. The result: many qualified college teachers trained out of the Southeast will not consider accepting a job in the region. A concrete indication of the South's problem is offered by a recent study of the faculty at the University of Minnesota. At any given time, a particular university such as the University of Minnesota is raiding other faculties, and in turn, other schools are attempting to lure away Minnesota's faculty. Measuring Minnesota's offensive success in raiding by an "attraction index" (number of offers accepted divided by number of offers extended) and Minnesota's defensive ability by a "retention index," it was found that both Minnesota's offense and defense were most effective against institutions in the South. Southern schools were the easiest to raid and the easiest to keep from raiding Minnesota. The rejection rate of offers from southern schools by the Minnesota faculty, for instance, was 29 per cent higher than for any other region.[15]

Along this line, several interviewees cited the pressures that had been applied to them while graduate students in the Middle West and East. In one instance a man's thesis adviser, having

15. Stecklein and Lathrop, *Faculty Attraction and Retention*, pp. 97-98.

previously expressed his anti-South attitude, telegraphed a mandate "not to accept a job in the South before returning to campus" to his advisee while the advisee was visiting on the southern campus. Upon returning, the adviser again tried to talk the man out of the job in the South. Though this man finally did accept the job in the South, there must be a far greater number of instances where anti-South pressures are successful in making a portion of the supply of college professors unavailable to the region.

To be cut off from a large part of the potentially available supply creates a serious problem for higher education in the South. Because the region qualifies relatively few college teachers compared to number of undergraduates, it has a great need to import. Teachers educated outside the region must be recruited. In 1951-52 the Southeast granted 15 per cent of the Bachelor and first professional degrees but only 5 per cent of the nation's doctorates. Although the situation has been improving rapidly (in 1959-60 the Southeast was granting 7 per cent of the nation's doctorates and about 14 to 15 per cent of the first degrees), the Southeast still demands more Ph.D.'s than it trains by about two to one.[16] A net in-migration of trained college teachers is still needed. At the current ratios, even if all recipients of Ph.D.'s from Southeastern schools remain, the region must persuade an equal number trained in other regions to settle in the Southeast. This need to import is magnified in universities which must hire Ph.D.'s from the very best graduate schools (normally not located in the South) if the new hirees are to teach at the graduate level. Of our sample, which includes a disproportionately high number of professors at institutions with graduate schools, over two-thirds (72 per cent) received their last degree from a non-Southeastern school.

In spite of the great need to import, except at these better known schools, the South remains relatively unsuccessful in its

16. Figures from U.S. Office of Education, *Earned Degrees Conferred by Higher Educational Institutions, 1959-60* (Washington: Government Printing Office, 1962) and U.S. Office of Education, *Biennial Survey of Education, 1950-52* (Washington: Government Printing Office, 1955), p. 48.

Table 4

Regional Salary Differentials by Type of Institution, 1961-62

Weighted Average Salary and Regional Salary
Differentials by Academic Rank and Geographic
Region[1] (9-10 Months' Basis)

Academic rank	Average salary		Regional salary differential (in $)	Salary in Non-South as a relative of the South[3]
	Non-South[2]	South[2]		
Universities				
Professor	$12,176	$10,279	$1,807	118.5
Assoc. Prof.	8,864	8,000	864	110.8
Assist. Prof.	7,242	6,628	614	109.3
Instructor	5,721	5,272	449	108.5
All Ranks	8,866	7,913	953	112.9
Liberal Arts Colleges				
Professor	$10,364	$8,317	$2,047	124.6
Assoc. Prof.	8,335	6,934	1,401	120.2
Assist. Prof.	7,097	6,077	1,020	116.8
Instructor	5,937	5,226	711	113.6
All Ranks	7,926	6,624	1,300	119.3

1. Average salaries weighted by number of full-time faculty members, AAUP data.
2. South includes Alabama, Arkansas, Florida, Georgia, Louisiana, Mississippi, North Carolina, South Carolina, Tennessee, Virginia, Delaware, District of Columbia, Kentucky, Maryland, Missouri, Oklahoma, Texas, West Virginia. Non-South includes all other states.
3. The relative for any given academic rank is calculated by dividing the average salary in the non-South by the average salary in the South.
Source: Peggy Heim, "Academic Compensation in the South: Its Present and Future," *Southern Economic Journal*, XXIX, 4 (April, 1963), 345. Printed by permission of the Southern Economic Association, copyright 1963.

recruitment attempts. Part of the problem is salaries. Southeastern salaries are lower than any other region in the nation. College teachers in the Southeast earn about 10 per cent less than teachers in other regions, with the differential between the North Atlantic and Southeast being considerably larger. The South cannot expect to have the same quantity of professors made available to it if it is not willing to meet the demand prices offered by competitive buyers. Additional professors will become available when the South is willing to raise salaries and thereby move to higher price-quantity equilibrium points. Groups of employers who are willing to pay a 10 per cent higher wage may be expected to get the lion's share of supply.

Table 4, which is a reproduction of a table in a recent *Southern Economic Journal* article by Peggy Heim, shows both the magnitude of this competitive disadvantage and the South's attempt to adjust partially to its disadvantage without committing additional resources to salaries.[17] By underpaying the groups of professors that are relatively less marketable (i.e., the professors at higher ranks), southern schools are slightly more competitive at the relatively mobile ranks, the instructor and assistant professor levels. At the highly competitive assistant professor level, for example, the salaries paid by non-South universities are only 8 per cent above the South, whereas the differential at the full professor level is over twice as large. Note also that the South-non-South differentials are lower among universities than liberal arts colleges. The colleges, which tend to be regionally oriented, do not feel the pressures of competition from outside the South as much as the universities. In the areas where it must, the South is making an attempt to compete. The Southeast is attempting to do something to correct its supply problem.

But according to southern observers, salaries are the easier part of the problem. The low opinion of southern schools in general and an impatience with the environmental laggardness are even more important factors in the refusals to accept jobs in the South. Higher course loads, poorer preparation of students, fewer research funds, poorer public schools for faculty children, more restrictions upon academic freedom, and fewer opportunities for consulting income, these are additional reasons why a large proportion of the supply available to the nation as a whole does not consider opportunities in the South.

17. Note that the Heim boundaries for the South are more inclusive than the ones used in this study.

Summary

Entry into academic labor markets grows out of a wide diversity of circumstances. Graduate students who have achieved or are near achieving their terminal degrees and students who have not yet completed their training; college professors who have outgrown their jobs or whose jobs have outgrown them; individuals trained to teach at the college level who wish to return to academia after a few years with business, with government, or even with a college in an administrative capacity; and individuals who have been "fired" or "laid off" against their wills, these are the groups that make up the labor supply. The supply of labor available to any particular recruiter is less than the supply to the market as a whole and varies depending upon how particular he is regarding salary, specialty, race, religion; how attractive he can make his position; and how much effort and money he can invest in the search.[18]

18. For additional comments on the subjects discussed in this chapter and the next, refer to Howard D. Marshall, *The Mobility of College Faculties* (New York: Pageant Press, Inc., 1964). Publication deadlines have prevented the incorporation of specific references into the text of the chapters.

V

DEMAND MEETS SUPPLY

The hiring process consists of three equally important elements: the existence of a demand for labor, the existence of a supply of labor, and the existence of a labor market. To work toward an understanding of this third element is the primary aim of this volume and the special mission of the remaining chapters. Before attacking the more difficult question of "why do people move through the labor market in certain directions?" in Chapters VI and VII, we shall direct our attention in the current chapter toward the question "how do people find or switch jobs?" Sandwiched in between, at the end of this chapter, we shall attempt to make more precise our definition of "a labor market." For the time being it will suffice to think of a "labor market" as the place where buyers and sellers of labor services come together or contract one with another.

The Lack of Information

A most obvious observation about academic labor markets is that they are not perfect. All candidates are not aware of all job vacancies; all hiring schools are not aware of all candidates. In practice, the ideal of perfect knowledge does not exist. Ignorance pervades academic labor markets. Demanders and suppliers are not communicating.

Both the words and actions of department chairmen point to the imperfection of communications. When queried about specific recruiting situations, the department chairmen felt that over 80 per cent of the time they hired before completing an exhaustive search of the market. Fifteen per cent of the vacancies were filled without knowing about any candidate other than the one hired. The chairman of a twenty-two-member economics department, which was seeking an associate professor to teach macro-economic theory, wrote seven graduate schools that together suggested only one man. This man was hired without knowledge of any other who might be interested. When hiring a specialist in ancient history, a large private school went no farther than a folder containing only two "mass feeler" letters from ancient historians. One of these two men was hired without further solicitation of names. Even some of the more extensive market searches resulted in the collection of no more than ten to fifteen "names of persons even remotely considered for the opening." Because of the high time and money costs of finding and investigating candidates and because of the competitive pressures that force chairmen to extend offers before their prospective candidates sign a contract with another school, department chairmen do not complete exhaustive surveys of the market. In most cases, employers select from a relatively small portion of the total number of candidates that might qualify for the job.[1] Typically, the available supply exceeds the known-to-be-available supply and the known-to-be-available supply is quite small.

Candidates evidence a similar ignorance of the market. As shown by Table 1, 46 per cent of the professors who were interviewed stated that, at the time they accepted their current job, they had no other job offer. About one-half of the professors without other offers did not even know of another job opening. Among the 54 per cent that did have other offers, more than one other offer was rare. Rare indeed was the historian at a small

1. This statement does not apply to very specialized labor markets. When the total number of qualified candidates is very small (e.g., the market for well-known sociologists specializing in Brazil), the few candidates that are considered represent a high proportion of the total number of candidates that might qualify.

Table 1

Knowledge of Alternative Job Opportunities

At the time they accepted their current jobs, interviewees	Number of Persons
Knew of no other job openings	20
Knew of other openings; no other offers	27
Had one other offer	23
Had two other offers	14
Had three other offers	9
Had more than three other offers	10
TOTAL	103

Source: Individual Interviews

denominational school who had chosen his present job, his first, from nineteen different offers.

Reflecting this lack of knowledge of alternative positions available are the many suggestions offered for improving the structure of the market as it exists today. Professors who have recently been job hunting have the distinct feeling that the present labor market does not bring all, or even a sufficient number, of the job alternatives to the attention of the hunters. Although detailed treatment of these suggestions will not be undertaken until a later chapter, it is relevant to cite their existence as proof that the communications within the market are far from perfect.

A final indication of the imperfection of communications can be drawn from the existing recruitment practices and the resultant distribution of professors. As we shall soon see, the typical practice is for a recruiting department to write several friends to solicit names of persons who might be desirous of teaching at the school of the recruiter. The fact that only a few letters are written to usually near-by friends suggests that many "possible" names will not be listed. Many willing candidates will never be made aware of the opportunity. As a result of these relatively narrow channels of communication, department faculties often become "lopsided," with little diversity. If, for example, the chairman of the history department received his Ph.D. from Columbia, when new staff must be added, he is likely to write back to Columbia for suggestions. The hiring of another Columbia man then increases the ties between the two departments. When a third man is to be hired, Columbia will, in all likelihood, again be contacted. Because all channels of communication are not well developed, the school must keep turning to the only major university out of the region with which it has established contact. An extreme example of what can happen in a situation like this is a history department at a state school in the South that is staffed by eleven out of eighteen men who not only received their last degree from the same school but also studied under the same man at their graduate school. Concentrations of Ph.D.'s would not be nearly so great if the academic labor markets were more nearly perfect. Thus, the existence of concentration is an indication of imperfection, an indication of lack of communication.

The implications of lack of communication and the resultant imperfections in labor markets are serious and for the most part undesirable. In a free enterprise economy, differentials in job attractiveness are relied upon to allocate labor optimally. The academic labor market is no exception. Each prospective professor should accept the job, among all possible alternatives, that offers the greatest net advantage or, in other words, is the most attractive. In order to fill staff needs, schools compete among themselves. Each school calculates the worth of a particular addition to its staff and extends an offer in accord with the calculation. The university or college where the new recruit will do the most good will extend the best offer and, thereby, successfully attract the candidate. The optimal allocation of labor is achieved because labor attaches itself to the demanders who value its services most highly. Whether or not schools actually make these fine calculations and candidates actually respond to small differentials in net advantage is, for the moment at least, immaterial. The point to be stressed is that the achievement of an optimal distribution of resources depends upon all resource buyers and all resource sellers knowing their markets. The resource seller (in this case a potential professor selling labor services) must be fully aware of the price that all will offer for his services and accept the offer of none other than the highest bidder. Though it is not alone sufficient, an awareness of alternative positions available is a necessary condition for the optimal allocation of labor. Professors cannot accept jobs that they do not know exist. As the communications in the academic labor market are less than perfect, the distribution of labor is less than optimal. In imperfect markets, the proper matching of demanders and suppliers is less likely.

Good communications are, therefore, important; yet, there are many evidences that the desired communication system is lacking in most academic labor markets. Why? What can be done? How can the flow of information be improved? To answer adequately these and other like questions, a thorough understanding of the present system of communication is a must. It is toward this task that the remainder of this chapter is devoted.

Prevailing Matching Practices

A great deal of insight into the operations of academic labor markets can be gained by studying how job seeking professors advertise their availability and how hiring schools make known "positions available." The problems associated with communicating availability in labor markets, especially those where there are a large number of relatively small and geographically scattered demanders and suppliers, are immense. In many non-academic markets that have many small buyers and sellers, the inherent problem of communication is eased by a commonly accepted liaison (a person or group of persons, an institution or an agency, a geographic location) which is responsible for consolidating information on demanders and distributing it, upon request, to suppliers, or vice versa. For example, savings banks receive the excess funds of many families and lend the money to many others. But for reasons that are primarily non-economic, no liaison has received general acceptance in the academic labor market. A commonly agreed upon centralized agency, whether formal or informal, has not yet, at least, developed. The market

lacks organization and commonness of procedure.[2] Present practices and procedures are a patchwork of partly effective techniques, each pursued in an attempt to make up for the inadequacy
of the others: a mixture of individuals contacting schools, schools
contacting individuals, and primarily parties making contact
through obscure liaisons. Each party is, in his own way, attempting to increase the range of choice by making others aware of his
need. Though they may be acting independently from one
another, and in many cases unknown to one another, they are all
working toward the same objective; to wit, an improvement of
communications and consequent improvement in the distribution
of labor in academic labor markets.

Methods of Advertising "Position Wanted"

Consider, for example, the activity of individuals desiring
new jobs. The ninety-two interviewees who were actually looking for a job when they found out about the one that they currently hold were asked: "What had you done to find another
position?" Their replies, as summarized in Table 2, allow us to

Table 2

Methods Used to Advertise Availability

Methods	Interviewees*
Informed Friends	95%
Contacted Graduate School	62%
Attended Professional Meetings	35%
Listed with an Employment Agency	16%
Consulted or Ran Want Ads in Professional Journals	23%
Wrote "Blind" Letters	27%

* Percentage of the ninety-two persons who responded to the question, "What
had you done to find a job at the time you located your present one?"
Source: Individual Interviews

characterize job hunting activity. Job seeking is essentially a task
of advertising, of making one's availability known to as many
potentially helpful persons as possible.

2. For a similar statement see Wilson, *The Academic Man*, p. 47.

The first step is to inform friends and professional acquaintances. Ninety-five per cent of the interviewees had made at least one contact of this type. Graduate students, whose professional friends and acquaintances are not well developed, must be satisfied with informing their former and present teachers of their availability and advertising among their fellow students who are already teaching at other colleges and universities. Persons switching between teaching jobs, who have had an opportunity to develop contacts on their own, can be more independent and ingenious. Besides alerting their former teachers and former graduate school colleagues, experienced professors typically inform co-authors, present and previous colleagues, fellow institute participants, acquaintances made at professional conventions, and former students. Even casual friends and acquaintances are informed. When job hunting, all but the very timid first job seekers quickly learn that a friend or a professional acquaintance is anyone whom they have met who might know something about a vacancy somewhere, or know someone who does.

Realizing that much of the conversation passing among "name tag" friends at the various professional gatherings relates to positions wanted and available, 35 per cent of our interviewees attended one or more conventions with the expressed purpose of finding a job. At these conventions both casual friends and good ones, if they have not been previously informed by a letter or a phone call, become knowledgeable about one's availability through conversation such as "The dean's getting on my nerves," "My load is too heavy to allow the time for research that I would like," "If you hear of anything that I might be interested in, be sure to let me know," "I want to move," or "Do you have a place for me?"

The job seeker whose helpful friends are few or who desires to teach at particular schools with which his friends have few contacts must make his availability known by other methods. Direct and quasi-direct notifications of availability, similar to application "at the gate" in the world of the blue collar worker, are used.

The least direct contacts are made by third parties. A job seeker typically draws up a list of schools at which he would like to teach and asks friends or acquaintances (such as his thesis adviser) who are better known or more likely to be recognized by the preferred school to make the contact. The letter may read: "I have a friend who is currently teaching at the University of Illinois who is quite interested in moving to Wisconsin. If you should have need for a methodology man, I would strongly urge that you consider his qualifications. A vita is enclosed."

The use of third parties when making direct contacts is, however, rare. Usually the applicant writes his own letters telling of availability. In this way his friends and acquaintances need to make a recommendation to only the schools that are really interested in hiring the applicant. The burden of job hunting is placed upon the shoulders of the person who will benefit the most from the new job. If the job seeker now holds some position, he is usually fairly selective of the schools to which he writes, contacting only those five to ten schools that he is most interested in. For a number of reasons which shall be identified later in the chapter, some first job seekers, panicked by the prospect of being without any job, write letters to almost all of the schools that they have heard of. These "buckshot" or "mass" letters, sent to department chairmen, are often no more than a mimeographed vita and a short covering letter informing the potential recruiter of the candidate's availability. Among the first job seekers interviewed, over 20 per cent sent out fifteen or more letters. One man sent fifty and finally received nineteen offers.

In spite of the loss of prestige associated with their use, a surprisingly large number of job seekers list their availability with a fee-charging teacher employment service (23 per cent of our sample had made this step in their searches) or with the employment service of their professional association (16 per cent of our sample). It is interesting to note, however, that even those who participate in these formal clearing houses have little faith in them. Names are listed more to insure that some job will be found than to find the best job available. Listing is regarded as job finding insurance. By the types of persons eventually hired by the larger schools, contacting an employment agency is generally regarded as either "incidental" or "a last ditch effort" in the job hunt.

Methods of Advertising "Positions Available"

While candidates are searching jobs by a wide variety of methods, the departments with vacancies are seeking candidates. After a department makes the decision to hire, and the dean approves, a candidate suitable to both the department and the dean must be located. Here again, personal and professional acquaintances are relied upon heavily. Either the department chairman or the department chairman and other members of the department will write, phone, or converse with their friends and professional acquaintances to see if they know of anyone who is qualified and might be interested. Feelers are sent in all directions. Letters are sent to graduate school professors, to former students, to acquaintances made at semi-professional and professional meetings, to friends made while serving the government or attending an institute, to former colleagues, to former fellow graduate students, and to relatives if in the same profession. Although many of the letters will prove to be fruitless, it is impossible to predict which one of these friends and acquaintances will know about a third party who is the best available for the job. Of course, the more contacts a department has, the more likely it is to learn about any given man.

To emphasize the stress placed upon personal contacts by the department chairmen, several quotations from the interviews are given below:

The only way to recruit is through personal contacts, a lifetime of personal contacts throughout the better universities in the U.S. My recruitment is done by personal contacts at meetings. I would not go to employment agencies.

Recruiting is a matter of contacts, getting into the network. Once you hire a man from Harvard this strengthens the contact. For you can always write how he's doing, and talk about him at the conventions. . . .

Contacts at other schools are our primary source of leads. Whenever we get a man from another school, he brings contacts with him. Whenever a man leaves here, we are sorry but it does mean that we establish still more contacts. Contacts are the thing.

As shown in Table 3, in over 70 per cent of the hiring situations discussed in detail with the department chairmen, some contacts were made with personal friends in the course of the search. All of the department chairmen said that they had, in some hiring situation, called upon friends for referrals.

Table 3

Methods Used to Advertise Vacancies

Methods	Department Chairmen*
Informed Friends	71%
Contacted Graduate Schools	90%
Made Contacts at Professional Meetings	35%
Listed with an Employment Agency or Used Want Ads in Professional Journals	14%
Consulted "Blind" Letters	29%

* Percentage of forty-nine department chairmen who responded to the question, "How did you go about locating the names of persons who might fill the vacancy?"
Source: Chairmen Interviews

Few department chairmen, however, rely solely upon good friends and acquaintances. Reasoning that the men who are researching and training teachers in any given field are the most familiar with the personnel available in that field, 90 per cent of the department chairmen with whom we talked about a specific hiring situation indicated that they had made some attempt to identify the most prominent schools and scholars in the field and to solicit names from these institutions and individuals. This method of advertising a vacancy was mentioned more frequently than any other.[3] To follow this technique, the initial step is the

3. In his study of 349 economics departments, Marshall makes a similar observation; that is, the most frequently pursued method of locating new personnel is by contacting graduate schools. Marshall also concurs in the unimportance of formal placement techniques. Marshall notes, however, a greater use of "blind letters" than the current study implies. See Howard D. Marshall, "The Labor Market for Economists," *The Review of Economics and Statistics*, XLV, 3 (August, 1963), 331.

identification of the experts in the field. Usually the hiring school has on its staff or at least knows someone who knows enough about the field to identify the experts, though the identification is obviously complicated by the fact that the man who would know the field the best is the very man who is being recruited. If the hiring school is filling a vacancy left by resignation, the individual who has resigned is often requested to aid in the identification of experts. In the words of a history department chairman from a private school with a twenty-man department: "In almost any field we can identify the top experts in the field, the men who keep their eyes and ears open at meetings to promising men in their specialty, the men who in many cases train the best of the new generation, the men who pick up the gossip about people in their specialty, the men who come to know the peculiar quirks of the individuals within their field."

Once the list of experts is compiled, ten to fifteen of the institutions and individuals are asked to suggest prospective candidates. The referrals received from the graduate schools, the specialists, and friends and acquaintances will typically vary widely in number, quality, and movability. In general, more referrals are received for the easier-to-fill positions. And, the number of referrals tends to be larger when the characteristics desired in the applicants are more vaguely spelled out in the letters requesting referrals. If, for example, the letters are quite vague, the referrers will suggest one or two men of various types (e.g., several graduate students and several assistant professors with three years' experience) and allow the requesting school a choice. Of course, many of the suggested candidates will probably have to be eliminated posthaste, and the number of serious candidates is no greater (perhaps fewer) than the number that would have been received if the requesting letter had been more specific. The broad approach that brings forth many names is sometimes referred to as the "buckshot technique," and the approach whereby the qualities desired in candidates are spelled out in detail in the letters to possible referrers is called the "pinpoint technique."

As for quality, the present study sheds very little light on the question raised by previous researchers, "are referrals geared to the quality of the requesting institution, with the better institutions receiving the better referrals?" Although one chairman at a "middle-quality" school, in an aside, commented that "The Ivy League institutions do send us the names of their *top* students . . . because [we are] their friends . . . [and] they recognize the fact that we are trying to develop our department. . . ," most of the previous researchers agree that the answer to the previous question is "yes."[4] For it is in the interest of every graduate school to place its graduates as well as possible. The reputation of a graduate school is dependent upon its graduates—where they are and how well they are doing—as well as its faculty. Knowing that the better schools will not accept their poorer candidates and fearing that their better candidates might be tempted by "ephemerally attractive" offers from poorer schools, the graduate schools tend to mention their best students only to their most prestigious customers. Also, the graduate schools see no point in frustrating the lower quality schools by letting them look at the candidates who are too rich for their blood. Too many referrals of this type may cause hiring schools to stop soliciting suggestions, and may reduce the market for the not-so-good candidates from a particular school. A case in point is that of a sociology department in a middle-sized, private, southern university that was no longer soliciting names from one of the northern state schools because all of the candidates that the northern school had suggested had, in past years, demanded unrealistically high salaries. Evidently these candidates were too good; their opportunity costs of accepting an offer from the southern school were too high. It probably would have been better if the northern school had referred some of its poorer candidates, candidates with fewer and less attractive alternative offers, to this particular school. Newburn, summarizing his observations made during an extensive study of personnel practices in state universities, suggests that even the requesting schools recognize that they will be discriminated against: "Those

4. In addition to those cited below, see, for example, Caplow and McGee, *The Academic Marketplace*, p. 168.

who can afford it ask for nominations of two or three of the top men; those who can be less demanding call for suggestions of *good* or *able* men, and the others just write and hope for the best."[5]

Whether the school is topnotch or second rate, unless it specifically requests the names of all persons who might be qualified for the position, the persons referred are relatively mobile. One of the history chairmen observed: ". . . they [the referrers] will usually suggest several names of persons just receiving their degrees, or persons that they think might be moved. Their conception of who might be moved is colored to some extent by their ideas concerning who should move, who is better than his institution, who is due for a promotion, who has a blockage problem. You won't normally be given the name of a man who is or should be completely satisfied in his current position." In most cases, the referrer has had some positive indication that the men he mentions are looking for a new job. The referrer is usually a former teacher or a personal friend or at least a professional acquaintance of the referred who has been told of the referred's availability. Here is where the advertising of one's availability, discussed earlier, pays off. The liaison makes the connection that is desired by all.

Although recruiting schools depend primarily upon liaisons— be they experts, graduate schools, or friends—occasionally other techniques of locating prospective faculty are used. These techniques supplement, rather than supplant, the referrals and tend to be used only when the candidates located by referral are not acceptable, either because they are not qualified or because they will not come. Since most referrers are associated with graduate schools and tend to think first of their recent graduate students, a department that desires to hire an older, experienced man who is competent but not famous is likely to find referrals received from graduate schools inadequate. In order to supplement the list, the recruiters attempt to infer for themselves who is qualified and

5. H. K. Newburn, *Faculty Personnel Policies in State Universities* (Missoula, Montana: Montana State University, 1959), p. 12. Multilithed for limited distribution.

who might be interested in moving. The indexes of periodicals, lists of new book titles, "news and notes" in professional journals, and summaries of research grant recipients contain the names of persons who are actively engaged in research. From here the recruiters must make some preliminary investigations concerning availability. By noting most recent promotions, analyzing blockage problems of these active men, and subjectively assessing the relative desirability of the men's present schools and jobs versus what the recruiters have to offer, some indication of movability can be gained. If the men are qualified and there seems to be some chance of getting them, they are contacted. The process is well summarized by the statement of a chairman of an economics department that is now undergoing a period of rapid expansion and is in need of several experienced men: "We searched the literature of the last five years, looking for men who had published decent articles in decent places who were at places where they could be moved or at ranks where they should be promoted." Incidentally, this department chairman located a man by this method.

In instances where qualifications are not quite so important and where the demands of the hiring institution are not so particularized, the process of direct search may be ordered differently. For example, one of the department chairmen was, at the time of the interview, planning to make offers to all members of the University of Mississippi's economics department that he regarded as qualified. He reasoned that after the crisis many of these men would be anxious to leave and could be attracted at a bargain price. Availability, rather than qualification, may be the first characteristic sought.

Another technique used to locate prospective professors is the same as that used by businessmen when they recruit graduating college seniors, the recruiting trip. Although this technique was used by only three of the department chairmen interviewed, all three spoke highly of it and intended to use it again. They point to a number of advantages of recruiting trips. Compared to on-campus interviewing, recruiting trips are less costly, less time-consuming, and more productive. If the hirer travels to the candidates' campus, one round-trip fare can expose the hirer to four or five prospective candidates: four or five round-trip fares would be required if the candidates were brought to the hirer. Because the interviewing trip can often be combined with other business, the marginal time cost to the department chairman is usually quite small. Because the time-consuming task of entertaining prospective candidates while on campus and the voluminous task of extensive correspondence is somewhat circumvented, the department chairman is able to more than make up for the time lost by making the trip. Because many prospective candidates who would not have been willing to give the time that would have been required by a trip to the hirer's campus are willing to give the hour or so required for an interview on their own campus, the hiring school is exposed to a greater number of candidates. For all of these reasons, it is not surprising that the interviewing schedules at the nation's leading graduate schools are becoming increasingly crowded.

Attitudes toward making use of the unsolicited letters received from candidates who are looking for a job vary. Most recruiters prefer to take the initiative. The fact that a man must seek a job in direct and obvious ways worries most recruiters and they would, therefore, prefer to be informed of a man's availability in more subtle ways. Nevertheless (because the department's marginal cost is so low), many department chairmen keep a file of the letters that they have received and consult this file when the need for a new staff member arises. In the particular hiring situations discussed with the department chairmen, 29 per cent said that they had looked over the letters. A chairman at one of the most prestigious schools said this about unsolicited letters: "We receive many letters telling of availability to work here at ———. Over half of these are from men currently teaching someplace else. I answer all letters. I don't regard them as a nuisance. I keep a list of those persons we might be interested in in the future."

Unsolicited letters from graduate *schools* also provide a

source of possible names. A few of the major graduate schools send out annually a list of the men who will be available for employment as of September of the following year. Most of these lists include only the basic details on newly graduated candidates such as degree expected, age, experience, and areas of specialty. It is suggested that recruiters request complete vitas for those persons in whom they are most interested.

Thirty-one of the more prestigious departments of economics, including all of the major graduate institutions, have developed a variant on this method. Every year, immediately prior to the national meetings, each of the schools submits a list of its graduate students who will be seeking jobs for the following September. These lists are consolidated and returned to each of the participating schools, normally known within the profession as the "cartel." Any member of the cartel may then share the list with non-cartel members, but non-cartel members do not receive the original, consolidated list. Each of the department chairmen in the four schools that are in both our sample and the cartel mentioned using this list as a basis for locating young faculty.

As a last resort, a department may list its opening with either the professional association, or much less likely, a commercial employment agency. The listing of a job with the "slave market" at the convention, in the employment bulletin or the professional journal, or with a commercial employment agency brings forth large numbers of low quality candidates, the candidates who have been forced to find jobs by methods that are not generally acceptable professionally, the candidates who are not sufficiently highly regarded by their friends and professional acquaintances to be recommended. There are exceptions, but this is the rule. As a whole, 14 per cent of the department chairmen in this study listed their jobs with the employment agency of their professional society; all but two were sociologists.

To summarize, both recruiting departments and job seeking individuals use many channels to make known their availabilities. The present communication system is eclectic, complex, and decentralized. Like Topsy, it has "just growed." At any time, at any place, from anybody, and by any means, a department may become aware of a qualified candidate, or a candidate, of an interesting position.

Success in Advertising

A rough indication of the effectiveness of the various job hunting and candidate hunting methods is offered by the ways in which individuals actually find jobs. Although an individual may use many methods to find out about jobs, the method used to find out about the job that he eventually accepts is the most relevant, the most successful. With this in mind, the individuals were asked, "How did you first learn about the job you now hold?" The response is summarized in Table 4.

The personalized nature of the academic labor market is emphasized. Contacts are extremely important. Friends were the most frequent source of promising leads. By letter, by phone, and in person, friends and acquaintances were the ones who had made nearly 50 per cent of our respondents aware of the jobs they now hold and this figure does not include the respondents' graduate school professors, many of whom are more friends than teachers.

Table 4

Channel by Which Current Jobs Were First Learned About

Methods	Interviewees
Friends, by Letter and Phone	34%
Friends, at Convention	12%
Graduate School Department (other than major professor)	23%
Major Graduate School Professor	11%
"Mass Letter"	7%
University Placement Office	4%
Commercial Teacher Placement Agency	1%
Professional Journal Want Ads	2%
Other	6%
TOTAL	100%

Source: Individual Interviews

Which friends and acquaintances are most likely to lead the candidate to the desired job is difficult to predict. Knowing someone personally at the hiring school can be extremely helpful, as indicated by the following incidents:

"The person who was leaving here wrote to me. We had worked together in 1951-52."

"The department chairman here is a personal friend. We had taught together at ——."

"The former department chairman had taught me when I was an undergraduate at another school."

"The dean's wife was a patient of my father who is a physician. One summer the dean visited my parents at their summer home. The job was mentioned."

"I first learned about the job while attending a meeting sponsored by the AFL-CIO, from the current dean who is a personal friend."

"Two of my former students were teaching at —— and told me of the opportunity."

"While teaching botany at —— I got to know the younger generation in the economics department through Newcomer's Club. At an August picnic I learned that economics needed another professor for September. Since my appointment in botany had not been renewed, I needed a job and got the one in economics."

"I wrote the chairman here at ——, who was a friend of mine, and asked if there was a position."

"A friend from graduate school was teaching here and found this job for me."

"A graduate school friend asked me if I wanted her job; she was leaving teaching."

Yet, it is not imperative that a candidate develop friendships with persons at hiring schools:

"While I was teaching undergraduates at Duke on a one-year appointment, a Duke graduate student told me of the opening at ——."

"[I learned about my job] at a Russian Institute through a friend who had taught at —— in the past and had kept up his contacts."

"A colleague of mine at Minnesota passed along a letter of inquiry that he had received."

"I learned from graduate school friends who were then working in

Washington that Professor X was leaving ——— and joining them in Washington. I then contacted ——— and got the job."

"A fellow graduate student of mine at Harvard had been given a letter from ——— telling of a vacancy. Since he wasn't interested, he referred the letter to me."

"A mutual friend of the department chairman and me, who was working at the Federal Reserve Bank, brought us together."

"[I found out about the job] through a friend who had a friend here."

Many candidates have found that "the people who know the right people" are their former graduate school professors. A majority of the candidates who did not find their current jobs through personal friends, or 34 per cent of all candidates interviewed, first learned about their jobs from either their major professor (11 per cent) or the department (23 per cent). The incidents cited below are illustrative.

"The ——— department had written to Princeton where I was doing graduate work, and Princeton had given them my name."

"I had written back to my graduate school, Columbia, and said I was interested in moving. Columbia relayed the message to Professor X, another specialist in my field, at ——— for whom I had recently written a chapter in a book he edited. Professor X contacted me."

"[I learned about my job] through a professor of mine at the University of California who had found out about it from one of his former teachers who was here."

"The department chairman [from ———] interviewed at my graduate school."

"——— contacted me. They had gotten my name through my graduate school, though I hadn't told them that I was looking around."

"My major professor referred my name to ——— who contacted me at the convention."

"My major professor was co-authoring a book with one of the ——— faculty members, who had told him about an opening."

Realizing that the repute of the graduate school itself is a function of the prowess and placement of their graduates,[6]

6. For a similar statement see Miller, *Exploratory Study*, p. 10. Also see Wilson, *The Academic Man*, p. 49.

graduate schools and individual professors within the graduate schools actively attempt to place and replace their graduates in the very best jobs that are available to them. Well-placed graduates are able to advertise the merits of their graduate school in circles that count, and the graduates themselves serve as signs that men from a given graduate school are placed well. This status seeking among graduate schools is not without merit. While attempting to achieve status, the graduate schools provide a valuable liaison in the decentralized academic labor market.

Taken together, 80 per cent of the professors interviewed had located their jobs either through friends or through their graduate school. Although 27 per cent of the candidates had sent "mass letters" and 29 per cent of the department chairmen had consulted them, only 7 per cent of the jobs accepted were located through this means of communication. Private placement agencies, journal ads, and university placement services were usually unproductive. Before passing judgment upon these means of locating jobs, however, it must be noted that all of the interviewees had found jobs in relatively well-known, large schools, the very schools that are least likely to need to refer to the secondary markets provided by formal placement services. If the sample had included faculty located at some of the less well-known schools, it is very likely that a greater dependence upon these more formal means of job location would have been in evidence.

The Rationale

Now that we are generally familiar with the ways in which jobs and candidates are sought and found, let us consider the whys. Why are jobs sought primarily through friends? Why do some job seekers pursue more methods of locating jobs than others? Why are some hiring schools satisfied with less than an exhaustive market search? Why do some candidates accept the first jobs offered without investigating opportunity costs? In order to understand the differential popularity of the various methods of employee initiated job seeking and to explain the differences in the usage of various techniques by doctrine, experience, and the like, a general rationale or theory for job seeking professors must be examined.

"Marginal reasoning" is the basis of the rationale. An individual professor will hunt new job opportunities as long as the (expected) marginal benefits to be gained exceed the (expected) costs of the hunt. That is, until the expected differential in "net advantage" between the "to be found job" and the "best job known and available" no longer exceeds the time and money costs of looking for the "to be found job," a job-seeking professor will continue his hunt. The expected gain must be greater than the expected cost. In terms of satisfaction units, the job at A State ("to be found job") must be predicted to yield at least (say) twelve more units of satisfaction than the job at B State (the best known and available alternative job), if the estimated satisfaction that must be sacrificed to find the job at A is twelve units. Letting "a" represent the units of satisfaction expected for a job at A (the "to be found job"), and "b" at B, and "c" represent the marginal dissatisfaction expected to be incurred in finding a job as good as or better than the job at A, $(a - b) =$ expected net yield. If $(a - b) > c$ then the job hunt should continue. Beyond the point where predicted marginal utility $(a - b)$ exceeds marginal disutility (c), a professor should accept the best known and available alternative (i.e., B) and stop hunting.

Thus, if a professor knows of no job, he will search by many and relatively unpleasant means, for the utility to be received from a subsistence income far exceeds the disutility associated with an intensive job hunt. As better and better jobs become known and available (b increases), improvement possible from further hunting $(a - b)$ decreases. And, as the less costly means of pursuing new jobs are used up, the dissatisfaction (c) of further hunts increases. Except for the overly optimistic candidate, there is a point well before the completion of an exhaustive market search where the expected net yields from continued searching cannot be justified in light of the anticipated costs of the search.

The same marginal principle explains why some methods of hunting jobs are used more frequently than others and why some methods are used before others. At each point in the job hunt and for each alternative method of hunting jobs, it is wise to stop and ask: "Do the expected gains from a further search exceed the anticipated costs?" For example, "How do the marginal utilities and disutilities compare if I try to learn about other job openings by writing my friends? . . . by informing my former thesis adviser of my availability? . . . by listing with a commercial employment agency?" If a net gain is expected by any method, the search should be continued. If the expected net gains are positive for several alternative methods, the method which is expected to yield the greatest net gain should be pursued. High yield-low cost methods will, therefore, be the first used.

It is interesting to speculate about the yields and costs of various methods. Although exact computations of yields are not possible, approximations are offered by Table 5. Persons who switched jobs would have naturally picked the job that appeared to offer the highest satisfaction. Since a relatively high percentage of the jobs chosen were found through friends and acquaintances, we might infer that jobs that are located through friends and acquaintances tend to be better than average and, by similar logic, that job vacancies that are first learned about from commercial agencies, mass letters, and university placement offices tend to be worse than average. The quality of jobs located through graduate schools tends to fall in between the two poles.

As for costs, with the exception of the fee-charging employment agencies, both the time and money costs of the various

Table 5

Estimated Yields and Costs of Various Methods
of Job Hunting (Rank Ordering)

	Estimated Yield	Estimated Cost
Friends	1	4
Graduate School	2	2
Mass Letter	3	3
Formal Agencies & Want Ads	4	1

methods of learning about vacant positions appear to be about the same. In each instance, a letter is written. The burdens of corresponding with several friends, of submitting one's name to a commercial employment agency or the professional association, of issuing a standard letter and vita to a large number of chairmen, and of contacting one's graduate school are probably about equal. But the cost differentials arise because of differences in opportunity costs. For example, the opportunity cost of contacting one's graduate school is relatively high; a person cannot forever expect his graduate school to be on the alert for new job opportunities for him. If he asks his major professor to seek opportunities for him but does not seriously consider the opportunities uncovered, except the El Dorados, the major professor will eventually become discouraged and may very likely reduce his efforts to locate new positions. Similarly, the social disutility associated with the use of commercial employment agencies and professional journal want ads increases the costs of using these means of finding jobs. Though it is not explicit, the social disapproval associated with the use of these agencies must be considered as a cost in the calculus.

The above observations on yields and costs are summarized in Table 5, where four of the major methods of job hunting are ranked according to absolute yield and cost. The facts that many of the most attractive jobs are located through friends and professional acquaintances, that a short letter to a friend or a brief word inserted into a conversation at the annual meetings costs little time and money, and that personal contacts are the most acceptable means of communicating in the market mean that jobs are first pursued through friends. Usually, when a person has developed many friends, his friends respect him and his friends are likely to be aware of the "good" jobs, the contacting of friends is all that needs to be done. As a first step for persons without so many fortunately situated friends and as a second step for persons who found that their friends were unable to locate the desired job, job seekers are likely to contact their graduate schools. Because of their low cost, mass letters are often used in spite of the relatively low absolute yields. Formal employment agencies, the lowest yield-highest cost method of job seeking are used only by persons with very unattractive alternatives. For an individual to seek out a formal employment agency, the "b" in the equation on page 106 (which represents the expected satisfaction from the best known and available job alternatives) must be very low. Otherwise, the high "c" (disutility of looking) will exceed the difference between a relatively low "a" and "b."

A group for whom the "b" is relatively low is graduate students, especially graduate students without Ph.D.'s. Since graduate students do not have a current job to fall back upon if their searches by the more acceptable methods of friends and graduate schools should fail to turn up anything of interest, they may be expected to be more active in seeking their jobs than experienced men, to use mass letters and employment agencies more frequently, and to pursue jobs by a greater variety of methods. The interviews suggest that this is the case. Compared to experienced professors, graduate students used 50 per cent more channels to find jobs. Moreover, graduate students resorted to the low yield methods of mass letter writing and listing with an employment agency more frequently.

Before attempting any further hypotheses concerning the differential in job seeking activity among various groups of candidates, let us consider the rationale for candidate seeking by employers. For the extent to which an individual needs to seek a job is to some degree dependent upon how actively employers are seeking him.

The rationale is quite similar to the one developed in the paragraphs above. Letting a^* represent the expected productivity (units of teaching and researching services) of the "to be found candidate" named A^*, b^* represent the expected productivity of the "best known and available" candidate named B^*, and c^* the expected productivity lost (in time) and disutility experienced in the course of finding a candidate as good as or better than A^*, a hiring school will continue its search for new candidates as long as $(a^* - b^*) > c^*$. If the expected change in productivity realized by hiring A* rather than B* does not exceed the marginal costs of pursuing A* rather than B*, then as long as B* is of acceptable quality the hiring school should search no farther. If, on the other hand, B* is below the minimal standards acceptable to the hiring school or if A* is expected to be sufficiently better than B* to justify the costs of an extended search, then the hiring school can maximize productivity by continuing its search.

Almost all hirers stand to benefit by some searching for candidates, for a search will almost certainly increase the number of candidates to be considered and it is very likely that the candidates located by searching will be better than the candidates that are known before a search is pursued. As Reynolds has shown, in labor markets with monopsonistic wage rates, job availability is a major determinant of labor supply.[7] By advertising the availability of a position, employers of college faculty will almost certainly increase the number of applications that they receive. Moreover, there are many reasons to suspect that the applicants that have been sought by the employer are generally better than the applicants that have themselves initiated the contact. At any given time, a school can compile a list of persons who desire teaching jobs simply by opening its mail, by reading the mass letters sent by job seekers and the open letter sent by graduate schools. However, the quality of the candidates on a list compiled in this manner is typically quite low. For the best candidates do not have to seek their own jobs. The best men are sought after. By the schools that are willing and able to recruit actively, the more qualified professors are located and hired before their availability is generally known. Only the prospective professors that have been located and rejected by the active recruiters find a need to make their availability known to the hirers who do not recruit. Self-seeking job hunters are the residue. Hirers stand to gain by recruiting.

The extent of recruitment is determined by the point at which the marginal loss due to the time and money expended in the

7. Reynolds, *The Structure of Labor Markets*, pp. 210-11.

search exceeds the marginal gain resulting from the man who might be found and willing to come at the same price.

Though the formula is simple enough, the application of the formula is complicated immensely by the immeasurability of productivity. Indexes such as course load and student load are woefully inadequate in that they fail to account for the administrative and research duties of college professors; on the other hand, more precise measures either require unrealistically meticulous diary-keeping or are pragmatically inoperative. Moreover, there is some question as to whether units of "students taught" and "research completed" are the true quantities that university administrators desire to maximize. Caplow and McGee suggest, for instance, that prestige in the eyes of their fellow educators is more important. The present author can do little more than raise the controversy. The theory developed here may be used with any quantifiable measure of productivity.

Whatever the productivity measure, guided by the principle that the expected marginal cost of recruitment should at no time exceed the expected marginal revenue, certain hypotheses can be formulated relating to the extent of recruitment of various types of faculty. When hiring in disciplines and at academic ranks where the candidates are advertising either their competence through publications or their availability through direct and indirect expressions of availability, we would expect that hirers would not need to put a great effort into recruiting. If a relatively large number or a relatively high percentage of the qualified, available candidates are easily identified, further recruitment cannot be expected to yield A* candidates who are much better than B* candidates. When the sample of candidates is large, the probability of an inordinately poor sample is small. Thus, we would expect departments to exert a relatively small amount of effort to compile a list of candidates to fill positions in disciplines where excess supply is relatively large, and correspondingly greater efforts in disciplines where candidates are scarce. Similarly, we would expect that at ranks where expected productivities are relatively more difficult to calculate (i.e., the lower ranks where prestige value of the persons has not as yet been determined), the effort exerted in recruitment would be less. Also, we would expect departments to search for new candidates first via the relatively inexpensive methods of contacting friends and graduate departments, and only in desperate situations by the professionally shameful and typically unproductive journal want ads and employment agencies.

Although the sample of responses from department chairmen is too small to establish any of the conclusions with statistical significance, the data suggest that each of these hypotheses might be confirmed by a larger sample. Graduate students, who are typically on the market in large numbers, were sought by relatively few, inexpensive methods. The efforts exerted when making appointments at the instructor level were minimal. Departments that had a large faculty, and therefore many informal contacts and a relatively large number of applicants, tended to exert less effort in recruitment than did the smaller, more isolated departments. More methods and more expensive methods were used to seek out associate professors than either assistant or full professors.[8] To locate qualified candidates in disciplines and sub-disciplines where there was a strong excess demand, hiring departments exerted extraordinary efforts. The high cost methods of working through formal employment agencies and professional journal want ads were used mostly by several sociology departments with dire supply problems.

The vigor of departments and candidates is complementary; where departments are active, candidates are not, and vice versa. When seeking to fill a position for which many candidates qualify (e.g., an assistant professor to teach modern civilization), without effort a department may compile an unmanageably long list of names. Solicitation of more names will stop long before the department has gained an exhaustive knowledge of all persons available. The sheer size of the supply available precludes the feasibility of a complete canvass of the market. Especially at the lower ranks where appointments are without tenure, the

8. Wilson, *The Academic Man*, p. 50. Wilson also notes that the associate professor is the least advertised of all ranks.

increase in net productivity likely to be derived from an extended search is not worth the cost. But the individual sees the situation from a quite different view. Whereas the department is large enough that it can carry a weak teacher for a year or two without damage, the acceptance of a job at an "undesirable" school may stunt an individual's career for many years. The individual candidate thus has an interest in pursuing job opportunities on his own to the point, as pointed out previously, where the expected marginal gains begin to be offset by the anticipated marginal costs.[9]

It is precisely in the areas where the hiring departments fail to make an exhaustive survey that job seeking individuals are likely to make their largest net gains. If an individual is one of ten specialists in Western Russian Agriculture, he may be relatively confident that he will be considered for any and all positions requiring such talent. But if the man is one among many persons available to teach Western Civilization, it is very likely that a particular school will not have considered his name seriously. There are simply too many others to consider. In such a case, it is in the individual's interest to make the hiring department aware of his availability and to make sure that the hiring department at least considers his name. The larger and more complex the market, the less likely a school is to consider a given name, and the more an individual has to gain by making his availability known.

By this rationale we would expect the job hunting activity by candidates to be greatest where employers are least active. The data collected from the 103 interviews with individuals suggest, but do not necessarily confirm, that our expectations are

9. The results of a survey of job seeking activity by Jerry L. L. Miller fit well into such an hypothesis. He observes (pp. 45 and 51) that in the physical sciences jobs are usually found by graduate students through their department chairmen; in the social sciences through some other member of the faculty at their graduate school (e.g., their thesis adviser); and that the mass letters are used mostly by students in the humanities. Notice that as jobs become harder and harder to find (the seller's market is strongest in the physical sciences and weakest in the humanities), the burden of job finding must be spread out over more and more people.

Table 6

Mean Number of Methods Used to Locate
"Positions Available" by Department, Experience, and Productivity

Group	Number of Methods Used[1]
Historians	1.31
Economists	1.06
Sociologists	1.06
Inexperienced Professors (no previous full-time college teaching)	1.46
Experienced Professors	1.09
Productive Professors[2]	.91
Unproductive Professors[2]	1.26

1. Hypotheses of no difference among departments, between experience levels, and between productivity levels could not be rejected by Kolmogrov-Smirnov one-tailed tests at 90 per cent confidence.
2. Professors were dichotomized into "productive" and "unproductive" according to the extent of their publications. For details, see Appendix E.
Source: Individual Interviews

correct. As expected, candidates seeking jobs in the relatively large markets for historians and in the markets for inexperienced faculty tended to use more, different methods to find new jobs. And candidates with unimpressive publication records (reflected by the productivity index), who would tend to be passed over without notice, sought new jobs by more methods than their more productive colleagues. But the differences between each of these groups and the relevant counterpart groups were not (by the Kolmogrov-Smirnov one-tailed test at a 10 per cent level of significance) statistically significant. From this we must infer that if there are significant differences in the levels of job seeking activity of individuals, these differences are reflected through the intensity with which jobs are sought via a given number of methods rather than through the use of a greater number of methods. For example, greater effort in job seeking is manifested by contacting *more* friends with greater regularity rather than by attempting to locate additional "positions available" by pursuing more methods such as listing with a commercial employment agency.

Formal Clearing Agencies

Let us pause here to consider in more detail the role of the formal employment agencies. Communications in academic labor markets are highly dependent upon individuals, institutions, and agencies acting as clearinghouses by formally and informally collecting information on "positions available" and passing the information on to the available candidates, and vice versa. Informal clearinghouses—friends, thesis advisers, and graduate department chairmen—are the cornerstones of the communication system. There is, however, a large segment of the market that has not been adequately served by these informal methods. In response to the need, a number of more formal clearinghouse arrangements have developed. University placement offices at colleges and universities with graduate schools have extended their services to students seeking positions in college teaching. Some commercial employment agencies are now placing college teachers; a few agencies (e.g., The American College Bureau) deal exclusively in college teachers.

In addition to the placement offices and commercial agencies, according to the *National Directory of Employment Services* (Detroit: Gale Research Co., 1962) more than one hundred disciplinary professional societies from the American Academy of Criminalistics (college professors in police science) to the National Association of Business Economists are now maintaining job clearinghouses for the convenience of their members. The American Sociological Association, for example, distributes to all its members a relatively well-accepted, bi-monthly *Employment Bulletin* which lists, in want ad style, positions available and positions wanted in the profession, such as:

V-608. New position in 3-man department of sociology and anthropology; Ph.D. with experience required; East North Central, growing state college; salary: around $8,000 for nine months, summer additional when available; September 1963. To avoid duplication with present staff specializations, please state specific areas of training.

A-M885. Multidisciplinary research, teaching, and/or administration; Sociology of American West, community, gerontology; Ph.D.;

PBK, Ford Fellowship, research grants; fourteen years teaching, research, administration, over thirty-five publications; North Central prefer California or Southwest; forty-three, married; available ninety days notice.[10]

Anyone interested in job V-608 and candidate A-M885 acknowledges interest by writing to the box number in New York City. The letter is then forwarded to the appropriate person. If the person who receives the expression of interest desires, he may reply to the letter or simply ignore it. For this service, institutions may list free and candidates who list are charged $1.00.

Other, non-disciplinary, professional societies such as the American Association of University Professors, Phi Beta Kappa, and the American Association of Emeriti, also provide some clearinghouse services. The AAUP, for instance, runs want ads in its quarterly journal. College professors seeking jobs in other countries can now check with organizations such as the Near East College Association and the Parisian based Institute of American Universities. Emigrant teachers can consult with the Masaryk Institute and the American Council for Emigres in the Professions as a start. Most religious sects, as well as several ecumenical councils, have appointed a person to make candidates aware of opportunities within their denominational colleges and to make the colleges aware of the candidates.

The U.S. Employment Service aids many professional associations by staffing *ad hoc* clearing agencies at annual conventions. In most of the disciplines where such convention clearing agencies (called slave markets) have been established, the agencies are a far more important factor in the market than the journal listings.

In spite of the large number of agencies, only a small percentage of the movement in academic labor markets is associated with these formal agencies. Too many recruiting schools and job seeking candidates have found that the quality of service provided is not commensurate with the costs. Like employment agencies which operate in the labor markets for blue collar

10. "Employment Bulletin," *Supplement to the American Sociological Review*, XXVIII, 4 (August, 1963), 1 and 5.

workers,[11] professional worker formal employment services have not been handling the more qualified candidates and the better jobs. Only the residue reaches the agencies. In markets where informal communications dominate and formal procedures are generally regarded as "unprofessional," only the jobs and candidates that have been studied when advertised informally and have found no takers are listed with the agencies and in the journals. Just as it is unethical for a dentist or doctor to advertise his services, it is not respectable for professors, the members of another profession, to advertise. Professors are expected to be inconspicuous in making their availability known. "There is a tendency in most fields for only the weakest candidates to use the services of a placement agency," note Caplow and McGee in *The Academic Marketplace*.[12] A similar conclusion was reached by Kenneth Browne in his 1942 study of Presbyterian colleges when he states that notices of candidates in education journals are "only occasionally or never used."[13] Logan Wilson observed that although formal placement services list many jobs, the lists include only unattractive jobs in the isolated and unknown colleges of Siberia.[14] Explaining this phenomenon, Kotschnig wrote, "Many professional workers who believe in professional organization are afraid of becoming stigmatized as people of inferior worth, unable to make their way without outside help. . . . This conflict leaves it indeed to the weaker members of the profession to apply for work through an agency. The vicious circle is completed by the employer then preferring to fill whatever vacancy he has to offer without resorting to the agency."[15] Millet refers to teachers' agencies as "A final recourse for the aspirant to a teaching appointment."[16] There is little doubt that the quality of

11. See, e.g., Reynolds, *The Structure of Labor Markets*, pp. 55-73, 269-74, for an evaluation of the role of employment agencies in blue collar labor markets.
12. Caplow and McGee, *The Academic Marketplace*, p. 120.
13. Kenneth Browne, *The Selection of Faculty Members for Church-Related Colleges* (Philadelphia: Kenneth Alton Brown, 1942), p. 84.
14. Wilson, *The Academic Man*, p. 50.
15. Walter M. Kotschnig, *Unemployment in the Learned Professions* (London: Oxford University Press, 1937), pp. 257-58.
16. Fred B. Millet, *Professor: Problems and Rewards of College Teaching* (New York: The Macmillan Company, 1961), p. 88.

the candidates and colleges that are currently making use of formal employment agencies is, by traditional professional standards, well below average. In terms of the model developed in the previous section, the A^*'s (best expected "to be found candidate") located through formal employment agencies are mediocre at best. Only schools and candidates whose B^*'s and B's (i.e., next best alternatives) are even poorer will consider listing their needs with a formal agency. In short, low yields discourage use of this means of locating jobs.

Although most are reluctant to work through formal clearinghouses because of the poor quality of products available, some are discouraged by the high costs. For an individual, listing involves several different types of costs. First, if a job is found through a commercial teachers' agency, he may be asked to assign up to 10 per cent of his first year's salary or if availability is advertised through a want ad the individual must pay for the ad. Second, time is involved. Listing may invite a barrage of inquiries from large numbers of inferior employers who have been forced to resort to the formal channels of communication. Much time must be spent expressing polite "appreciation for your interest" and declining. Third, as mentioned above, use of formal channels of communication is stigmatized. An individual who resorts to these channels must count as a cost the loss of self-esteem and the esteem of others resulting from the admission that he must revert to these means of finding a job.

For the school, time and prestige are the major costs. A department that lists an opening obligates itself to an endless stream of correspondence, an inhuman schedule of interviews, and an almost unmanageable responsibility for rejecting candidates without insult. One of the Southeastern department chairmen interviewed reminisced with us about the year that he listed an opening in the "slave market" at the convention. According to his report, the phone was ringing when he first placed his key in the door of his hotel room and it never stopped until the morning after the three-day convention was over. His interview schedule was so tight that he had to have all his meals sent up to his room. He was not only unable to listen to any of the papers delivered but also found that his heavy interviewing schedule did not allow time for attending cocktail parties and gossiping with friends in the lobby. After it all was over, he had talked with nearly seventy-five prospects. The position was eventually filled by a man who was not at the convention.

Use of formal clearinghouses also costs a department dearly in terms of the prestige lost. To advertise publicly a vacancy is to admit defeat publicly. With the possible exception of university placement bureaus, resort to the formal clearinghouses to find candidates is generally considered as a conspicuous expression of either the inadequacy of the department as a place to work or the incompetency of the department as a recruiter of personnel. Members of the profession are likely to take note and to be, in the future, more reluctant to refer promising candidates to the advertising school. In this sense, advertising is self-defeating. In order to preserve anonymity, most of the "positions available" listed in the pages of professional journals are blind. Interested candidates respond to a box number rather than the school. But listings in the slave markets, with teachers' agencies, and with university placement offices are conspicuous.

As Caplow and McGee note, "The function of placement bureaus in the recruiting process of major universities can be summarized by saying that prestige is attached to the non-use of their services."[17] Many of the comments from the department chairmen interviewed for the present study indicate similar attitudes. For example:

We never use the AEA [American Economic Association] employment service. The AEA service is helpful to me. I know who *not* to look at by noting who is moving through the market by this means.

This is a second quality market. The best graduate students never use it. First rate institutions aren't going to list openings here. There is an onus on the association employment bureau now.

It's unsafe to use commercial placement bureaus. Only the dregs of the market are listed with such agencies. I'd rather cut out courses

17. Caplow and McGee, *The Academic Marketplace*, p. 120.

than take a chance with these people. Almost all of them have a record of some maladjustment in the past.

To use the bureaus is to sacrifice prestige.

Despite the high costs associated with their use and the poor candidates and positions moving through formal clearinghouses, these houses provide a vital and much needed service to some schools, a service for which they have received very little recognition in the literature which concentrates upon evaluating their usefulness in terms of the needs of the more prestigious institutions. The informal channels of communication work efficiently to move information on jobs and candidates among the major universities, the top twenty-five schools. And the informal channels appear to provide a relatively free flow of information among the major universities and the smaller schools. For instance, if the dean at a small denominational college is seeking to locate a man who is willing to interrupt his graduate studies and accept an appointment at the instructor or perhaps assistant professor level, he can write to his friends at the major graduate schools and normally locate the man he needs. Where the informal channels do not suffice is among the smaller, non-major institutions. Men currently teaching at one non-major college are generally ignorant of positions available at other non-major colleges, and the recruiting schools are similarly unaware of the available candidates.

The non-major colleges are the institutions that have the most to gain and the least to lose by using formal methods of candidate-hunting. Without the large staffs with the many contacts that the larger, major universities have, without the financial resources of the larger schools, without the many unsolicited inquiries about available positions that naturally come to the departments in the better known institutions, the smaller schools have a real supply problem. Their horizons are narrow. Known candidates are few. The best of the two or three known and available candidates (B^*) is, by simple laws of probability, not likely to be as good as the best of the ten or twelve candidates which a larger school can select. B_1^*, the best candidate known by the larger school, is likely to be better than B^*, the best candidate known by the smaller school. Assuming that the best candidate referred by a formal clearinghouse to both the larger and the smaller school is the same (A^*) and that the costs of using the employment agency (c^* and c_1^*) are the same, it is more likely that $(a^* - b^*) > c^*$ than $(a^* - b_1^*) > c_1^*$ because $(a^* - b^*)$ is greater than $(a^* - b_1^*)$. In other words, by making use of formal clearinghouses, the smaller school is more likely to improve upon the quality of candidates available, for it had fewer qualified candidates to select in the first place. Yet this is not the only reason to expect formal clearinghouses to be more useful to smaller schools. The assumption that c^* and c_1^* are the same is unrealistic.

The loss of prestige associated with the use of formal employment agencies is probably the greatest single cost to the hiring schools. For the better schools that are dedicated to researching and writing, to maintaining their prestige ratings in the eyes of the best known scholars, and to attracting the very best students, the use of formal methods of finding faculty would be an admission of defeat and, therefore, would result in serious prestige losses. But for the smaller schools that by emphasizing teaching rather than research have already lost the "respect" of the scholars, that admit to financial difficulties, that are interested in attracting good but not necessarily the very best students, the stigma attached to the use of formal clearinghouses is not so harmful. For the school that starts from a relatively lower point on the prestige scale, the prestige costs of using formal methods of employee-seeking are lower; c^* is less than c_1^*. This, of course, emphasizes the positive difference between $(a^* - b^*) - c^*$ and $(a^* - b_1^*) - c_1^*$. Smaller universities and colleges are more likely to make use of the formal clearinghouses both because they have more to gain and because they have less to lose.

The small amount of empirical information available suggests that prevailing practices are consistent with the above reasoning. Stecklein and Lathrop, in their extensive study of the University of Minnesota, note that at the less prestigious Duluth campus nearly one-third of the appointees had found their jobs via a professional agency whereas at the Twin Cities campus, the main campus of one of our top twenty-five universities, less than one-twentieth of the appointees had found their jobs in this manner.[18] In general, individuals whose experience is with the smaller, less prestigious schools show far less disdain for the formal clearinghouses than scholars such as Caplow and McGee and Wilson who are most familiar with the major institutions.[19] Observers of the labor markets for engineers and technicians and for clerical workers have noted that the smaller employers who cannot afford to hire their own staffs use the formal employment agencies more than the larger employers, even though the larger employers employ more people.[20] All of the previous studies with which this author is familiar tend to confirm that the smaller, less prestigious departments are the ones that turn to formal candidate-locating facilities in time of need.

Further confirmation is offered by the present study. When the fifty Southeastern department chairmen were asked "How did you go about locating names of persons who might be qualified to fill your vacant position?" eleven of them indicated that they had used some type of formal service such as a university placement office, a commercial teachers' agency, or the want ads in professional journals. As shown in Table 7, almost all of these chairmen were from small departments located in the less prestigious schools. None of the chairmen from the larger departments (eleven or more full-time staff members) had found it necessary to use formal methods to locate personnel whereas nearly half of the chairmen from the smaller departments (ten or fewer full-time staff members) had felt such a need. A dichotomization by the quality or prestige points up the fact that only two out of the twenty-six department chairmen in the more prestigious schools (and one of these was captaining an extremely weak sociology department) had used formal clearing-

18. Stecklein and Lathrop, *Faculty Attraction and Retention*, p. 15.

19. See, for example, "The Selection of Faculty Members" in John Dale Russell (ed.), *Problems of Faculty Personnel* ("Proceedings of the Institute for Administrative Officers of Higher Institutions," Vol. 26 [Chicago: University of Chicago Press, 1946]), p. 18.

20. See, for example, Henry C. Thole, *Shortage of Skilled Manpower: Implications for Kalamazoo Businessmen* (Kalamazoo, Mich.: W. E. Upjohn Institute for Community Research, 1958), pp. 22-26.

Table 7

Use of Formal Methods of Locating Candidates by
Department Chairmen—By Department Size and School Quality

	Number of Department Chairmen:		
	(1) Used Formal Method(s) of Locating Candidate	(2) Did Not Use Formal Methods	(3) Percentage Who Used Formal Method
Larger Departments (staff of 11 or more)*	0	26	0%
Smaller Departments (staff of 10 or less)*	11	13	46%
Higher Prestige Schools*	2	24	8%
Lower Prestige Schools*	9	15	37%

* Hypothesis of no difference was rejected by Fisher exact probability test at 95 per cent confidence.
Source: Chairmen Interviews

houses, whereas more than one-third of the heads of department at less prestigious schools had done so. Because of the low quality of the candidates listed by formal means, the adequacy of informal means of communication, and the requisite sharp drop in prestige rating, the chairmen recruiting for the larger departments in the more prestigious schools condemn the formal clearinghouses as unnecessary and useless. Facing the reality that they must be satisfied with less than the very best quality candidates, recognizing that the quantity of candidates that can be located by informal methods is not sufficient, and realizing that the professional hex placed upon the use of formal methods will not do further damage to their prestige rating, the department chairmen in the smaller departments at the less prestigious schools not only fail to condemn but also actually make use of the more structured methods of communicating demands and supplies. University placement offices, want ads in journals, slave markets, and even commercial teachers' agencies play a constructive role in academic labor markets. That over 1,500 different organizations are now providing such services to this or that group of professors is itself a strong indication of the need. The accepted, informal methods of job and candidate hunting that are efficiently allocating personnel among the major universities are not now, and probably will not be in the future, functioning effectively in the hinterlands. The formal methods must not be shunned just because the major colleges and universities do not need them. There is a need. There is a strong need for not only the preservation but also the development and improvement of the techniques currently in use, the formal as well as the informal.

The case for further development of the formal modes of communication is a strong one. In addition to the fact that it is infeasible for the informal channels to withstand the overload of moving all professional workers between jobs, there are many advantages of handling mobility through professional societies and other centralized clearinghouses. First, the anonymity of centralized employment services has its advantages. If a school is not interested in a candidate who responds to a "blind" ad (school not identified specifically), no hard-to-write and time consuming letters are necessary. The school never needs to identify itself. Similarly, candidates do not need to spend their time writing to schools in which they are not interested. Second, by increasing the number of candidates and jobs that any individual school or person has to select from, formal services strengthen the probability that a really desired job or desirable candidate is among those considered. More exhaustive market searches are enabled. Third, the use of formal clearinghouses enables a department to minimize nepotistic themes. In the current market where personal friendships are the only accepted means of communicating, a recruiter's horizons are limited to those of his friends. Small school recruiters, whose relatively few friends are concentrated in a few schools, cannot easily extend their recruitment beyond these limited contacts. As a result, many departments (as cited above) become top heavy with Ph.D.'s from a given university or group of universities. Finally, centralized clearinghouses minimize the required reserves of unemployed. In every market, academic labor markets much less so than in many, there exists a group of marginally employable persons who are usually without jobs but may be called upon in an emergency. Every market must have such a labor reserve in order to insure continuity of production. If there are many small employing units (e.g., many departments), each with a given probability that it will need "emergency personnel," each employing unit must maintain its own reserve. But if the reserves are pooled, the number of persons in the reserve can be lessened without lessening the adequacy of the reserve; for it is very improbable that all of the pooled employers will demand maximum work forces during the same period. The maintenance of such a centralized pool requires a centralized clearinghouse.

Some disciplines, such as French and sociology, have already developed centralized clearinghouses which have gained at least limited acceptance. Some graduate schools, such as Columbia[21] and Wisconsin, have well-developed programs for the placement and relocation of their graduates. If the highly decentralized system of American higher education is to meet adequately the challenge of increasing enrollments, efforts such as these must be furthered, and other disciplines and graduate schools must be encouraged to find new ways of maximizing the allocation of professional labor, especially among the smaller and less prestigious schools.[22]

Defining the Labor Market

Now that we have a better understanding of the types of job seeking and candidate seeking activity that exist in the academic labor market, let us return to a question posed at the beginning of the chapter, "What is an academic labor market?" Is there a

21. Harrison Hoblitzelle, "Teacher Placement: A New Frontier," *Graduate Faculties Newsletter, Columbia University* (December, 1962), pp. 4-5.

22. The nature and role of institutional intermediaries will be revealed by a nationwide study of newly appointed college teachers in 78 disciplines and in 2,000 different colleges, universities, and junior colleges. This study, which is being conducted by the Department of Economics at the University of North Carolina at Chapel Hill under the direction of the author, is sponsored by the Office of Manpower, Automation, and Training of the U.S. Department of Labor and is to be completed by September, 1965.

single, or are there many, academic labor markets? If there are many, how is one market delineated from another?

In blue collar worker labor markets experts agree that the "most important boundaries between labor markets run along geographical lines" and therefore define a labor market area as that geographic space that has a centrally located cluster of industry or other source of employment and that forms a community in the sense that a great majority of the people who are in the labor force maintain both their places of employment and their places of residence in the area.[23] But geographically defined labor markets make little sense for professional workers. The labor market for professors is not limited by commuting times and common residences, for geographic mobility is characteristic of most professionals. Few professors are willing to restrict their horizons to institutions within commuting distance. It is rare for a professor to change jobs and not change residences. A study of the faculty joining the staff at the University of Minnesota between 1956 and 1958 indicates that over half of the new professors were drawn not only from other cities and other states, but also from other regions. Twenty per cent came from institutions in the West, 12 per cent from the South, 18 per cent from the East, 4 per cent from other countries, and only 45 per cent from other midwestern institutions.[24] The statement made by Anantaraman, based on his nationwide survey of 280 prominent economists (71 per cent of whom had moved across regional boundaries at some point in their careers), that "the market for economists is truly national in scope . . ."[25] appears to be applicable to all groups of professors. Academic labor markets are truly national in scope.

Our interviews with department chairmen emphasize the geographic breadth of the market. The candidates considered for jobs in the Southeast were drawn from all quarters. In 62 per cent of the hiring situations discussed in detail with the chairmen,

23. Leonard P. Adams and Thomas W. Mackesey, *Commuting Patterns* (Housing Research Center Publication No. 1; Ithaca, N. Y.: Cornell University, 1955), especially pp. 40-42.

24. Stecklein and Lathrop, *Faculty Attraction and Retention*, p. 97.

25. Anantaraman, *Mobility of Professional Economists*, p. 30.

Table 8

Regional Distribution of Men
Considered and Hired (N = 50)

Geographic Areas	At least one of the men considered was located in	Man Hired: was previously located in	Man Hired: received last degree from school in
Same state	12%	8%	2%
Southeast (but not same state)	60%	38%	32%
Middle West	62%	32%	20%
Southwest and Far West	58%	14%	12%
Northeast and Middle Atlantic	48%	4%	4%
No Information	—	4%	30%

Source: Chairmen Interviews

one of the candidates seriously considered was presently located in the Midwest. Comparable percentages for other regions of the country are 48 per cent in the Northeast and Middle Atlantic, 32 per cent in the Far West, 16 per cent in the Southwest, and 60 per cent in the Southeast. In only 12 per cent of the cases was even one candidate located within the state. Of the men actually hired a majority came from outside the South; only 8 per cent came from within the same state. These figures are summarized in Table 8.

Because professors are not willing to change teaching specialties and because there are relatively few job opportunities in college teaching within most geographic areas, labor markets are balkanized by teaching specialties, not by geography. Separate labor markets exist for physicists, for economists, for historians; not for Southeastern professors, Midwestern professors, and Far Western professors. A faculty member is first a member of his profession and second a college professor, not vice versa. Professors trained in different disciplines are poor substitutes for one another. A sociologist is qualified to teach sociology, and sociology alone; not chemistry or English or education. For each different type of service there is a separate market. Since the academic labor market is so heavily balkanized into fine sub-markets by discipline, the number of persons who would be willing and able to teach at any given institution without changing residence is quite small. Supply is limited and inelastic.[26] Consider, for example, the following extreme situation.

If the four thousand Ph.D. sociologists were evenly distributed throughout the U.S., each sociologist would be, on the average, about ninety miles away from his nearest colleague. Of course, the assumption of even distribution is highly inaccurate, for Ph.D.'s cluster near universities and colleges which are themselves clustered. As unrealistic as this example is, however, it does serve to highlight the very small supply of labor available to a hiring school if it restricts its horizons to the "local" labor market. When choice in the "local" labor market is so limited, the hiring institution can usually make substantial improvements in quality by extending itself to other geographic areas. In terms of the model developed earlier in the chapter, if the best of the locally available personnel (B^*) yields b^* productivity, there is a high probability that a^*, the productivity of A^* who is "to be found" in another local labor market, will be considerably higher; therefore, the ($a^* - b^*$) is large enough to justify a fairly high c^*.

Every employer can overcome a shortage of specialized labor in one of two ways: spend more money in recruiting efforts (e.g., search in other local labor markets, agree to pay transportation costs of workers between markets, offer higher inducements to workers) or hire worker X without the specialized qualifications and train him in the specialty. For many semi-skilled jobs the latter is a feasible option. But for academic jobs, because of the long gestation periods required, the special capacities needed, and the great responsibilities given to even beginning teachers except at the large graduate institutions, in-service training is too costly. The costs of training are so high that most institutions have found that it is less expensive to recruit in other local labor markets, even if transportation costs and inducement-to-move increments must be paid. As the skill requirements for the vacant job increase, the costs of training a person to fill the job also increase, and importing the skill from other localities becomes more and

26. Caplow and McGee, *The Academic Marketplace*, p. 168.

more attractive.[27] In short, the high yields to be achieved by importing and the high costs of developing adequate substitutes from locally available supply cause employers to cross geographic boundaries more frequently than occupational ones in order to overcome the inherent problems of small supply in the highly balkanized labor markets. Academic labor markets are, therefore, national in scope.

Having documented and rationalized the breadth of geographic boundaries in academic labor markets, qualifications are in order. The outer boundaries of the markets are national. Within the national market, however, there are many regional sub-markets, usually represented by regional professional associations (e.g., the Southern Sociological Society). Insofar as they can be identified at all, the national markets are loose confederations of regional sub-markets. Although almost all schools find that they must go beyond their local labor markets to locate personnel qualified to fill faculty posts, it is neither always necessary nor desirable to conduct a search on a nationwide scale. Extensive nationwide talent hunts are expensive. In some cases, schools cannot justify the marginal cost of extending the hunt beyond a given geographic area. At any time, a hiring school knows of a B^* (the best available and known candidate for a given job) and a series of A^*'s. That is, it has a series of expectations of the types of faculty it could find if it extended the hunt to various sub-markets; for example, A_1^* if the hunt were restricted to the state; A_2^* for the Southeastern region; A_3^* for the Southeastern region and the Midwest; A_4^* for the Southeastern region, the Midwest and the Northeast; and so forth. There also exists a set of disutilities associated with hunts of various magnitudes: c_0^* is associated with finding B^*, c_1^* with A_1^* and so forth. Normally, both the a_i^*'s and c_i^*'s increase as the search is extended: a more extensive search will turn up a

27. F. Theodore Malm, "Recruiting Patterns and the Functioning of Labor Markets," *Industrial and Labor Relations Review* (July, 1954), pp. 515-17, notes that the geographic area of recruitment tends to expand as labor requirements become more specialized. The results of his California survey indicate that employers recruit manual, clerical, and sales workers locally whereas managerial and professional workers are recruited nationally in about 20 per cent of the cases.

better candidate and will cost more. The geographic extent of the search is determined by the "i" that causes $(a_i{}^* - b^*) - c_i{}^*$ to be maximized. A higher "i" indicates a more extensive search. If, for example, there is no $A_i{}^*$ for which $(a_i{}^* - b^*) - c_i{}^*$ is positive, then it is clearly in the best interests of the hiring school to hire B^*, as long as he meets the school's minimal qualifications. A search will be conducted if, and only if, the expected greater productivity offered by the "to be found candidate" is greater than the expected cost of finding him. If $a_{i+1}{}^* - a_i{}^*)$ exceeds $(c_{i+1}{}^* - c_i{}^*)$ then the search will be extended.

To ask under what circumstances limited and national talent hunts are likely to occur is the same as asking under what circumstances might we expect the $a_i{}^*$'s to be increasing more rapidly than the $c_i{}^*$'s, in absolute terms. If a school has been able to consider a large number of candidates, it is less likely to change a^* significantly than if only a few candidates have been considered. For example, we would expect that a school hiring graduate students, a relatively large group, would not extend its searches as far as a school looking for a full professor in some obscure speciality in sociology. The colleges that are less interested in specific specialities and more tolerant of faculty without Ph.D. certification will find a larger supply in a given region and may, therefore, be expected to revert to the national market less often. On the other hand, the large graduate institutions that are seeking professional prestige and hiring professors to teach future professors must view a given supply more selectively and are more likely to need to view the supplies of faculty in other regions in order to attain a sample of the desired size. Also the larger schools and departments with more contacts everywhere, including other regions, find national recruiting less expensive and more fruitful than the small schools without the contacts.

In order to test the validity of these a priori expectations, our fifty department chairmen were asked "Where were these candidates [that you considered for the job] from?" The country was divided into five sections: Southeast, Southwest, Midwest, Northeast, and Far West. If the chairmen indicated that they had considered a man from the region, it was assumed that recruiting had been done in that region and if the department chairmen had not considered a man from a region, it was assumed that there had been no recruiting in that region. Each time a department chairman mentioned one or more candidates from a given region, that region was awarded a point. Thus, if a chairman said that the department had considered two men from the Southeast, four from the Midwest, and one from the Far West, each of the three regions was awarded one point to indicate that recruiting had taken place in the region. Compilation of the fifty interviews indicates that 109 points were awarded in all, or that on the average each department had recruited in slightly over two regions of the country. As expected, the extent to which departments recruited in regions outside the Southeast varied according to their needs and abilities.

Table 9 indicates these differences. Second and third quality schools were far more provincial in their recruitment than the schools in the top quality class. Eighty-five per cent of the points awarded to top quality schools were for recruiting outside of the Southeastern region, whereas the comparable percentage for the poorer schools was sixty-five. Similarly, the smaller departments

Table 9

Location of Recruiting Activity for Selected Groups

Group	Percentage Recruitment Done in the Southeast
{ By six best[1] schools in sample[2]	15%
{ By twelve other schools in sample[2]	35%
{ Graduate student hired[2]	32%
{ Non-graduate student hired[2]	23%
{ By large (14+) departments	23%
{ By small (8—) departments	32%
{ By economists	32%
{ By sociologists	27%
{ By historians	25%

1. The method used for rating schools is explained in Appendix D.
2. Hypothesis of no difference was rejected with 95 per cent confidence by Chi Square.

Source: Chairmen Interviews

tended to restrict themselves to the Southeast more than the larger departments. Furthermore, schools were less likely to extend recruiting efforts outside the Southeast when filling a position for which graduate students qualified than when seeking a man with experience. Although the disciplinary differences in non-Southeast recruiting efforts proved to be statistically insignificant, the findings summarized in Table 9 tend to confirm our expectations.

These data and several unsolicited comments made by persons in the interview suggest that academic labor markets are balkanized more at the lower than the higher echelons. The markets for professors willing and able to teach in the top twenty-five schools in the country are truly national markets. Nationwide professional association meetings, intra-twenty-five faculty and graduate students' swaps,[28] exchanges in the journals, and joint appointments on nationwide committees keep the channels of communication open among the best known members of the professions. The horizons of the professors located at these twenty-five top schools are nationwide. They are, in a sense, in positions that allow them to look down upon the American higher educational system and see only the peaks. The colleges nearby are, to these talented few, the nearest sister institutions who also belong to the "exclusive twenty-five club." Both as recruiters and candidates, the professors at these institutions operate in a fairly efficient, national market. The market is not unmanageably large, for there are only twenty-four other schools "worth" keeping track of. Logan Wilson's observation about graduate students is generally applicable to faculty as well: "placement will not be in a university of higher repute than the one from which he [comes]."[29]

In contrast, both candidates and recruiters from the less well-known schools operate in a primarily regional market. For the recruiter from one of these lesser schools who does not have the financial backing that allows him to be particular, there are many

28. See Bernard Berelson, *Graduate Education in the United States* (New York: McGraw-Hill Book Company, Inc., 1960), p. 113.

29. Wilson, *The Academic Man*, p. 49.

candidates to select from within the region. To extend the hunt beyond the region would be to collect more names than could be handled and to increase the expense of recruitment unnecessarily. Moreover, such an extension would be relatively costly, in that the administrators from these less well-known schools do not circulate as widely and since there would be fewer mutual acquaintances, the evaluation of the persons suggested would be relatively more expensive and less reliable.   Similarly, the mediocre candidate can find all the opportunities that he has the time to evaluate *within* the region. To branch out into another region of the country is foolish when his "best opportunities [are] in an institution within the sphere of influence of his university or department."[30] It is uncommon for a man to move across regional lines when he changes from one poor or mediocre university to another. The national market is primarily a "top quality" market.

Summary

In determining what methods and how many methods to use to locate jobs (candidates), candidates (recruiters) are guided by the following principle: seek out new job opportunities (candidates) only if the new opportunities (candidates) are expected to be not only better than the opportunities (candidates) presently available but also enough better to justify the costs of the search. If the less costly and more effective methods of locating jobs (candidates) through friends and graduate school contacts fail to present promising leads, less personalized and usually less effective techniques such as mass letters and formal clearing houses must be considered. Whether or not these additional techniques will be pursued will depend upon how probable it is that a better job (candidate) will be found, how much better the job (candidate) is expected to be, and how unpleasant the process of finding the better job (candidate) is expected to be. For every candidate (recruiter) there is a point, usually well before an exhaustive study of the market has been made, beyond which the expected costs exceed expected benefits.

30. *Ibid.*

For the candidate, this point is likely to be reached sooner in markets where recruiters are more active. When the hiring university is both willing and able to make a rather complete survey of the labor market, a candidate who has done relatively little to advertise his availability will probably be located. The kinds of labor markets in which this happens are the ones where there are strong excess demands for labor (e.g., Slavic Historians), relatively few candidates qualified for the positions (e.g., a position at one of the "high" prestige universities), many well-financed recruiters (e.g., large departments recruiting for well-endowed schools), and clear and definite indexes of ability (e.g., full professors with long records of publication). In contrast, the markets unserved by the employer-dominated locating system are where candidates are plentiful, diverse, expensive to locate, and difficult to evaluate and where the recruiters are few, poverty-stricken, and uncommunicating. In markets such as the latter, the burden of bringing demand and supply together rests squarely with the candidates; candidates must make employers aware of their availability, for otherwise they are likely to go unnoticed in the sea of applicants.

The very small markets can be adequately served by employers seeking candidates. Slightly larger labor markets can, with some help from job-seeking candidates, also operate efficiently and effectively. The informal methods currently in vogue suffice. As the number of candidates and recruiters that must be serviced by the market increases and the market consequently becomes more and more complex, there is an increasing need for the development of a centralized clearinghouse, a place where the needs of candidates and recruiters can be matched. In the past, the relatively few institutions who were qualifying persons for teaching at the college level were able to provide such clearing services. In the future, however, when teachers are being qualified by hundreds of institutions, even more centralization would seem both desirable and necessary.

Job and candidate seeking in today's academic labor markets is a curious hodgepodge of mostly informal channels of communication. Due to promotion from within and nepotistic hiring practices, many jobs and candidates never reach the open market. Academic labor markets are in many ways similar to black markets, markets in which personal friendships, special contacts, and connections play a vital role. Neither the locus nor the boundaries of these markets can be defined with precision, though it is apparent that the balkanization of the markets is more occupational than geographic. Supply meets demand at almost any time and place, in almost any way.

VI

SCHOOLS EVALUATE PROFESSORS

After locating the candidates that might qualify, the hiring college faces the decision, "Which one is the fairest of them all?" To which candidate should an offer be extended? Selection requires evaluation. Evaluation, in turn, demands the gathering of facts and opinions about the candidates and the identifying of selective criteria. This chapter concentrates upon the information gathering-evaluating-selecting activity of employers.

Information Gathering

Information gathering is selective. Because the obtaining of reliable information on candidates is both difficult and time-consuming, most recruiters pursue a "gather-cut-gather-cut-gather . . ." pattern. To start, a small amount of information is gathered on all possible candidates, for example, educational backgrounds. On the basis of this scanty information, the least promising candidates are dropped. More information is collected on the remaining candidates, for example, recommendations. Based upon the recommendations, another cut is made. On the remaining candidates more information is collected, another cut is made, more information is collected, another cut is made, and so forth until the field is narrowed to one. The whole procedure stresses expediency. To avoid the burdensome task of collecting a great deal of information on many candidates, all but the two or three most promising candidates are dropped from consideration at a relatively early stage. Insofar as extensive information is gathered on any candidate, it is gathered only on a few of the most promising.[1]

Referrals and Vitae

In the early stages of evaluation, when many candidates are under consideration, the types of information that are utilized the most are the types that are the easiest to collect. Reliability is sacrificed for the sake of expediency.

Since one of the more obvious characteristics of a prospective candidate is how his availability became known to the hiring school, a first cut is often based upon the source of the referral. How was his name referred to the hiring school: by the recommendation of a respected scholar in the field? by a mass letter? by a journal want ad? If, for example, a candidate's availability has been advertised by formal means, many schools will investigate no farther. Reasoning that formal means of advertising are used only by the relatively poor candidates, the candidate will be cut immediately. Similarly, it is reasoned that the most prominent referrers suggest the most qualified candidates and cuts are made accordingly. By ranking the referrers, by eliminating the mass letter, by not reading the want ads, and by not soliciting suggestions from the less prestigious graduate schools, many candidates that were located or would have been located if these channels had been pursued are implicitly, if not explicitly, eliminated from consideration. The practice is justified on the probabilistic conviction that there is a relationship between the quality of candidates and the means by which their availability is advertised.

Another easily obtained indication of the relative merits of prospective candidates that is used in the early stages of the gather-cut-gather-cut process, when a large number of candidates

1. Note in Table 3 that departments that attempted to investigate thoroughly four or more candidates tended to do a less complete job than departments that limited their information searches to three or two candidates.

must be evaluated, is a man's vita. On a single page, a man's vita summarizes his personal characteristics, his educational background, his professional work experience, his closest professional acquaintances, his fields of interest, and his research productivity. If a hirer wishes to discriminate against women, or Negroes, or candidates over age forty-five, the list of possibly available and potentially acceptable candidates can be reduced without further investigation. By analyzing educational background, the department can gain an indication of the quality and character of the candidate's training. From the information on education and expressions of fields of interest, the hiring department can infer how well each candidate would fit the particular opening. The titles and places of publications offer a further clue to interests and suggest the quality and extent of the candidate's research work. The renown of the men that have agreed to write recommendations for him and the relationships of the recommenders to the candidate are indicative of what and how well a candidate has done in the past. By noting the schools where the candidate has taught in the past and the number of times he has switched jobs, a hirer can make a reasonable estimate of how long the candidate will remain at his school.

Vitae have their limitations. It is interesting to note that hirers only reject, they do not accept, candidates on the basis of their vitas. Department chairmen acknowledge that vitas can be deceptive. Though instances are rare, two chairmen cited cases in which a candidate had falsified the information contained on his vita; for example, one candidate had listed a Ph.D. degree that he had not received. More common than intentional deceit is unintentional deception. Candidates who appear to be superior on paper often, in the later stages of investigation, are revealed to be weak. One candidate's vita indicated that he had trained under some of the best and most respected men in his field. Upon investigation, the hiring department learned that the candidate had done very poorly under these men and that the respected men regarded the candidate as a poor risk. In another instance, a candidate listed a Ph.D. from a school that had a very respectable department of history. Only after further investigation did the hirer learn that the candidate had received his degree from the relatively weak School of Education, not the history department.

Indicative of the department chairmen's attitudes toward vitae is the observation that all of the chairmen who had located more than three candidates for their vacancy eliminated some of the least promising candidates on the basis of vita information, but only three chairmen regarded the vita as the "most important technique of investigation." From the candidate's viewpoint, impressive paper, though usually necessary, is not sufficient to get an offer.

Recommendations

For the candidates with the more promising vitae, recommendations are sought. Persons listed by the candidate on his vita are contacted first. Except in the rare instances where the candidate has misjudged his recommenders' opinions of him, these candidate-oriented letters of recommendation are filled with praise. Since all candidates have carefully chosen the people who they believe will place them in the most favorable light, the recommendations received from persons suggested by the candidates are often viewed with distrust. Many departments solicit the letters on the small chance that one of the recommenders will point out some of the shortcomings of his candidate; if all comments are favorable, the letters are disregarded. Some of the larger, more prestigious departments do not even contact candidate-oriented recommenders.

The great distrust with which candidate-oriented recommendations are viewed is well illustrated by excerpting some quotes from our interviews with department chairmen:

Only the most optimistic are asked to write recommendations.

Formal recommendations from previous employers are really not reliable. I know that when we want to get rid of a man we'll give him the highest recommendations to assure that someone else will take him.[2]

Recommendations from present employers can't be trusted, for when they want to move a man along many chairmen will give him the highest of recommendations. A case in point is a full professor, the ex-chairman of the economics department at his former school, who came to us with glowing recommendations but had no classroom ability at all. We let him go after one year.

I'll not volunteer negative information on a man unless the receiver of the recommendation is a personal friend of mine. It just doesn't pay to go out on limbs.

Some graduate school professors are willing to say almost anything to get job hunters out of their hair.

I wrote to [the man whom a candidate had listed as a recommender], who had been his graduate instructor. His recommendation was very high. I'll never forgive him. Though professionally competent, the man [the candidate] is personally obnoxious.

You can't depend much upon most recommendations. . . .

Hiring department chairmen recognize that authors of candidate-oriented recommendations are much more likely to hurt the inquiring department that they do not know than the aspiring candidate whom they do know. It is not that recommenders are not honest; they are simply not frank. When in doubt recommenders give the candidate the benefit.

Recognizing the unreliability of the recommenders suggested by the candidate, hiring departments usually investigate on their own. They search their own recommenders, employer-oriented recommenders. Although the hiring department is unlikely to know the specific recommenders listed by the candidate, in most cases mutual acquaintances can be identified. The academic world is a small one: many people are known to each other. Therefore, the hirers may know someone who has taught the candidate, who is teaching on the same faculty, who went to graduate school with the man, who has heard the man deliver

2. For a similar statement see Gordon C. Godbey, "On Reducing Faculty Losses," *Liberal Education*, XLVI, 4 (December, 1960), 452.

a paper at a convention, or who knows people who know the candidate. From these mutual acquaintances confidential and hopefully candid evaluations are solicited. These contacts are usually made by long distance phone or in person in order to overcome the natural reluctance of recommenders to place negative comments in writing and, thereby, submit themselves to the legal possibilities of libel proceedings. Unlike employee-oriented recommenders, recommenders who know and respect the hiring department are, in the words of one chairman, "reluctant to stick you with a loser." They are more likely to consider the interests of the department as well as those of the individual. Even though employer-oriented recommenders may not know the candidate quite as well, a positive recommendation by a mutual acquaintance usually carries more weight than glowing tribute from a person who has been hand-picked by the candidate.

The importance of the mutual acquaintance recommendation as a source of reliable information cannot be overstressed. As shown by Table 1, this was cited most frequently as the most important information source in the fifty hiring situations discussed in detail with the department chairmen.

Even recommendations from friends are, however, not always to be trusted. When using recommendations of any type, one must always be reading between the lines for true meanings, guessing at the sincerity of the recommender, and assessing the

Table 1

Technique of Investigation
Believed to be the Most Important by the Department Chairmen

Technique	No. of Chairmen
Recommendation from *Mutual* Acquaintance	14
Recommendation from *Candidate's* Friend or Acquaintance	7
Candidate's "Paper" & Publications	3
On-Campus Interview	13
Knew Candidate as a Personal Friend	6
No answer	7
TOTAL	50

Source: Chairmen Interviews

validity of the recommender's judgment. How well does the recommender know the recommended? Does he know him personally as well as professionally? Is the relationship so loose that the recommender is reluctant to blackball the candidate on the basis of a casual acquaintance even though he suspects inadequacies? Also, how familiar is the recommender with the hiring school's setup and does he respect it? It is a custom to gear recommendations to the receiving school. If, for example, the same candidate asks for a letter to an Ivy League school and a state teachers' college, in most cases the candidate will be given a better recommendation to the lesser school. The recommender is not really being dishonest. To both schools he is writing a recommendation in terms of the standards of the school. Where standards are lower, the candidate is made to look better. Whether or not the ends justify the means is a moot question: the practice does exist and since it does the answer to the question, "What does the recommender think of us?" can be important.

On-Campus Interviews

Many department chairmen, indeed most of those interviewed, before hiring invite the more promising candidates to visit their campus at the school's expense.[3] Our survey of the larger schools in the Southeast indicate that between two-thirds and three-fourths of all college teachers hired above the level of instructor made one or more visits to their new campus before signing a contract. As described by the individuals whom we interviewed, there is no comon format for on-campus interviews. They range from one to three days in length; some visits are intricately planned whereas others are quite casual. Arrangements may include a social gathering with the members of the depart-

3. Sixteen of the eighteen schools (89 per cent) studied paid interviewing expenses at least as frequently as "sometimes." This figure is comparable to that reported by the College and University Personnel Association upon the basis of a 122-institution study in *Personnel Practices in Colleges and Universities* (Champagne, Ill.: College and University Personnel Association, 1958), p. 121.

ment and their wives, a visit to the library, a general tour of campus, an exploration of housing facilities, a tourist's introduction, a session with the school's top administrative officers, and so forth. The candidate may spend most of his time with the department chairman or he may be passed around among the members of the department who may ask the candidate about his research, or ask for help on their own research, or give the candidate a "fair" impression of what teaching there is like and answer as many of the candidate's questions as they can. At the schools that are good enough to require it, the candidate may be expected to present a paper to a seminar of faculty and graduate students. In general, the formats of on-campus interviewing trips appear to follow the needs and interests of the schools and candidates involved.

Attitudes of department chairmen toward the necessity and purpose of on-campus interviews before hiring vary from "there's nothing more important than an interview on the grounds, for either party" to "interviews are not worth the trouble." Some departments envision the on-campus interview as a time to evaluate the candidate; others, as a time to put on the hard sell and make sure that the candidate will accept the job when offered; and still others, as a time simply to confirm the decision to hire that was reached by the department by other techniques of evaluation prior to the visit. These diverse viewpoints are reflected by the statements of the three department chairmen quoted below:

THE PURPOSE OF ON-CAMPUS INTERVIEWING IS EVALUATION: The on-campus interview is the point at which we make our most extensive investigation and judgment. Every sociologist sees the candidate individually. In the interviews, we pursue the strong and weak points mentioned in the recommendations. Can we live with the man, personally and intellectually? We see how he responds at cocktail parties, which is important here. . . . While he is still on campus, we meet, compare notes, and reach a decision.

THE PURPOSE OF ON-CAMPUS INTERVIEWING IS SELLING: There is an element of selling in the campus interview. . . . Any candidate

I'm seriously interested in I always take home for dinner and cocktails and show him how well a professor at ———— can live. On the way we wander through the nicest residential sections and I tell him how much the houses cost. . . . The important thing is to make a man feel that he'll be happy here. . . . [I always make the] "we're decent guys" pitch.

THE PURPOSE OF ON-CAMPUS INTERVIEWING IS CONFIRMATION: Impressions during an interview are questionable. It's good for a man to see [our setup here], but for evaluation we are dependent upon what men say that have known him over a longer period of time. The interview situation is too artificial, too strained, too high-pressured to tell much. In the last analysis we depend upon recommendations.

The view expressed in the first quotation above, that on-campus interviews are a valuable and essential technique of evaluation, is held primarily by the smaller, especially the denominational, schools that stress teaching rather than research. In these schools the qualities that can be best judged in the interview situation such as personality, ability to get along with other people, political leanings, religious beliefs, and ability to communicate orally are more important than in the larger, less personal setting of a state university. The way that a man will conduct himself among his colleagues and the types of relationships a man will develop with his students are crucial to the smaller schools. Realizing that it is impossible to judge how well a candidate will fit into a specific position without knowing both the position and the prospective candidate, the smaller departments advocate using the on-campus interview as a means of getting to know the candidate. In contrast, for institutions that are more interested in knowing the "research potential" of a candidate (an ability that is more or less independent of time and place and that is best evaluated by persons who have known and worked with the candidate for a period greater than two or three days) and are not particularly bothered by radicals, agnostics, and obnoxious personalities, there is less need to base an evaluation upon the types of information collected in the course of on-campus interviews.

Table 2

Number of Persons Interviewed on Campus

No. of Candidates Interviewed on Campus	No. of Instances Cited by Department Chairmen
None	8
One, including candidate hired	24
Two, including candidate hired	9
Three, including candidate hired	4
Four, including candidate hired	1
One, excluding candidate hired	2
No answer	2
TOTAL	50

Source: Chairmen Interviews

Indications are that the views expressed in the second and third quotations are more common than the first view. It stands to reason that if a department envisions the on-campus interview as a means of choosing one candidate over others, at least two candidates must be brought to campus for comparison. To bring only one implies that the hirer is already relatively sure of the man he wants and is either seeking confirmation or an opportunity to convince the chosen one that this is the job for him. Since, as shown in Table 2, in 60 per cent of the instances where on-campus interviews were conducted, the man hired was the only one interviewed on campus, we may infer that on-campus interviews are used primarily for selling and confirming purposes. Candidates are first ranked on the basis of information gathered from vitae and recommendations. Then, in order of rank, the candidates are invited to campus and offered the job until someone accepts.

There is little doubt that on-campus interviewing is an effective way of getting to know a candidate. But what department can, every time a vacancy must be filled, afford the time that two, three, or four of these visits would require? Because of the heavy demands upon faculty time, on-campus interviewing is reserved for only the most promising. Before inviting any candidates on campus, most schools have, at least tentatively, made their final cut. There are exceptions but this is the rule.[4]

4. Table 1 shows that thirteen department chairmen regarded on-campus

Knowledge About the Man Hired

All information gathering is directed toward one end, the enabling of the selection of the one best candidate. Ideally, before selecting the best candidate, the employer should learn all pertinent facts and opinions about all candidates. In practice, the hirer's knowledge is grossly incomplete and imperfect.[5] The hirers themselves acknowledge their ignorance. When asked "what did you not know about the man you hired at the time you hired him that would have been pertinent in judging his qualifications for the job?" only five of the fifty department chairmen indicated that they knew all that they should have known. Some of the things listed as not known by different department chairmen were the hired's teaching ability, future research productivity, ability to work independently, degree of ambition, reactions to particular teaching situations and environments, temperament, personality, way of life, physical appearance, political views, religious convictions, and college grades. In one instance a foreign-born man who had difficulty speaking English was hired without the hirer knowing about the difficulty. Another chairman mentioned an appointment he had made without knowing about two of the appointee's previous teaching jobs and without knowing about the appointee's past record of major mal-

interviewing as the *most* important of the investigatory techniques, a finding apparently contrary to the above statement. However, eight of these thirteen chairmen had interviewed only one person, which suggests that even these chairmen are using on-campus interviewing more to confirm their choice of a given candidate than to differentiate among two or more alternative candidates.

5. At first it would seem that employers in academic labor markets, who have extensive recommendations, numerous opinions of interviewers, and a personal knowledge of the candidate, are in a much better position than employers in blue collar labor markets who must choose among alternative applicants for unskilled jobs on the basis of fifteen-minute interviews and terse information contained on standard personnel forms. But the advantage is apparent only. Academic employers do have more to judge by, but they also have more to judge for. The characteristics that hirers of academic manpower must assess are more subtle. Where the personnel manager must determine dependability, physical strength, and skill level, the department chairman must predict research potential and effectiveness as a classroom teacher. The information available to the department chairman is not nearly adequate. The things that cannot be committed to paper, and are therefore not usually known, are the very things in which the recruiters of professors are the most interested.

adjustments. Other department chairmen had made appointments without knowing about the appointees' consuming interest in race relations, impending divorce, physical handicap, distance away from the Ph.D. degree, and forced move from previous job. Since one would expect the hiring department to be more knowledgeable about the man that is actually offered the job than about other candidates who were considered for the job but did not receive an offer, if hirers are not knowledgeable about the hired, it is reasonable to expect that hirers are also not knowledgeable about the almost hired. There is a wide discrepancy between the ideal and the actual.

One might ask, "why are employers willing to hire without a full investigation?" The answer is that the anticipated improvement in decision-making ability does not justify the additional costs of collecting the information: the marginal costs exceed the marginal benefits. Further information on any given candidate is sought only as long as the value of the increased knowledge is expected to cover the time and money costs of getting it.

The marginal cost-marginal benefit principle explains why schools investigate some candidate more thoroughly than others. The values and costs of information gathering differ widely. If, for example, a hirer attaches great importance to personality or if preliminary information gives some indication of undesirable personality traits, the value of additional information on personality would be quite high and further investigation would probably be justified, even if the investigation were rather costly. In contrast, another school that does not value personality as high, or the same school evaluating a "less suspicious" candidate, would be less able to justify the use of equally costly techniques. Other examples can be structured to illustrate why differences in the cost of gathering information would cause an employer to investigate one candidate more thoroughly than another, even though there were no differences between candidates in the anticipated value of the new information.

According to this principle, we would expect employers to know more about candidates when the value of collecting additional information is high and the cost, low. To test this expectation, we have developed a rough measure of how much the hirer knew about the candidate at the time of hiring, the Knowledgeability Index, and applied it to the data gathered from interviews with the Southeastern department chairmen.

The Knowledgeability Index is a ratio. For each "yes" answer to the six questions listed below, one point was added to the numerator of the index. One point was added to the denominator for each of the questions answered. Thus, the maximum numerator and denominator were both six. A larger Knowledgeability Index reflects greater knowledgeability, the maximum score being 1. The questions, which were asked of the department chairmen, in slightly different form, are:

1. Did you know at least four of the five following things about the man hired: ability as a teacher? ability as a researcher? ability as a student? personality? adjustability?
2. Did you know why the hiree left his previous job (if he had one)?
3. Did you know the hiree's salary at his previous job (if he had one)?
4. Did you know if the hiree was considering any other offers at the time you extended yours?
5. If so, did you know the salaries involved in the other offers?
6. Was the hiree interviewed on campus?

A Knowledgeability Index was computed in each of the hiring situations discussed in detail with the department chairmen. The thirteen situations where the department chairmen were poorly informed (Knowledgeability Index less than .45) are compared with the thirty-seven situations where the chairmen knew the man hired relatively well (Knowledgeability Index greater than .45) in Table 3.

These data are consistent with the principle that employers investigate candidates more thoroughly when there is more at stake. When hiring at the associate and full professor levels, where mistakes cannot easily be corrected because of tenure pro-

Table 3

Knowledgeability of Chairmen by Previous Location of Man Hired,
Academic Rank of Man Hired, Number of Candidates Investigated,
Size of Hiring Department, and Discipline

Characteristic	Chairmen Were Well Informed About the Candi- date. (K.1. > .45)[1]	Chairmen Were Poorly Informed About the Candi- date. (K.1. < .45)[1]
Assistant Professor Hired[2]	22	12
Associate or Full Professor Hired[2]	14	1
Hired Came from Southeast[3]	20	4
Hired Came from Outside Southeast[3]	17	9
School Considered Only One Candidate[4]	3	3
School Investigated Two or Three Candidates[4]	19	3
School Investigated Four or More Candidates[4]	15	7
Departments with 14 or More Staff Members[4]	11	6
Departments with 8-13 Staff Members[4]	13	3
Departments with 7 or Fewer Staff Members[4]	13	4
History Departments[4]	11	7
Economics Departments[4]	14	1
Sociology Departments[4]	12	5

1. For an explanation of the Knowledgeability Index, see page 148.
2. Hypothesis of no difference was rejected by Fisher Exact Probability Test at 95 per cent confidence.
3. Hypothesis of no difference could not be rejected by Chi Square or Fisher Exact Probability at 95 per cent confidence.
4. Hypothesis of no difference was not tested.
Source: Chairmen interviews

visions, departments were very careful to investigate thoroughly before making an offer. Only one associate or full professor, a man from England, was hired "blindly." In contrast, at the assistant professor level, where mistakes are not so costly, over one-third of the appointments were made without full investigation. To cite another example, a priori one would expect that the additional value of investigating a candidate who is the only one known would fall off rapidly after a minimal degree of competence had been established. The data again affirm expectations. In situations where the choice was between a single candidate and no candidate, investigations tended to be much less extensive than in those where the merits of several candidates had to be weighed.

On the cost side, the data are less consistent with our hypothesis that less information is gathered when the costs of gathering are larger. One would expect that since the costs of investigating candidates who are farther away is greater, less would be known about these candidates when hired. Although it is true that hiring departments were poorly informed about 35 per cent of the candidates hired from points outside the Southeast compared to only 20 per cent of the candidates located within the region, the difference is not statistically significant. The difficulties of evaluating candidates over long distances were not insurmountable. Also, the fact that larger departments can more easily undertake extensive evaluations because of the many contacts they have makes one expect that larger departments would know more than smaller departments about the men they hire. If anything, the opposite is true: 35 per cent of the hiring into larger departments was relatively "blind" compared to only 27 per cent for the smaller.

In light of these observations, we conclude that departments do not weigh the value and cost factors equally. If it is important to have an as-accurate-as-possible evaluation of a candiate, hirers seek out the information desired regardless of reasonable cost. Even though thorough investigations are more expensive for smaller departments, the smaller departments pursue them with even greater regularity because with such a small staff they cannot afford to hire a new man who is incompetent or a misfit. The marginal benefits exceed the marginal costs.

Criteria for Selecting Candidates

Regardless of the volume of information that has been compiled on the candidates, choices are eventually made. Candidates are judged. Decisions are reached: to offer the job to this candidate, not to extend an offer to those candidates, or to delay the extension of any offer because none of the known and available candidates measures up to minimum standards. A relevant question is: On what bases are these decisions made? Or what are the criteria used to select some candidates and reject others?

Fred B. Millet, president of the University of Miami, in his book, *Professor: Problems and Rewards of College Teaching*, states that these criteria are (1) probable effectiveness as a teacher, (2) past and future productivity as a scholar, (3) reputation as a specialist and appropriateness of specialty for a given position, and (4) personal qualities such as compatability and stability.[6] In a very similar typology in the *Academic Man*, Logan Wilson identifies ability in research, ability in teaching, quality and character of professional training, intellectual caliber, capacity for leadership, originality, personality and character, general reputation, and probable future performance as the relevant criteria upon which candidates are evaluated.[7]

The similarity of these lists reflects unanimity among scholars of university administration concerning the factors that should be considered when selecting college faculty.

There are, however, differences of opinion regarding the stress placed upon each selection criterion. The cleavage between administrators at the smaller, less known liberal arts colleges on the one hand, and at the major graduate institutions on the other, is perhaps the most dramatic. The former stress the importance of choosing candidates who are good teachers, responsible citizens, and versatile instructors willing and able to teach different subjects. Our interviews with department chairmen indicate that hirers from these schools are willing to compromise on the research interests and abilities of candidates if they can attract a candidate who has an intense interest in students, a commendable "way of life," and a winning personality. To quote one of the chairmen from a small, denominational school: "All other things equal, I'll hire a Baptist. . . . We would never hire an atheist. . . . We are not interested in having a man who simply meets his classes and dashes off to write another journal article. We want our faculty to take an interest in the students, to get to know the students. . . ." In contrast, at the larger universities, where contacts are more professional than personal, compatibility, citizenship, and religious commitment are less important.

6. Millet, *Professor*, p. 92.
7. Wilson, *The Academic Man*, p. 54.

These schools emphasize ability as a productive scholar, depth of knowledge in a specific subject area, and again ability as a teacher. When necessary, hirers of university faculty appear willing to compromise on personality in order to obtain a top-flight research person. Scholarly productivity is desired because institutions build their reputations on the research and because the graduate level teaching needs of these schools require men who are real specialists in their areas, men who are researching at the frontiers of their subject areas. At these universities ability and willingness to teach a number of different courses is not a requirement because high enrollment in all courses and a large staff permit men to teach only in their specialty.

Universities, like colleges, are anxious to hire good teachers. Contrary to the popular images that colleges hire teachers and universities hire researchers, our Southeastern study indicates that the higher prestige universities are at least equally concerned with good classroom teaching. Compared to the schools in the lowest third, six times as many of the departments in the top quality grouping of schools listed teaching experience as a necessary requirement in candidates considered for jobs. Time was taken to investigate candidates' teaching ability almost three times as often by top quality departments than by lowest quality ones. The top quality schools do not have lesser standards regarding the in-classroom teaching abilities of the faculty they hire. Rather, in addition to the teaching ability requirement, they demand research ability. The universities demand more research ability, not less teaching ability. Both colleges and universities demand good in-classroom teaching. Out of the classroom, universities want research, colleges want more teaching.[8]

Regardless of which criteria are stressed, because the measures of qualities such as teaching ability, research ability, and personality are so imprecise, it is often necessary to differentiate among candidates on the basis of more measurable though less

8. An interesting contrast is provided by the statements of Caplow and McGee, *The Academic Marketplace,* p. 164, for the universities, and the Dean of Administration at Brothers College (Lankard, in Russell, *Problems of Faculty Personnel,* pp. 11-15) for the colleges.

important criteria: for example, connections. To quote Logan Wilson, "Although the candidate with a high record and unqualified recommendations from competent judges stands a better chance than the less meritorious, between eligible individuals of apparently equal ability and training, preferment is always shown for 'connections.'"[9] Favoring those with connections makes sense. The evaluation process is subject to three primary sources of error: (1) a candidate may be honestly overrated by those who know him well, (2) a candidate may be intentionally overrated in an attempt to make him more marketable, and (3) the change in environment occasioned by the change of job may undesirably affect the candidate in an unpredictable way. By hiring men with connections, there is reason to believe that type two errors are reduced significantly, for a recommender who might be willing to oversell a candidate to a stranger would be reluctant to do the same when the recommendation is addressed to a personal friend. If the hirer has a strong aversion to risk, connections may be a dominant criterion for choice.

Candidates' supply prices (the amount of salary demanded) are another measurable choice criterion. Hirers view salaries as costs. Since schools must allocate limited resources among many demands, other things equal, preferment is shown toward less costly candidates. If schools were not concerned with costs, all would demand the very best professors. Because schools are cost conscious, differences in supply prices provide a convenient and logical basis for selection.

Still another criterion in the selection calculus is "anticipated availability." Hirers try to avoid the extension of an offer to a candidate who is certain to turn down the offer. Investigating persons who will not accept the types of offers that can be extended is very costly and to be avoided whenever possible. If, for whatever reasons, a candidate is investigated but not hired, then another candidate must be investigated. A second investigation roughly doubles the costs of investigation over what they would have been if the first man had been hired. In addition to these direct costs, opportunity costs are involved. In the

9. Wilson, *The Academic Man*, p. 51.

academic labor market, time is crucial. Open season on professors is relatively short; in most disciplines men are investigated and hired between Christmas and Spring vacations. Yet the hiring procedure is quite lengthy. The completing of application forms, requesting and receiving of recommendations, scheduling of on-campus interviews, deciding on the advisability of making offers, and considering of these offers by the candidates take at least a full month. During this month the hiring school is losing opportunities, for other candidates are being considered and signed by other schools. If a school spends the months of January-March contemplating offers to various candidates who are later found not to be interested at the compensation offered and therefore not hired, the school then, in April, faces a real problem of finding and attracting someone who has been left, someone who has not already been signed by a competitor. It is a wise policy to give candidates under serious consideration an indication of the type of offer that will probably be forthcoming if they are chosen so that the candidates have an opportunity to indicate what offers they will not consider.

Salary Determination

The determination of faculty salaries is carefully clothed in secrecy at most institutions.[10] Time and time again, when individuals (and even department chairmen) were asked to discuss what they knew about salary determination they replied: "That stuff's top secret here," or "That's the dean's business."

The American Association of University Professors with its annual salary studies has made heroic strides toward unveiling the results, if not the process, of salary determination. But even now a number of universities will not provide average salary data to the AAUP, and still others provide the data only with the stip-

10. There are many exceptions to the general rule. At one of the state schools surveyed, for example, professors were paid one of sixteen salaries and the number and rank of professors at each salary level was general knowledge of the entire faculty. At another school, a small denominational college, several faculty members pulled from their files detailed statistics on faculty salaries which had been compiled and distributed by the administration.

ulations that they not be published in identifiable form. Ignorance remains. When asked "what guidelines were used to determine the salary offered [to a particular candidate]?" one of the department chairmen we interviewed replied, "The university officials have an image of what a man of certain rank and experience ought to be paid, and they are always ready to point out that my image exceeds their limit. What their image is based upon God only knows."

Unfortunately, our study offers little insight into this relatively unexplored area, since the one aspect of hiring that department chairmen tend to know the least about is salary determination. It is the deans who are primarily responsible for setting faculty salaries for both old and new faculty. Even so, on the basis of an analysis of the comments made by department chairmen, it is possible to identify and discuss some of the factors that deans must consider when determining compensations.

Guidelines for Salary Determination

Responses of the department chairmen indicate that the guidelines used to determine the amount of salary offered are primarily three: (1) the salaries of present faculty in the same department and sometimes the same institution, (2) the salary necessary to get the man to accept the offer, and (3) the salary that the hiring school can afford to pay.

The salaries of some professors are determined almost entirely by the salaries of present faculty. Several department chairmen indicated instances where they had hired associate and full professors and paid them the median compensation at the rank. When hiring at the assistant professor level, department chairmen stressed the importance of preserving "a comfortable gap between the new man and the men who have been here awhile." Several chairmen cited instances where, even though the higher administration was willing to offer a larger salary to the new recruit, the offer was not extended because the new man would have been brought in above the present earnings of "comparable" men hired in previous years and the resulting salary structure might have caused morale problems. The marginal cost of raising the salaries of the men hired in previous years, an obvious solution to possible morale problems, was too great and could not be sold to the higher ups: the paying of higher salaries to all men on the staff is considerably more costly than offering the higher salary only to the last man hired. Salaries have been rising so rapidly that professors have come to expect newly hired faculty to start at a higher rate than they did, but the old faculty do not tolerate starting salaries which are higher than their current ones.

Salary setting is also guided by necessity, the necessity of getting a man to accept an offer. About one-third of the chairmen made statements such as we paid him "what we had to pay to get him," "the minimum salary needed to attract" and "what we could get him for." In predicting how high an offer must be in order to get a man to accept it two indexes are used: (1) the man's previous salary and (2) the salary that the man could be earning elsewhere. Recognizing the reluctance to move at a decrease in salary, a majority of the department chairmen hiring men directly from other jobs in college teaching asked the candidate what he was earning presently and then either matched or bettered it. In only one instance was a man offered a salary known to be lower than the one he was currently earning.

Since the candidate may compare two new offers rather than one new offer and his current job, some attempt is usually made at estimating what the candidate would be offered by "comparable" schools; for example, a nearby school of the same type, or, less important, the same size. Though it is rare to ask a man what he has been offered by another school, there are many ways of estimating this offer. Salary statistics published by the Office of Education, National Education Association, American Association of University Professors, and others are a start. Confidential salary studies exchanged among administrators at selected schools (e.g., the AACSB survey of business school salaries and the cartel survey of salaries in thirty-one leading economics departments) provide more specific and more useful data. By picking up scuttlebutt at conventions, noting the offers received by one's own staff and own graduate students from other schools, reading the "want ads" in the journals and at the convention slave markets, and soliciting published salary studies from other schools, a wealth of comparative salary data can be collected. Department chairmen, especially in the departments where salaries are above the university average due to a tight market situation, will often arm themselves with these data when justifying what might seem to be an unusually high salary offer to the dean.

Funds are limited. The dean, who must have his eye on the total financial situation, is the ultimate guardian of the salary funds and he must always keep in mind that a salary offer that is higher than necessary at one point may prevent him from making a high enough salary offer when filling another position. Deans must economize funds where feasible. Limits of salary offers must be established to avoid overspending in one area; yet these limits must be high enough to enable recruitment of personnel of the desired quality. In the opinion of the department chairmen, in 50 per cent of the hiring situations discussed, the dean's upper limit was within fifty dollars (per year) of the lowest offer the hired candidate would have accepted. Candidates turned down offers because the salary was too low in only 12 per cent of the situations. This indicates that, at least in their own opinions, hirers are fairly effective in their attempts to estimate "minimum acceptable offers."

Intra- and Inter-University Comparability

Two forces often working at cross purposes when deans are setting limits on salary offers are the demands to maintain comparable salaries in all departments of the university and to maintain salaries in each department that are competitive with similar departments in other schools. Considering themselves both members of their scholarly disciplines (e.g., historians) and members of the faculty at a particular school, most professors are dually aligned. Two labor markets, one professional and the other institutional, are relevant for each person. Each person has, therefore, two "orbits of coercive comparison" or two groups with which to compare salaries. History professors at the University of Illinois, for example, expect to be paid about the same as comparable historians at the University of Maryland *and* as comparable mathematicians at the University of Illinois. The problems arise when the "comparable salary" in one market differs from the "comparable salary" in the other, and this is very likely to be the case. Professors of comparable abilities in two disciplines have different scarcity values; for example, mathematicians are in shorter supply relative to demand than historians. Whereas competitive bidding among universities may require that a school offer at least $9,000 for a bright mathematician, a historian of equal promise but less bargaining power may be hired for $7,500. What is happening is that other deans are deciding that in their particular situations the value of the product contributed by one more mathematician is greater than that of a historian. Of course, the differential in economic or scarcity value is not directly related to the difference in the "real value" of the two individuals. Whether or not a particular dean agrees with this judgment rendered by the collectivity of all employers, he must face the differential and account for it if he wants to hire any mathematicians. If he has sufficient funds a dean may pay $9,000 to both, but regardless of the sufficiency of his funds he must pay at least $7,500 for a historian and $9,000 for a mathematician. He cannot pay both $7,500. Too often the dean is forced into a dilemma.

There is little agreement among the department chairmen interviewed as to how this dilemma should be resolved. On the one hand, there are those who argue for intra-university comparability:

Intra-university [pay] differentials create too much internal dissension.

Annoying as it may be to recruiters in scarcity fields, you wouldn't have a can of worms if rates and step increases were not comparable. It is intolerable to have intra-institution inequities.

Professors are more conscious of the salaries of other people on this campus than salaries on other campuses.

I am not greatly impressed with the idea that you have to pay mathematicians more. . . . This seems like a fallacious argument.

Our people are very professionally oriented, yet they compare salaries with others at [his university]. If sociologists at [his university] are paid more than most [professors in other departments] at [his university] though less than the "going rate" in the profession, they are more likely to forgive than if they are paid more than other sociologists but less than colleagues in other departments. In the former case, they are sympathetic that the university is doing all that it can; in the latter, they feel that they aren't getting a fair shake. Here you have two sources of relative deprivation; both are important.

I know that an historian at Davidson gets paid $2,000 more than I and feel sorry, but not mad. If a [his college] sociologist is earning $2,000 more, I get hopping mad and bee-line for the Dean. . . . It is not the money but the principle of the thing.

As a rule with exceptions, the proponents of *intra*-university comparability are at the smaller, less prestigious, denominational schools. See Table 4 on page 160. The very schools that expect institutional commitments from their professors are the ones that believe institutional comparability to be more important.

The data in Table 4 also indicate that department chairmen are looking out for their own staffs. Since both economists and sociologists tend to be paid salaries slightly above the average in most colleges of arts and sciences, their salaries would tend to be lower if professors in all departments were paid on the same basis. On the other hand, the salaries of historians would tend to be higher under a policy of intra-university comparability. Reflecting their departments' self-interest, a higher percentage of historians than economists and sociologists felt a need for salary comparability along institutional lines rather than disciplinary.

Outvoting the proponents of internal consistency by a greater than two-to-one margin were the chairmen expressing the view

Table 4

Department Chairmen's Opinions on the
Relative Importance of Same Salaries Within University
Versus Same Salaries Within Disciplines, by Selected Groups

Grouping	No. Advocating Comparable Salaries in all Universities for each Discipline	No. Advocating Comparable Salaries in all Disciplines for each University
By Quality of School—		
Highest Prestige Group[1]	15	3
Middle Prestige Group[1]	12	4
Lowest Prestige Group[1]	5	7
By Size of School—		
Largest Third[1]	12	1
Middle Third[1]	15	7
Smallest Third[1]	5	6
By Type of School—		
Private[2]	13	10
Public[2]	19	4
By Department—		
Economics[2]	12	2
Sociology[2]	11	5
History[2]	9	7

1. Hypothesis of no difference was rejected by Chi Square with 95 per cent confidence.
2. Hypothesis of no difference could not be rejected with 95 per cent confidence.
Source: Chairmen Interviews

that pay rates should be professionally rather than institutionally oriented.

Intra-university equity is widely recognized as desirable but widely ignored in practice. One must succumb to the necessities of recruitment, even at the sacrifice of internal consistency within his own department.

It comes down to the practical matter of moving people. Money must be placed where the [excess] demand is.

If everyone within the university is equitably treated in terms of what they could be earning elsewhere, they will be satisfied and the internal problems will solve themselves.

Though within university consistency is desirable, being competitive is to the greater welfare of the university in the long run.

If you stick to internal consistency [by paying all professors of the same rank same salaries], a cheapening of the rank in various tight fields must develop.

To maximize the quality of the total faculty, assuming fixed financial resources, price discrimination must be used. This may not be the most ethical way to operate but it's the best.

As an economist aware of the cost savings that can be achieved by dividing markets and as a pragmatist, the *professional* orientation of pay scale makes the most sense to this author. Psychologists, and for that matter deans, may disagree.

The Importance of Mobility

Another way in which deans may divide the markets for faculty personnel and thereby allocate optimally their limited funds is on the basis of the relative mobility of professors. Consider the hypothetical case where, within the department of sociology, there are two individuals equally valuable to the department, both worth (say) $9,500. One of the men has been at the school for fifteen years and developed many friends, purchased a home, and nurtured a special research institute. Although this man knows that his "free market" value is $9,500, both non-vested professional interests and emotional ties to his current school cause him to accept a salary as low as $8,000 without moving to another school. He is in a sense willing to accept $1,500 psychic income in lieu of the same amount in real income. The other man, who does not attach value to teaching at his current institution per se, would move if paid much less than his market value of $9,500. Deans, realizing these differential preferences, tend to offer higher salaries only when they must. As a result many faculty are "exploited."[11]

11. Exploitation of the very top men in the field is especially common, but for a different reason. Top men in their fields are certainly worth more than the $25,000 to $30,000 that they are paid, for they bestow more prestige on their schools than an entire corps of less known scholars. If hirers followed a strict marginal revenue product salary setting policy, the salaries of these men would be considerably higher. But in actual practice, a school does not need to pay a man

The practice of exploiting where feasible and paying the competitive rate where necessary has tended to contract the salary differentials among different schools more at the lower than the higher ranks. At the assistant professor level, where there is active competition among schools for faculty, a school cannot afford to allow its salaries to get too far out of line. Therefore, the salaries offered by different schools are quite similar. Salary policy is dominated by the competitive necessity of attracting personnel to particular schools. Once settled at a particular school, faculty are continually deepening their institutional commitments and correspondingly weakening their professional ones. Eventually they become oblivious to outside offers. At this point, the university no longer needs to worry about losing faculty and may channel its salary funds to other professors who are in danger of being lost to a higher bidder. At these upper ranks, where the oldtimers tend to be concentrated and where the amount of inter-university competition for faculty tends to be small (except at the very best schools), salary differentials tend to be much larger. A few wealthy schools can afford the luxury of maintaining "equitable" salary differentials among ranks, whereas the less well-to-do schools depend upon psychic income to fill the gap left by the redirection of funds.

The greater similarity of salary levels at the lower ranks is well illustrated by the American Association of University Professors' salary studies. According to rough calculations from the data published in the summer of 1962, the mean deviation of average compensation paid by the 545 schools surveyed was

---

any more than his best competitive offer. Assuming for the moment that professors choose jobs on the basis of salary only, Harvard needs to pay a famous historian only a few dollars more than any other school to keep him.

On the other hand, even though most universities and colleges are not paying famous professors as much as they are truly worth, these same professors are usually receiving some "economic rent." A man is receiving "economic rent" to the extent that his current compensation exceeds that of the best alternative. Except in the scientific and some of the quantitative social scientific disciplines where the demands for Ph.D. trained personnel outside teaching are high, professors are earning more teaching than they could in any other profession. For example, there are very few things that an English professor can use his training for other than teaching. Schools, in most disciplines, are paying teachers more than is necessary to keep them in teaching.

$1,494 among full professors but only $236 among assistant professors.[12] Even after allowing for the fact that full professors' salaries are higher than assistant professors' by dividing each mean deviation by the average salary for the rank, the percentage mean deviation for full professors (15.2 per cent) is over four times as large as that for assistant professors (3.3 per cent). In accord with the expectations of economic theory, salaries are most diverse where potential mobility is the lowest, for without potential mobility there is no strong force pushing wages together.[13]

That schools try to pay as little as necessary at all ranks, and that the lower ranks are the most responsive to market scarcity, has resulted in an observable tendency for academic salaries to be raised, in the words of Caplow and McGee, "from the bottom up."[14] The results of this phenomenon are again observable in the AAUP data. The AAUP rates the "average compensation" level at each of the four academic ranks from "AA" (good) down to "G" (terrible). The rank at which schools tend to receive their lowest rating indicates the faculty group that is being compensated least adequately. In 1961-62, 88 per cent of the lowest ratings were at the relatively immobile ranks of associate and full professor. The modal rating at the assistant level was "B," two ranks above the modal rating at the full professor level. The salaries of associate and full professors are just now feeling the effects of the forces that have been causing a rapid upward movement in the salaries of assistant professors and instructors for many years.

12. In order to make these calculations, frequency distributions of the grades assigned by the AAUP to various schools were determined, one for full professors and one for assistant professors. Each school classified as (say) "B" at the assistant professor level was assumed to be paying the average of all schools classified as "B-B" ($7,316) as shown in their Table 4. A weighted average, using the relevant figures in the frequency distribution as weights, was then computed. Source: AAUP Bulletin, Vol. 48, No. 2 (Summer, 1962).
13. Clark Kerr, "The Balkanization of Labor Markets" in E. Wight Bakke et al. (ed.), Labor Mobility and Economic Opportunity (New York: Massachusetts Institute of Technology and Wiley, 1954), p. 106; J. R. Hicks, The Theory of Wages (New York: The Macmillan Company, 1935), p. 79.
14. Caplow and McGee, The Academic Marketplace, p. 212.

Salary Determination

If the limited investigations of salary determination in academic labor markets justify any generalization, it is that price (salary) is, except at the very wealthy institutions, supply oriented, not demand. Because the products produced are neither measurable nor priceable, the marginal value products or value of professors' services can be only roughly determined. This determination is so speculative that it is generally considered to be a very unreliable guide to salary determination. Who is to judge the relative values of the services of historians and mathematicians? of researchers and teachers? In lieu of an accurate measure of value, salary setters have turned to the competitive labor market where scarcity values are determined. The differences in salaries therefore reflect differences in the levels and shapes of supply schedules in the various disciplinary sub-labor markets.

Summary

Hirers generally prefer candidates who are good teachers, good researchers, and good persons. If a hirer is unable to attract a person with all three of these desired qualities because of budgetary limitations, the tastes of the candidates, or the demands for an equitable salary structure by the hiring institution's present faculty, the small college hirer is prone to acquiesce in his insistence upon ability as a researcher whereas the large university hirer is prone to sacrifice one of the other characteristics.

The process by which the good candidates are separated from the not-so-good is well described as a gather-cut-gather-cut process. A small amount of information is gathered on many candidates, the least promising are eliminated from consideration, on the more promising candidates more information is gathered, another cut is made, more information, another cut, and so forth until the field is narrowed to the one best candidate. In the initial stages, the information that is relied upon is gathered because of its ease of collection, not its reliability. Vitae and candidate-oriented recommendations are commonly used here. As the selection process proceeds, employers solicit opinions from their friends who are not necessarily listed by the candidates as recommenders. The on-campus interview is typically restricted to the most promising candidates.

In spite of all this information gathering and evaluating, our study indicates that hirers are amazingly ignorant about the men they are hiring at the time contracts are signed. The benefits gained by investigating candidates thoroughly are simply not commensurate with the high costs of investigation.

VII

CANDIDATES EVALUATE JOBS

At the same time that hirers are deciding which candidates to make what offers, the candidates are deciding which offers to accept from whom. For the candidate, like the employer, the location of alternative opportunities is only the first step in the many staged decision-making process that eventually results in a new job. After locating the jobs available, the candidate must thoroughly investigate and then evaluate them according to the factors that he feels are most and least important in a job. One job must be chosen; all others rejected.

Like the great majority of jobs, positions in college teaching cannot be accurately evaluated without actually spending time on the job. There are too many intangibles to consider. Non-personal exchanges by mail and phone, personal interviews with some of the faculty at annual meetings, and even extended campus interviewing trips offer little more than an indication of what a job will really be like. Prediction of how a new professor will react to his peers, his superiors, his students, his work environment, his social setting, his home situation, and ad infinitum is virtually impossible until the new man has spent at least several weeks on the job. The candidate has no sure way of determining the sincerity, honesty, or completeness of his new employer when he describes the job and its responsibilities.

In spite of these difficulties, the typical professor probably knows more about his job at the time of acceptance than the typical laborer, since he has more free time available for investigating, greater financial resources for providing subsistence during the hunting period, and greater mental abilities of the type required when investigating, evaluating, and choosing among several partially known alternatives. For most professors the evaluation of job opportunities is a continuously pursued avocation that reaches its epitome when contemplating seriously a change of jobs. Besides his presently held job, the typical job-seeking professor knows of at least two other openings. Even when he is not seeking a new job, the average professor becomes aware of a large number of alternative employment opportunities. Among the professors interviewed, about two-thirds of the men who had been at their present location for at least one full year had received, on the average, one or more job offers per year. Although many of these offers can be readily identified as undesirable, many others demand extensive information gathering and evaluation before they can be rejected. To choose properly, each offer must be compared with all other offers of new jobs, all developing offers of new jobs, the present job, and the minimally acceptable job. An improper choice means that the professor is less satisfied than he would be in another position (especially if he learns of his mistake). The dissatisfaction may eventually result in additional turnover, a process that is costly to the economy as a whole as well as the individual and his employers.

It is the intent of this chapter first to identify and evaluate the various methods used by candidates to collect information about specific, known openings and second to examine the criteria used to select the one best opening. The format of the chapter follows closely that of the one previous.

Information Gathering

Job talk is typically rather vague and often misinformed. Since the liaisons are not professionals, are not themselves interested in the opportunities they describe (they would pursue the offers themselves if they were), are carrying information on so many jobs that the specifics tend to become confused—the person from whom a candidate learns of an opening does not usually know all the details that someone really interested in the job would have to know. The liaison does little more than make the candidate aware of the opportunity.

The candidate must then, upon hearing of the possibility of an opening, decide whether or not the opening is worthy of further investigation on his part. To investigate too many positions is to expend time and energy needlessly. Thorough investigation for its own sake deserves ridicule. For there is little point in learning the minute details about jobs that are, on the basis of preliminary information, very unlikely to be better than the best known and available alternatives or about jobs that are not going to be offered to the investigating candidate. Yet, the investigation of too few or the wrong job opportunities may result in the candidate's acceptance of a position that is significantly poorer than the best available.

Why some jobs are investigated and others not, why the investigation of some jobs is carried further than that of others is not immediately evident. We can only hypothesize. Candidates probably use what amounts to a marginal analysis. If the expected marginal returns from the investigation of a particular job option exceed the expected marginal costs, the job is investigated. If not, the job is dropped without further consideration. Returns are high if preliminary evidence suggests that the job is one that would probably be offered to the candidate, the job is better than any other known alternative, and the techniques of investigation contemplated will greatly expand an originally small knowledge of the job. Costs are low if the techniques of investigation contemplated take little time and money.

Though the decision to investigate a job at all is made only once, the decision to investigate a job more thoroughly is made time and time again. Each time the decision is made, one less technique of investigation is available for further investigation and, hopefully, more is known.

Table 1

Methods Used by Individuals to Investigate Job Offers

Method	Percentage of 103 Candidates Who Used the Method When Investigating Their Current Job*
Polled Friends, Acquaintances, or Graduate School Professors	48%
Interviewed Prospective Employer	51%
Consulted Library Statistics and/or College Catalogue	34%
Other	19%
Did Nothing	9%

* Total percentages exceed 100 because one individual could use several methods.

Source: Individual Interviews

Friends

The high yield-low cost methods of information gathering are the first and most frequently used. As shown in Table 1, before accepting new employment many candidates (48 per cent) seek the opinion of a friend or acquaintance who personally knows something about the school or the staff. The opinion may be that of the friend of a friend in the middle of the hotel lobby at the annual meetings, of a former colleague either in graduate school or after, or of a respected teacher. This person may have taught there, known others who have taught there or nearby, gone to school there, done research with men from there, etc. He can, in an objective and detached way, interpret the subtle pros and cons of the position and is often able to answer many of the specific questions that the candidate may have been reluctant to ask his prospective employer. Since it involves little more than writing several short letters or looking someone up at the annual meetings, the gathering of information from these personal sources is almost costless.

The value depends in large measure upon the closeness of the "information sharer" to the particular department within the hiring school and the strength of the friendship between the candidate and the informant. The fact that a trusted friend who is close to a situation is such a valuable resource when evaluating jobs explains to some extent why so many candidates seek jobs through friends. Many candidates have evidently found that it is easier to locate a reliable informant who knows about a good job than to locate an apparently good job and then find a reliable informant to confirm the "goodness."

Published Statistics

Since they tend to know fewer helpful informants, the younger, less experienced candidates moving relatively long distances to smaller departments supplement their information about prospective jobs by consulting various published statistical data pertaining to the hiring school. College catalogues are studied to determine course offerings, the educational background of the faculty, the age structure within the department, and the general structure of the university. From educational reference books data such as student-faculty ratios, financial statements, and library holdings are obtained. A few study the AAUP salary ratings.

In order to place the use of published data in proper perspective it should be noted that although 34 per cent of our sample indicated that they had studied in detail one or more of these statistical guides, the studying of statistics is regarded as a poor substitute for other, more reliable methods of learning about jobs. Only one of the candidates interviewed felt that the studying of data was the single most important method of information gathering and she used no other. The statistics that are available are often outdated and deceptive. And the aspects of jobs that are most important to a majority of professors cannot easily be distilled into statistical form. Published statistics can indicate the number of volumes in a library but the specialist desires to know the holdings in his particular area. The study of the publications of the current faculty can give some indication of research interests and competence, but how these research interests will supplement those of the candidate cannot be determined until the two individuals exchange ideas.

On-Campus Interviews

Only through personal confrontations can personality fits be noted. Visiting the campus is the only way to determine the interaction of an individual with the environment, the climate, the school, administrators, and future colleagues. Thousands of little questions, no one of them crucial but when taken in total quite important, can be resolved only by a campus visit. Because they have grown used to it, the hiring department may fail to mention that offices are shared, that secretarial services are sorely lacking, that so-and-so in the administration is not at all sympathetic to the department, that 172 stairs must be climbed before the candidate reaches his office, or that Saturday classes and heavy committee loads are typical. By spending a day or so on the campus the answers to many of these questions will be self-evident without asking, and other questions will come to mind.

It is not surprising that on-campus interviewing was both the most frequently mentioned and most highly trusted method of gathering information on a particular job, in spite of its high time costs to the individual.[1] Fifty-one per cent of the interviewees had made visits to the hiring campus prior to their acceptance of the job, and over 90 per cent of the campus visiting group regarded the visit as the *most* helpful means of information gathering. Over 10 per cent of the candidates volunteered the statement that they would not accept a job without an on-campus interview, a percentage that would have undoubtedly been significantly higher had a specific question been asked. Although the hiring schools generally regard interviewing trips as an opportunity to confirm a decision previously reached, the visitor uses this opportunity to make his decision. In light of these findings, it might be relevant for the schools that are not now paying expenses for interviewing trips to re-examine their policy. It

1. A detailed description of on-campus interviews is given in Chapter VI, pp. 142-45.

seems that the universities and colleges that are prone to cutting expenses in this way are the very ones that can least afford to neglect the possible recruitment of qualified faculty for lack of transportation expenses.

Temporary Appointments

One other method of information gathering deserves mention more because of its probable popularity in some fields in the future than its use at the present time: the acceptance of an acknowledgedly temporary appointment at a school with the intent of considering the desirability of settling permanently. Opportunities for semester and year long campus visits have been increasing in recent years. More leaves of absences are being granted to professors who desire to spend a year freed from the responsibility of meeting classes and who are enabled to do so without financial sacrifice due to increased contractual research and additional foundation funds or non-contractual research. The absence of this regular faculty member affords an opportunity for a candidate to come in, teach the researcher's courses, and look the school over. Similarly, increasing enrollments during the summer months, a period when many members of the permanent faculty choose not to teach, is also affording greater opportunity for the long-term type of campus visit. By actually experiencing the teaching situation, the candidate can observe and judge the more subtle aspects of the job for himself. To test out each possible job is really the only effective way of being an intelligent job shopper.

Yet shopping by job switching is very costly. Since a change of teaching jobs almost always involves the physical relocation of home as well as work, a person accepting a semester or year appointment must bear the time, trouble, and expense of moving to and from every temporary appointment. Every year that is spent on temporary appointment is a year that seniority is not being accumulated at the school where the candidate finally settles, unless of course the temporary appointment is at that school. In many cases, there are also opportunity costs associated with the acceptance of temporary appointments. These costs are especially high for emerging graduate students. Most graduate schools feel some responsibility for placing a man in his first job and are willing to exert large efforts to see that their students are placed well. Once the students have been first placed, however, the sense of obligation frequently lessens. There is a new crop of students to be concerned about. Thus, for an emerging candidate, to accept a temporary appointment as his first is to squander his one best chance of getting help from his graduate school in finding a job.

In contrast, for the professor whose best alternative job is the one he currently holds, job shopping by a temporary appointment while on a leave of absence from his present school allows him to investigate thoroughly other opportunities without sacrificing the availability of a good job.

State of Knowledge at Time of Hiring

How much is known about a job before it is accepted? At what stage do the marginal costs of further investigation apparently exceed the expected returns? How effective are the various techniques of investigation? In order to answer these and related questions in terms of our sample of Southeastern economists, sociologists, and historians, an index (the Ignorance Index) has been developed. This index, which indicates the extent to which individual candidates are uninformed or misinformed about the jobs they accept at the time of acceptance, was computed for each individual from the answers given to the six following questions:[2]

(1) At the time you accepted this job did you know about the following items: salary? academic rank? hours of classroom teaching? courses to be taught? extent of library facilities? office facilities? fringe benefits? quality of students? promotion possibilities? congeniality of staff? availability of research monies? salary advancement? availability of secretarial services? committee duties?

2. A more detailed statement is included in Appendix C.

(2) If not, did you realize that you were accepting the job unaware of these matters?

(3) Did you visit the campus?

(4) Do you now feel that any subjects were "discreetly not mentioned" previously to the time you accepted the job?

(5) Would your decision to come here have been different if you had known more about the position?

(6) Did you know at the time you accepted the job if other candidates were being seriously considered?

To obtain an index number, the number of answers reflecting ignorance about the job was divided by the total number of questions answered.

Extent of Ignorance

Among the 103 individuals answering, the median index was .24. Thirty-six persons answered three or more of the questions in a way that implies ignorance about the job at the time of acceptance. Nearly one-fourth of the candidates felt that something had been "discreetly not mentioned," usually internal rifts among department members and conflicts between the department and university administrators. Discreet lack of mentioning the hours and courses to be taught, office facilities, expiration of research grants, and impending departures of certain key staff members were also reported, but less frequently. Over one-third had accepted the job unaware of their lack of knowledge on salient features of their job. This group not only did not know about their job but also they were not aware of their ignorance. Fourteen interviewees, about one-seventh, would not have accepted their positions if they had known more about them. Information was far from complete.

Nature of Ignorance

Very few candidates accept jobs without first knowing salary, academic rank, and the teaching load. These are the vital descriptive statistics that are easily stated, readily interpreted, and strictly comparable. In the very early stages of negotiations, tentative figures are exchanged with the hope that instances where the candidate's desires are irreconcilably higher than the hirer's intentions can be identified before too much time and effort is expended.

Since information on the less quantifiable aspects of compensation such as fringe benefits, salary advancement, and promotion possibilities is more difficult to obtain and compare, it is collected less frequently as shown by Table 2.

Table 2

Knowledge of Individuals About Specific Aspects of the Job They Accepted at Time of Acceptance

Items	Percentages of 103 Interviewees Who Knew About Item
Salary	96%
Academic Rank	95%
Hours of Classroom Teaching	93%
Courses to Be Taught	77%
Extent of Library Facilities	73%
Office Facilities	71%
Fringe Benefits	67%
Quality of Students	64%
Promotion Possibilities	61%
Congeniality of Staff	60%
Availability of Research Monies	56%
Salary Advancement	49%
Availability of Secretarial Services	48%
Committee Responsibilities	44%

Source: Individual Interviews

On matters relating to research such as the availability of research monies and the extent of library facilities, only the candidates who are considering positions at the high quality institutions (especially sociologists) are well informed.

Regarding teaching opportunities, candidates are amazingly unfamiliar with many specific aspects of the jobs they accept. Over one-fifth of our interviewees did not know what courses they would be teaching and more than one-third had nothing more than a vague impression of the quality and potential of the students they would be teaching. The administrative duties that the candidate would be asked to assume outside the classroom were unknown to a majority of the candidates. A majority of the candidates failed to inquire about secretarial services and less than three-fourths of the candidates knew where their new office would be and what equipment would be made available.

In general, candidates know about those aspects of the job in which they are most interested and those which are most easily discovered. Research oriented faculty may not know about the quality of the students, but they will look for low teaching loads, plentiful research funds, and adequate libraries. Professors attaching themselves to the smaller colleges, where mobility tends to be lower, are more likely to have information on promotion possibilities, fringe benefits, committee responsibilities, and the quality of students. Almost all professors know salary, rank, and hours taught.

Variations in Ignorance

An analysis of average Ignorance Indexes by sub-populations shows that some groups of professors are more knowledgeable about the jobs they are accepting than others. As a rule, the amount of information collected on the job accepted varied inversely with the number of jobs considered. When candidates considered several alternative job offers each of the options was examined with less care than when only one offer was considered. Historians, operating in the market where excess demand was the lowest, knew more about their jobs than economists or sociologists. Graduate students, untrained in what to look for in jobs, were not as well informed as persons switching teaching jobs. And finally, candidates who first learned about their jobs through impersonal means (e.g., formal placement agencies and mass letters) were not as well informed as persons accepting jobs located through friends and teachers.

Deciding upon a Particular Job

Information gathering cannot go on forever. At some point the most contemplative job changers must, on the basis of information available, choose among job opportunities. One must be chosen; the others sacrificed. The reasons why professors choose particular opportunities rather than others is a matter of vital concern to many different groups of people including university administrators who must attract and retain professors as employees, and economists who seek to confirm or deny hypotheses suggesting economic motivations for job choice. From this concern has resulted a number of studies, most of which shall be referred to frequently in subsequent pages.

A Caveat

Before proceeding, however, a caveat is in order. Ferreting out true human motivations is an extremely difficult and sophisticated process. In many instances a person does not himself know why he does what he does, and even when the individual knows his true motivations he is often reluctant to parade them in front of a social scientist, especially if his motivations are not the accepted ones. Although the former problem is less troublesome when dealing with a highly educated group such as college professors, the latter problem is probably more troublesome. For the more educated are more aware of which motivations are acceptable and better equipped to conceal the unacceptable ones. Among college professors, for instance, remnants of the legendary scholar seeking for truth with the abandonment of concern for any more than the necessities of subsistence in the world of material goods may very well cause present-day professors to conceal the importance of money as a motivational force. They may feel something of a traitor to the profession if they admit reverence to such suburban objectives as a larger car, a better home, or a more expensive fur.

Thus, if a professor is asked "On what bases do you choose among alternative jobs?" he is more likely to answer in terms of the criteria that he *thinks he should* use rather than the criteria that he *actually does* use.

In order to overcome this inherent difficulty faced in all motivational studies, several techniques were used. First, each professor was asked to think in terms of a specific, recent job change. Rather than asking what he "would do if," we concentrated upon "what he did do when." By questioning after the fact, theoretical and wishful answers were minimized. Professors were asked to state past experience, not hypothesize future behavior. By selecting a sample of only recent job changers, assurance was gained that most respondents would remember what their thoughts were and would not have to make them up. Also, by questioning after the fact, more specific answers could be demanded and from these answers internal inconsistencies could be more readily identified, pursued, and often corrected.

Second, the answers to direct questions were checked for consistency against the answers to indirect questions. For instance, the professor who desired to hide his true, salary-based motives might, with perseverance, respond "correctly" to questions such as "Would you say that salary was a major consideration in the job change?" and "What was the primary reason for switching positions?" "Why did you choose this job rather than one of the others?" and "What made you decide to stay here (rather than accept another opportunity that was offered)?" Yet, his true motives might still be uncovered by indirect questions such as "What are the advantages and disadvantages of your present job?" "What did you regard as the advantages and disadvantages of your previous job?" "If the salary of everyone on the faculty at your school were cut by $1,000 would you start looking for another position?" "If you are now looking for another job, have you specified in your own mind what minimal requirements this job must meet?" and many, many others. By repetition of closely related questions, it was possible to approach the true motives.

Finally, the answers given by the interviewees were checked against observable facts. On each individual a coterie of facts on such matters as age, educational background, fields of interest, publications, rank, change in rank from previous job, change in salary from previous job, hours taught on previous and present jobs, and so forth was accumulated. In the course of the interview, a man's answers were related to these facts. For instance, if a man said that the primary reason he switched jobs was because his previous salary was too low and we later discovered that his previous salary was greater than his current, he was asked to reconcile these two facts.

Admittedly, in spite of all these precautions, some professors have concealed their real motives, either intentionally or unintentionally. This then is the caveat: the conclusions in the next pages are valid only insofar as we were able to identify the true motivations of the professors that were interviewed. It is reasuring to know that, with very few exceptions, the interviewers were impressed with the apparent sincerity of the interviewees. Many of the interviewees talked freely about their experience. Their attitude was well expressed by several persons who stated, after the interview, that they welcomed this opportunity to help them see what their true motives for moving were and regarded the interview as somewhat of a confessional.

The Ideal Job

One additional preliminary comment seems in order. Professors, with different likes and dislikes, seek different things in their jobs. An "ideal" job from the viewpoint of one man may become available because another man has decided to leave it for other employment, supposedly better. No two professors, just as no two human beings, will judge employment on exactly the same criteria. The number of different factors that can enter into a job-choice decision is almost limitless—ranging from the climate to kinship, teaching loads to golf club membership requirements, religious affiliation to fringe benefits, publishing outlets to the local school system. It shall be our task in the remainder of this chapter to: (1) identify the factors that professors consider when choosing among jobs and indicate the overall importance of each; (2) distinguish among the factors that draw persons to new jobs, the factors that keep persons in old jobs, and the factors that cause old jobs to become intolerable; and (3) note and explain the differences in preference patterns of certain identifiable sub-populations of professors such as sociologists versus economists, veterans versus neophytes, Ph.D.'s versus non-Ph.D.'s, publishers versus non-publishers.

The attractiveness of professional appointments depends upon the working and the living aspects of the opportunities; that is, upon the characteristics of the jobs themselves and the characteristics of the environments in which the jobs place the professors. As a rule, better jobs carry higher salaries, more extensive fringe benefits, greater opportunities for earning additional income, higher academic rank, more adequate research facilities, fewer administrative responsibilities, and brighter students. The most attractive jobs are in departments and universities that command the greatest respect. Friendlier and more competent colleagues and more sympathetic and capable administrative officers increase job attractiveness. Better secretarial facilities, more extensive research equipment, larger and better equipped offices, more publishing outlets, greater research assistance, and closer parking lots are characteristics of better jobs. As for the environment, better appointments are nearer recreational facilities, cultural opportunities, relatives, and previously established friends. Better public schools, more desirable climates, and lower costs of living make for better jobs. Friendlier, more prosperous, and more progressive communities enhance job attractiveness. Communities with the "college atmosphere" generally appeal. These are the characteristics that all professors prefer in jobs: a finding that is not at all surprising.

Unfortunately, "ideal" jobs are non-existent. Any given employment opportunity carries with it some, but not all, of the desired qualities. For instance, a job at State University may pay well but require too many hours of teaching too many different courses. Or a job may pay well, require few hours of teaching, but be located in a city not to the candidate's liking. Though most professors can agree upon the characteristics of the ideal job, substantial differences of opinion appear when professors are required to choose the job characteristics and environmental characteristics that are the *most* desirable. This is in fact what professors are asked to do when selecting jobs. They must decide, for example, whether they would prefer a lower teaching load and lower salary to a higher teaching load and higher salary.

The Selection Process

To suggest that professors actually sit down with pencil and paper and note exactly how many dollars in salary they would be willing to sacrifice in order to get a job with three hours' lower teaching load or in order to get a job in a community that they like would be extremely deceptive. Job rating is casual. The professor is not an exception to the general rule that job evaluation and job seeking is rather a haphazard process. The uncertain end product from painstakingly comparing the satisfaction and dissatisfaction that he anticipates receiving from every component of a job, as contrasted to the corresponding components of every other job under consideration, is simply not worth the tremendous expenditures of time required. The actual process by which jobs are usually selected is far more practicable.

The selection process is primarily one of elimination. First, as mentioned in earlier chapters, many jobs are not chosen because of the paucity of information about them. In addition to the many open positions that never come to the attention of a job seeker due to the grossly imperfect channels of communication in most academic labor markets, a large number of jobs are eliminated without serious consideration because what is currently known about the openings is too little or too unreliable and the time and money costs of collecting more information are too expensive. Thus, the first criterion used in selecting (in this case eliminating) jobs is "uncertainty." Turning this around, one of the criterion for selecting a job is that the candidate, at some stage in the decision-making process, develop a relatively clear and reliable image of the job.

The second hurdle in the selection process relates to minimum characteristics, features that a job *must* have in order to be considered by the candidate. These characteristics are usually readily identifiable from a distance and without investigation. For instance, most professors will not consider jobs carrying a salary below what they are currently earning. That is to say, below present salary the marginal rate of substitution of dollars for a lower teaching load, for a better community, for more research facilities, or for more friendly colleagues is zero. No matter how good the job is in other ways, it will not be seriously considered if the salary is below a certain point. Similarly, jobs that require reductions in academic rank are usually eliminated without further investigation. Many professors will not consider jobs in certain parts of the country. Few professors will consider teaching outside their general field of specialty. Academic personnel will rarely consider a job outside teaching. Very few professors will consider a job at a university that does not have complete and guaranteed academic freedom.

For some professors the minimal characteristics of a job are quite specific. One man interviewed said that he would not consider a job at a school that was not connected with the Teachers' Insurance and Annuity Association. Another man stated he would live no place other than a given city. The point is that by specifying certain features that jobs must have, a large majority of the job openings of which one becomes aware can be eliminated with relatively little effort. This avoids much time-consuming investigation.

As a rule, the first two cuts narrow the field of possible job opportunities to no more than five, and more typically to two or three. From this point the selection process is painstakingly difficult. The ideal, an absolute measure of the net satisfaction that would be received from each opportunity under consideration, is not practicable: among other things, the variables to be considered are too numerous and diverse. Rather than attempting job comparisons on the basis of all relevant variables, it is our distinct impression that most professors select no more than five key factors by which to make their final job choice. The opportunities under consideration are contrasted and compared, selected and rejected, on the basis of these key factors. Key factors are aspects that the candidate regards as important, though not essential, in his job and environment. The selection of key factors is unique to each individual and dependent upon the individual's tastes, foresight, disposition to assume risk, experience and training, and such. For example, would-be professors who received their undergraduate training in a small, liberal arts college often insist upon teaching at a similar institution; boating enthusiasts insist upon jobs that place them near water suitable for boating; and graduates of prestigious graduate schools sometimes insist upon locating in a "publishing atmosphere."

It is necessary to emphasize, however, that the factors upon which jobs are selected (the key factors) are not always the factors that mean the most to the persons selecting the jobs (the most important factors). Certain aspects of jobs may be extremely important to the selecting individual up to a point, and considerably less important beyond that point. In such a case, this job aspect serves as a minimum constraint rather than a key factor. For instance, a professor may have decided that he is unwilling to live outside the Southeast, that he is unwilling to accept a salary lower than the one he is now receiving, that he must teach in a liberal arts college, or that academic freedom must exist in the college in which he teaches. To this professor these aspects of his job are so important that he will not consider any job that violates them. In terms of our oversimplified model, jobs not meeting these criteria would not have passed the second cut. The point is this: since these factors were taken into consideration at an earlier stage in the decision-making process, they are not considered at this stage. They are not so-called key factors. The distinction between minimal factors and key factors is an important one, especially when interpreting the results of this study. When an individual is asked why he accepted one job rather than another, he is likely to identify only the key factors, since both jobs had met his minimal criteria.

The key and most important factors differ in another way. Key factors, which are to be used to differentiate among jobs, must be more or less measurable. In contrast, the most important factors are sometimes not at all measurable. For instance, an individual may regard the right to plan his teaching and research independent from the control of a superior as one of the most important characteristics of a job. Yet, this cannot be measured. Matters such as interrelatedness of research interest, *esprit de corps* among one's prospective colleagues, and compatibility in community life are subject to the same limitation. Even though a person might regard these as most important, unless he were willing to assume a great degree of risk in the accuracy of his measurements, it is unlikely that the factors would be determinative in the final job choice.

And, in still another way, key and most important factors differ. Recall that "key factors" are the characteristics of the jobs under consideration that, in the final analysis, provide the basis for choosing one and rejecting the others. If the jobs are "equal" in regard to a factor (e.g., all jobs carry the same rank or the same salary or the same teaching load), no matter how important the factor may be, it cannot be used to differentiate among the jobs and is, therefore, not a key factor. One job cannot be chosen above another on the basis of salary if both jobs carry the same salary.

At first thought it appears that two (and especially more than two) jobs would rarely be "equal" in regard to any given factor. In fact this may be true, but in practice it is not. Most job characteristics are so difficult to rate that a large range of error must be allowed. For example, from the viewpoint of a person who has seen the jobs in two-day interviewing trips, the jobs are likely to appear equal in regard to the quality of students, the competency of colleagues, and so forth, even though they are not. When the jobs under consideration appear to have equal quantities of a given characteristic and all jobs are generally regarded as "acceptable," the characteristic is not a key or determinative factor, no matter how important it is. The would-be but undifferentiating key factor is supplanted as a basis for decision-making. This process probably results in an understatement of the importance of factors that tend to be regarded as equal. The process does, however, result in more accurate decision-making.

Having sketched the decision-making process, let us now turn to a detailed discussion of the various factors that enter into the decision. Due to the methodology used to collect the data, concentration must be placed upon the "key" factors, though some attempt is also made to identify the factors that are more appropriately regarded as minimum constraints.

Location

The role that location plays in the selection of jobs by professors is best understood by referring to Table 3. Each column in this table summarizes the answers to a slightly different question asked of our sample of Southeastern social scientists. Two figures appear in each column: a percentage and a rank. The 37 per cent in row 1 of column 1 indicates, for example, that 37 per cent of the 71 persons who indicated why they chose their current job instead of a competitive offer mentioned "location" as a factor. The ranks order the percentages by columns: rank one indicates the most frequently mentioned job characteristic in answer to the question at the top of the column.

The various columns of the table tell: why professors who had previous jobs switched (column 3), why professors who had several different job offers to choose from at the time they chose their present job made the choice they did (column 1), why professors who had recently received job offers from other schools decided to stay at their current job instead of accepting one of the offers (column 4), and for professors who are now seeking new jobs what characteristics new job offers must have before they receive serious consideration (column 2). By noting the relative strength of each factor at each stage of the decision-making process, it is possible to get a fairly well-defined idea of what extent and in what way the various factors influence the migratory patterns of professors.

Turning now to a consideration of "location," note that "location" is first ranked in column 1. This means that professors who

Table 3

Factors Stressed in Job Selection Decisions, by Stages in the Decision-Making Process[1]

Job Characteristics	(1) Why Did You Choose Your Present Job Rather Than Other Offers You Had at the Same Time?[2]		(2) What Are the Minimal Characteristics of Any New Job That You Would Consider at This Time?[3]		(3) What Were Your Primary Reasons for Switching Academic Jobs?[4]		(4) Why Did You Decide Not to Leave Your Present Job by Accepting Another Offer?[5]	
	Per cent (N = 71)	Vertical Rank	Per cent (N = 37)	Vertical Rank	Per cent (N = 67)	Vertical Rank	Per cent (N = 55)	Vertical Rank
Location	37%	1	43%	3	13%	6	29%	1
Reputation of Department and University	31%	2	49%	2	15%	4	20%	3
Work Duties, including Courses Taught	23%	3	22%	6	22%	2	27%	2
Salary	18%	4	68%	1	13%	6	11%	4
Colleagues, Congeniality and Competency	13%	5	3%	9	9%	8	2%	9
Number of Classes and Teaching Load	10%	6	41%	4	9%	9	5%	7
University Administration	10%	7	13%	7	28%	1	2%	8
Research Emphasis	7%	8	35%	5	13%	6	7%	6
Opportunities for Growth and Advancement	7%	9	0%	10	19%	3	9%	5
Academic Rank	1%	10	13%	8	6%	10	0%	10

1. The percentage figures in each of the four columns are computed from different bases. In each case the base refers to the total number of professors who answered each particular question. Thus, the 37 per cent in column one indicates that

37 per cent of the 71 persons who answered the question, "Why did you choose your present job rather than other offers you had at the same time?" mentioned location as one of the influences.

2. This question was addressed only to persons who had had more than one job offer to consider at the time they accepted their present job.

3. This question was addressed only to persons who were looking for another job at the time they were interviewed.

4. This question was addressed only to persons who had had academic employment immediately prior to their present job.

5. This question was addressed only to persons who had received, and rejected, offers from other schools while at their present job.

Source: Individual Interviews

---

faced the decision of which among several job offers should be accepted said that they had been influenced by the geographic location of the various offers more often than any other factor. Over 35 per cent of the 71 southeastern social scientists who had a choice of job offers at the time they accepted their current job listed, without prompting, some aspect of the physical locations of the various offers as one of the reasons why they chose the job they did.

As shown by column 4, geographic location was also the factor most frequently mentioned in decisions to reject offers from other schools. Twenty-nine per cent of the professors who had given serious consideration to a competitive job offer since teaching at the school where they were interviewed and had finally decided to remain commented that the geographic location had influenced their decision. And, among professors desirous of leaving the institutions where they were interviewed (and where they were teaching currently), over 40 per cent said that they would not move unless the new job was desirably located geographically (column 2).

The geography of jobs does have a strong influence upon the migratory patterns of professors. It is interesting to note, however, that most of the effects are "pull" and "keep," not "push." "Location" ranks sixth in importance among the factors that cause men to switch jobs, as shown by column three.[3]

3. Conjecturing upon why "location" is not an important "push" factor, two reasons come to mind. First, it is unlikely that a job will ever be accepted in a location that one regards as unacceptable, for most of the factors that influence the acceptability of locations (e.g., climate, size of town, nearness to relatives and friends, nearness to recreation facilities) are knowable before acceptance is

The reasons for preferring one geographic location to another are as numerous as the reason-givers. For new teachers with unfinished dissertations, it is important to be near their graduate school. Experts in the history of the southern United States, professors with research interests in the sociology of the South, and economists with specialties in the economic development of the Southeastern region are for obvious professional reasons constrained in their job choices. Nearness to recreational facilities is stressed by outdoor enthusiasts. (One professor we interviewed rejected an otherwise better offer in order to be near National Park facilities.) School systems and community cultural activities such as concerts, art exhibits, and live theatre are also important to some. Many professors stress climate in their job choice. Some professors like to teach in large cities because of the cultural facilities, the night life, the opportunities for outside income, or the anonymity that can be achieved. Others insist upon teaching in quaint college towns. Closeness to other academic institutions and to transportation facilities that can carry them to professional meetings and consulting engagements is emphasized by still others. The proximity of one's job to one's relatives is also considered: some express their preferences in terms of "nearness to" and others, "distances away from." Some jobs are taken in order to be near old friends. Still other professors accept jobs with the intention of making new friends in new parts of the country. There is no general rule, except that geographic location is an extremely important influence upon job choice. A small sample of the comments made by our interviewees is cited below:

Reported a scholar of church history, "Here at [a denominational college] I am near the state historical library, and the State Baptist Historical Society is on campus. This location affords an opportunity for my wife, who is a nursing instructor, to work. When I first came with an unfinished thesis, ——— was closer [than the other schools that extended offers] to my graduate school."

given. (This point is developed in the text on the next page.) Secondly, it is likely that, in lieu of norms of human behavior, any given location will become more rather than less acceptable as a person gets to know it better by living in it.

A textbook writer in economics accepted his current job because "it was the only offer in the South and I wanted to remain in the South."

A middle-aged economist who had suddenly had his job with a federal government agency terminated said that "my only criterion for a new job was that it be in the same city." He didn't want to move and disrupt his school-age children.

Commenting on his motives for returning to the university in the state where he had been born and raised, an economist stated, "I had prior connections with the town and the area. I knew the people who could introduce me to other people. I longed to get back to the lakes and the terrain that I knew as a boy."

Reported a sociologist who had accepted a job at a middle-prestige state university in the Deep South, "I left Minnesota because the climate caused me to be dreadfully sick."

A historian, who had a better reputation than his school and had several good job offers, explained why he turned down the offers in the following way: "With Wisconsin, it was a question of a good university versus palm trees, swimming pools, and a comfortable and accustomed life. . . . With the University of Washington, the West Coast is too far away from everything."

Another historian, who was located at a university in a large town commented: "I was attracted to the big city. A large town allows one to get lost. A big city is cosmopolitan, cultural. It allows one to develop interesting and stimulating friendships outside the university community. This is not a college town and that's what I like about it."

The importance of location stems from the fact that it is one of the few factors relevant to job choice that differs substantially and noticeably among jobs. When a professor has narrowed the job possibilities to the two or three that he considers best and is faced with the task of ranking there is usually very little basis for differentiating among jobs. The jobs often offer similar salaries, ranks, teaching loads, and teaching assignments. Although the jobs may differ in advancement potential, desirability of university administrations, competency and congeniality of colleagues, these differences cannot be known without actually try-

Table 4

Factors Stressed in Job

Diochotomizing Characteristics[1]	Percentage of Subgroup	
	(1) Loca- tion	(2) Repu- tation
Characteristics of Individuals:		
Economist (35)	69%*	43%
Sociologist (32)	44%*	28%
Historian (35)	40%*	29%
Junior Faculty Member (73)	51%	33%
Senior Faculty Member (28)	54%	32%
Highest Degree from Southeast (33)	64%	27%
Highest Degree not from Southeast (70)	46%	36%
Ph.D. Holder (80)	54%	36%
Non-Ph.D. Holder (22)	45%	18%
Publisher (42)[2]	57%	40%
Non-Publisher (50)[2]	44%	30%
Characteristics of Current Employers:		
Among Top 6 Schools Surveyed (35)[3]	31%*	47%*
Among Bottom 6 Schools Surveyed (31)[3]	58%*	16%*
Mean Salary Exceeds $9000 (25)[4]	28%*	16%
Mean Salary Is Less Than $7500 (20)[4]	55%*	30%
Characteristics of the Move to Current Employer:		
Knowledgeable about New Job (42)[5]	48%	21%*
Not Knowledgeable about New Job (61)[5]	56%	41%*
Original Offer Was Accepted (63)	48%	37%
Negotiations Changed Offer (39)	59%	28%
Only One Offer Considered (47)	47%	32%
More Than One Offer Considered (56)	55%	32%
Move Did Not Improve Salary (17)	53%	18%*
Move Improved Salary (10)	40%	80%*

1. The figures in parentheses refer to the absolute number of professors in the subgroup. The 69 per cent in column one means, for instance, that 69 per cent (or 24) of the 35 economists mentioned location.

2. Professors are rated according to their Productivity Indexes, see Appendix E.

3. Schools are graded by their Quality Indexes; see Appendix D.

4. Salary figures are taken from the *AAUP Bulletin*, Summer, 1962.

Selection Decisions by Subgroups

that was, at some stage, influenced by the following factors:

(3) Work Duties	(4) Salary	(5) Job Potential	(6) Teaching Load	(7) Adminis- tration	(8) Research Emphasis	(9) Col- leagues	(10) Academic Rank
20%	54%	20%	26%	20%	14%	17%	6%#
31%	44%	9%	28%	37%	16%	22%	16%#
37%	31%	23%	23%	23%	29%	29%	6%#
29%	44%	21%	26%	16%*	23%	22%	9%
36%	46%	11%	25%	54%*	11%	25%	9%
30%	36%	12%	24%	18%	6%*	24%	9%
30%	47%	20%	26%	30%	26%*	21%	9%
31%	46%	18%	24%	30%	23%	23%	9%
23%	32%	18%	27%	9%	9%	23%	9%
33%	50%	19%	26%	40%*	19%	24%	12%
32%	40%	16%	22%	16%*	22%	22%	6%
33%	56%*	14%	31%	28%	31%	22%	11%
26%	26%*	19%	29%	29%	10%	29%	0%
36%	56%	20%	24%	32%	31%*	12%*	8%
35%	45%	30%	25%	35%	0%*	45%*	5%
29%	26%*	14%	24%	26%	11%*	31%	2%*
31%	56%*	20%	26%	26%	25%*	16%	13%*
27%	41%	17%	22%	19%*	24%	24%	6%
36%	49%	18%	31%	38%*	13%	21%	13%
23%	32%*	15%	15%*	27%	15%	17%	9%
36%	54%*	20%	34%*	30%	23%	27%	9%
24%	35%*	18%	12%	29%	12%	29%	18%
30%	80%*	20%	30%	30%	20%	50%	0%

5. Professors are graded according to their Ignorance Indexes; see Appendix C.

* The percentages in the couplet or triplet are significantly different from one another, at the 95 per cent level of confidence according to Chi-Square (if all cells > 5) or Fisher-Yates (if one or more cell > 5).

Significance of difference could not be calculated.

Source: Individual Interviews.

ing out each job. The factors that are both differentiating and determinable, though they may not be the most important factors, are the ones on which the job choice must be based. It is here that "location" is crucial. Although competition may bring the salaries offered by a large city school in the North and a middle-sized private institution in the South into equality, neither institution can hide or alter its location. Because of these non-erasable, substantial, and determinable differences among jobs, geographic attractiveness is one of the key factors in job selection.

The extent to which particular groups of professors emphasize location in their job selection can be seen by studying Table 4. By various subgroupings (e.g., economists versus sociologists versus historians) this table shows the percentage of professors that mentioned location as an influence upon job selection at *any* stage in the decision-making process. In making Table 4, each subgroup of professors was dichotomized into two groups: those who had replied "location" to one of the four questions listed at the top of Table 3 and those who had not. The percentage of the total group who had is the figure cited in column 1 of Table 4. Thus, 69 per cent indicates that 69 per cent of the 35 (which appears in parentheses) economists interviewed had mentioned location as a minimum factor, as a key factor, as a factor important in job switching, or as a factor important in the decision to stay on a particular job.

The most definite differences in stress upon location can be seen to be between professors now teaching at high quality—high paying schools as opposed to those at the poorer quality—lower paying schools. The former group tended to stress salary, research emphasis, and reputation at the sacrifice of location. There are many indications that the latter group was more interested in climate, general atmosphere, and a way of life; thus location.[4]

Consistent with these observations were the findings of both

4. The only other significant difference in the group that stressed location and the group that did not is their discipline. Economists indicated a greater concern for location than either sociologists or historians. The difference may be explained by the desire of economists to be near consulting opportunities, though we did not test this hypothesis.

Miller and Stecklein-Lathrop. The professors of the University of Minnesota, an institution that would receive our highest quality rating, seemed to be less concerned about location per se than the widely diversified (in terms of prestige ratings of their graduate schools) sample of graduate students surveyed by Miller. Concerning locational factors, University of Minnesota professors said that they are considered more frequently than any of thirteen factors. They went on to say, however, that the consideration of location is not nearly as intense as several other factors and that location is rarely the primary determinant of a job choice.[5] In contrast, Jerry L. L. Miller, surveying 59 Southeastern graduate students who were in the process of accepting their first academic jobs, notes that 75 per cent of these men expressed some regional preference (usually for the Southeast) and 20 per cent of the men stated that the regional preference would in no case be compromised; the region was a minimum constraint by our model. Although quantitatively other factors were mentioned more frequently (e.g., load, advancement) by the Miller sample, the unwillingness to compromise location was unique, suggesting the qualitative significance of location for this group of college teachers.[6]

Rank

Because differences in rank among roughly *comparable* opportunities are rare and because professors are unwilling to sacrifice other job characteristics that they regard as more important in order to attain the questionable increase in prestige associated with higher rank, academic rank is rarely crucial in job choice decisions.

In the final stages of decision-making, it is rare for the job under consideration to carry different ranks. Ranks do differ, but not among comparable jobs. Lesser schools, attempting to compensate for the undesirable monetary and workload features of the positions they offer, often make appointments at ranks higher

5. Stecklein and Lathrop, *Faculty Attraction and Retention*, pp. 125 and 19-20.
6. Miller, *Exploratory Study*, pp. 39-40.

than the candidate "deserves." To cite an extreme case, one of our interviewees had turned down a full professorship at a small, mountain college to accept an appointment at a state university. He is teaching less and earning more, but his rank is that of assistant professor rather than full professor. Similarly, the great graduate schools of the North and West sometimes hire at a rank lower than the majority of accredited colleges and universities.

Offers carrying academic ranks higher than "deserved" should be regarded with suspicion.[7] The stature attached to rank cannot be transposed among institutions. At a given school, a full professor is in some ways regarded as superior to an associate, and an associate superior to an assistant. But, since the standards for attaining various ranks differ by schools, a full professor at School A cannot be adjudged superior to an associate at School B. Different schools have different calibrations on their rank structure. Rank is not, therefore, a symbol used to differentiate among the quality of men at different schools. As a prestige symbol, rank is intra-collegiate, not inter-collegiate. The status associated with rank is significant, if at all, only within one's own institution (and perhaps institutions that are generally regarded as comparable).

Since the true status value of academic rank is unique to the institution that offers it and cannot be readily evaluated by an outsider, rank per se is rarely a determining factor in the job choice decision. In our survey of Southeastern social scientists only one man mentioned that he accepted his present rather than another job because it offered a higher rank. Answers to other questions suggest that insofar as rank per se has any significance in the employment decision, it is a minimum constraint rather than a key factor. As shown in Table 3, rank is one of the least important factors in professorial job selection, at all stages. Offer-

7. Statistics compiled by the National Education Association ("Instructional Staff Practices and Policies in Degree-Granting Institutions, 1953-54," *Research Bulletin*, Vol. 32, No. 4 [December, 1954], p. 163) are in accord with the hypothesis that smaller schools cheapen rank. Nearly 34 per cent of the faculty members teaching at nonpublic colleges with enrollments under five hundred are listed as full professors whereas the comparable percentage for municipal universities is only about 19 per cent.

ing confirmation to our results, Stecklein and Lathrop in their survey of the reasons why persons accepted appointments at the University of Minnesota note that, among the thirteen factors studied, rank had "no influence" more often than any other factor except one.[8] Rank is significantly omitted from the lists of factors affecting job choices that have been compiled by other researchers.

A distinction should be made, however, between rank per se and the privileges and implications that rank sometimes carries. Rank per se is only a status symbol; it cannot buy groceries, as the saying goes. Rank, as a symbol of status, is confined to one's own campus and therefore of only limited significance. But rank may signal more than intra-campus status differences. For instance, on many campuses the rank of associate professor carries with it the right of tenure, a partial guarantee of job security. Many professors, especially ones who have reached or passed beyond their years of peak productivity, will not consider opportunities that do not guarantee tenure. Along this line, Caplow and McGee suggest that a primary motive for migration among men on the way down is the attainment of security and authority. The security aspect of this duo-motive could be attained through tenure.

Rank, and rank change, may also figure significantly into attempts to push unwanted professors to other jobs. Although it is impossible to compare ranks between campuses, the relative ranks and change of ranks within campuses, especially within departments at a given school, is a valid though sometimes unjust measure of relative esteem and prestige. If, for instance, two men with similar training and experience are hired into a department in the same year at the assistant professor level and, after two years, one of the two men is promoted to associate and the other is not, this definitely implies that the promoted man has a greater future at that school. It may well suggest to the man not promoted that he should start looking for another job, either because he is not as highly regarded or because there is a blockage problem (a senior professor in his area). In a similar way, ad-

8. Stecklein and Lathrop, *Faculty Attraction and Retention*, pp. 125 and 19.

ministrators often use effectively positive rank changes to keep men on their staffs.

To summarize, although the intra-campus prestige and the security provisions that rank sometimes symbolizes do influence the migration of professorial manpower, rank per se is not a criterion on which new jobs are chosen and rejected.

Work Duties

College teaching jobs differ widely. One school may ask its professors to emphasize teaching and classroom lecturing, another may require primary emphasis upon research and writing, and still another may desire many hours of counseling and administration. Differences in the distribution of courses that are to be taught and the mixture of teaching-research-administration are a major influence upon the choice of jobs. Indicated by the second place rankings of "work duties" in Table 3, the faculty members in our sample tended to remain at the job where they were doing what they wanted and tended to leave jobs where the duties were unappealing. These results confirm those of earlier studies. Miller found that "time to work in area of own interest" was an "important" factor in the selection of a particular job more often than any of the twenty-two other factors listed.[9] Every graduate student surveyed regarded the workload features of his new job as important. Professors who had recently accepted positions at the University of Minnesota, answering the questions of Stecklein and Lathrop, noted that "the nature of the position" was the third (of thirteen) most important influence on their decision to accept the appointment.[10] In his more general study of faculty at thirty-two Minnesota colleges and junior colleges, Stecklein's subjects listed "I could teach in the field of my choice" more often than any other as the reason for choosing their present staff affiliation.[11]

9. Miller, *Exploratory Study*, p. 40.
10. Stecklein and Lathrop, *Faculty Attraction and Retention*, pp. 125 and 16-17.
11. Ruth E. Eckert and John E. Stecklein, *Job Motivations and Satisfactions of College Teachers: A Study of Faculty Members in Minnesota Colleges*

How can this great concern for work duties be explained? Part of the explanation lies in the type of people that are attracted to college teaching careers. College professors are significantly different from persons in many other occupations in at least one respect: they are willing to exchange some of the satisfactions that money can bring for the nonmonetary satisfaction of their work. Many professors could, without any further training, switch to jobs outside of teaching at considerably higher rates of pay; yet they do not. This economically "irrational" behavior suggests that professors, as a group, are perhaps less concerned with what they take home in compensation for having worked than with what they are doing while working. According to a survey of professors at thirty-two Minnesota colleges, people that remain in college teaching like their jobs not because of the appreciation and the rewards, not because of the working conditions, but because of the nature of the work itself. The joys of transmitting knowledge, observing students' growth and success, associating with college age students, working and studying in one's own field of professional interest: these are the reasons why teachers like teaching.[12] From this and many similar surveys, it is safe to infer that the persons who choose college teaching as a career place a greater-than-ordinary stress upon what they do when they go off to make the dollars to pay for the groceries.

Since college teachers stress the "nature of the work" when choosing an occupation, it is not surprising to find that the "nature of the work" is also considered when selecting a particular job within teaching. Certain attractions are common to all teaching jobs. No matter where a person teaches, he has an opportunity to observe intellectual growth, associate with young people, and share knowledge. But teaching jobs do differ. For instance, some jobs ask teachers to share very general knowledge (e.g., a man trained in history might be asked to teach Western Civilization

("OE-53009, Cooperative Research Monograph No. 7"; Washington: Government Printing Office, 1961), p. 31.

12. Ruth E. Eckert, John E. Stecklein, and H. Bradley Sagen, "College Faculty Members View Their Jobs," *American Association of University Professors Bulletin*, Vol. 45, No. 4 (December, 1959), pp. 520-21.

to freshmen and an art course), whereas other jobs require the sharing of specific knowledge (e.g., a man trained in history might be asked to offer a graduate course in the history of Chinese Art between 900 and 1200 A.D.). Different teaching jobs offer different proportions of classroom instruction, individual instruction, research, and administration. The quality of students and the interests of students are not the same at different schools.

Our study of Southeastern social scientists indicates that of special concern to professors are the courses they will be asked to teach. One of the most coveted assignments in teaching is a graduate level course. Most professors feel that the greater challenge, higher prestige, and closer tie-in with their own research interests more than offset the greater preparation time requirements of graduate level courses. As a rule, professors prefer to specialize in the classroom, to concentrate upon the two or three courses that they are best qualified to teach. Very few professors would even consider teaching in more than one general area of knowledge (e.g., sociology, art, and physics) or in an area of knowledge different from their graduate school training. In the sociology versus art sense, the courses to be taught provide a minimum constraint upon the types of jobs any given college professor will consider. As specialties become more narrowly defined, preferences are not as strong. In the industrial sociology versus social psychology sense, the courses to be taught are often key factors, rarely minimum factors.

The desire for specialization is also understandable in light of the savings achieved in preparation times. If two sections of one course are taught, the total time that must be spent in preparing the lectures is considerably less than when two different courses are taught. If two different courses are taught, the more closely related the two courses are, the greater the transferability of lecture preparations and general background reading. And finally, if the closely related or same courses that are taught are in the same areas as one's research interests, a triple-barreled economy of scale is achieved. No wonder professors are advocates of specialization.[13] No wonder over 20 per cent of the interviewees that actually switched from one teaching job to another were motivated by the greater attractiveness of the courses that they would be asked to teach at the new assignment. Of the social scientists interviewed, in free response approximately one-fourth stated that one of the reasons they chose their present job instead of any of the alternatives was that the courses that they were asked to teach were either fewer,[14] more to their liking, or both.

A few of the quotations from the interviews with persons who emphasize work duties in their job choices are the following:

A productive, young Ph.D. in economics "wanted to stay away from smaller colleges where there would be little opportunity for work with graduate students and for research."

An emerging expert in financial economics and business cycles viewed favorably "the opportunity to teach both business and economics" offered by a high-prestige school and chose the job for this reason.

A young, promising historian related that he chose not to teach at a well-reputed, liberal arts college because "the university job [which he accepted] allowed me to teach graduate courses in Modern Indian History."

A new Ph.D. from the University of Minnesota had accepted his first job at a middle-prestige university because "it allowed me to spend most of my time teaching English History which is my special interest."

A historian who was a specialist in the Far East moved from a small liberal arts college to a Southeastern university because "[the

13. On the other hand, few professors seek complete specialization. Among the social scientists studied, most of the men interviewed were, regardless of rank, keeping in touch with the field in general by teaching at least one section of the introductory or survey course.
14. There is a difference between teaching fewer courses and teaching fewer hours. A professor teaching two sections of one course and one section of another may have the same nine-hour load as a professor teaching three different courses, but the former is teaching fewer courses. Similarly, a professor teaching three two-hour courses has a lower teaching load than one teaching three three-hour courses, though the number of courses taught is identical.

university] offered an opportunity to specialize, to do something in my own field."

By specializing in an area of learning where his skills are most fully developed, a professor is able to feel that he is maximizing his time and consequently maximizing his contribution to knowledge and society. If his present teaching assignment does not engender such a feeling, he is likely to seek a change.

Teaching Loads

Our interviews indicate that job changers are far more concerned with the composition of their teaching loads than the number of hours taught per se. Since 1955 there has been a decidedly downward trend in the number of hours that college professors are asked to spend in classrooms. The once standard twelve- and fifteen-hour teaching loads have been, in most of the schools surveyed, reduced to nine and twelve and in a few instances six. Contributing to these reductions are efforts of teacher organizations such as the American Association of University Professors and special accrediting associations such as the American Association of Collegiate Schools of Business. The main reason, however, is the effective demand for more research.

Public and private organizations are channeling unprecedented sums of money into university research. In the social sciences, organizations such as the Social Science Research Council, the Ford Foundation, the Carnegie Foundation, and a multiplicity of government agencies are stimulating research in everything from the culture of Uganda to the most desirable curriculum for high school economics courses. The National Science Foundation, National Institutes of Health, and other agencies and organizations provide even more extensive funds to professors in the natural sciences. If universities have always appreciated the importance and value of faculty research, it is only now that, at least partially, the financial means are being provided to pursue the desired goals.

To an extent greater in some fields than in others,[15] the new accent upon research is enabling the individual professor to have the choice of a career emphasizing research as opposed to one emphasizing teaching.[16] Prior to the popularity of research professorships and reduced teaching loads, all professors were asked to teach the same number of hours. Those choosing to do research had to fit it in between classes. A large share of the active researcher's time had to be channeled into teaching in order to make a living, no matter what the researching teacher might prefer to do with his time. Today, in the natural and to a lesser extent the social sciences, it is possible for professors to accept and to be compensated for research work in lieu of high teaching loads. The option between six hours teaching and research on the one hand and twelve hours' teaching and no research on the other is a live one. Within our sample of eighteen Southeastern universities, for instance, the average load for beginning assistant professors in sociology ranged from six hours at one institution that expected research to fifteen hours at one that did not. Similarly, the teaching loads of professors of the same rank at the same school varied by as many as nine hours due to acknowledged differences in research activity.

In spite of the large differentials in teaching loads among institutions, the job seekers we interviewed regard the "hours of teaching required" as one of the less important considerations in the job choice decision. Table 3, column 3, indicates that in decisions to switch jobs "teaching loads" is next to least important of the ten listed factors. Similarly, teaching loads are rarely decisive when choosing among alternative new jobs (Table 3,

15. Professors in fields such as mathematics, where research funds are plentiful, are experiencing faster reductions in teaching loads than professors in fields, such as history, where research funds are not so plentiful. At several of the surveyed schools, sociologists and economists are averaging teaching loads that are three to six hours lower than those in history.

16. Universities are now hiring many Ph.D.-level personnel to work only as researchers. These researchers, who are usually paid with funds that the university is receiving to complete specific projects, have no official contact with the students. They teach no courses; they do not counsel students; and they are not responsible for curriculum. They are simply research workers who might as well be working for a private firm.

column 1): only 10 per cent of the 71 professors who had more than one job offer to choose from named "teaching load" as a key factor. The only significant influence of teaching loads per se in migratory decisions is a negative one. In this era when the general trend of teaching loads is downward, few professors will even consider accepting a new job that requires more teaching than their present one. Succinctly, higher teaching loads keep applicants away, but lower teaching loads do not necessarily attract.

Why do professors show so little concern for teaching loads? In the first place, "teaching loads" is one of the job characteristics that tends to be "equal" for all the offers considered. Although teaching loads do vary among schools, the differentials are concentrated among groups of fundamentally different types of schools (e.g., the small liberal arts colleges versus the technical schools versus the major universities) and are relatively rare within groups. For instance, the offers received by a new Ph.D. seeking a position in a liberal arts college are unlikely to differ by more than three hours (from twelve to fifteen). The same is true of offers from research-oriented universities (from six to nine) and other types of institutions. If a professor were deciding between an offer from a liberal arts college and an offer from a research-oriented university, the teaching differentials would be large enough to deserve serious consideration. But this is rarely the type of choice that is made. As shall be more fully documented later in the chapter, most professors have a fairly well-defined idea of the type(s) of schools at which they will accept jobs. Most of the offers they solicit are from the same type of schools. It follows that the teaching loads attached to the offers they receive are about the same also. Teaching load differentials are, therefore, little help in discriminating among the offers; the differentials are not sufficiently large to make one job preferable to another.

Second, one gains the impression from the interviews that among professors, even those with the higher teaching loads, there is a realistic acknowledgment that lower teaching loads mean not less work, but different work. Universities hire men to teach six rather than twelve hours so that their faculty can have more research time, not more leisure. If teaching is not expected, research (or administration) is. Among our interviewees, the most active researchers were teaching the least, and vice versa. Grouping professors in five categories on the basis of research productivity and then in five categories on the basis of hours taught, it was noted that, without exception, the groups of more productive professors were teaching less. The rank correlation coefficient between the two groupings was one.

In the teaching profession, a lower workload is a will-o'-the-wisp. The meaningful choice is between "a research emphasis" and "a teaching emphasis," not high and low work loads. To use teaching loads per se as a criterion for job choice is to stress the means to a desired end rather than the end itself. High teaching loads are desired as a means of avoiding the necessity to do research; low loads, as a means of freeing time for research. Since reduced teaching loads is only one of several means of gaining more research time, it is more sensible for a person desirous of researching to seek a job where research is encouraged (by whatever means) than a job where research is encouraged by a specific means (i.e., reduced teaching loads). Besides lower teaching loads, more research time can be achieved through teaching fewer courses and maintaining the same load, teaching courses that are more closely related to each other and to one's research interests, hiring graders and secretaries to reduce the burden of menial tasks associated with teaching, and insisting upon an adequate salary so that it is unnecessary to consume valuable hours performing little-related tasks in outside employment. Though teaching load is important as a means to an end, it is not a key factor in most job choice decisions because professors wisely seek the end itself.

Research Emphasis

Teaching and research require different talents and offer different rewards. A good teacher must be friendly, inspiring, humane, interesting and above all verbal. It is his responsibility to organize and interpret the thoughts of scholars in his field so that this body of knowledge becomes meaningful to his students. The researcher must be methodical, original, and literary; for he is expected to furnish new raw materials to teachers. As for rewards, the teacher cherishes his associations with young people and shares his students' feelings of accomplishment as they grasp new concepts and learn that which was previously unknown to them.[17] The teacher receives constant reinforcement from his students: a facial expression showing enlightenment, a word of appreciation, a well-written examination, or perhaps a newspaper story relating some new success of one of his students. The rewards from research are more self-centered. Stature as a scholar is achieved through research, not teaching. In teaching excellence is difficult to recognize and receives little "off-campus" publicity. But in research the standards of accomplishment are more clearly defined, the judgers of quality are more refined and trusted, and the product can be transported among campuses. Satisfaction is dependent upon accomplishment, and accomplishment is less assured than in teaching. The researcher is rewarded by an inner knowledge that he has contributed new knowledge to mankind and by the applause and statements of praise from those sophisticated enough to appreciate his contribution.

It is not surprising that tasks requiring such different skills and offering such different rewards should be favored by different individuals. Most college professors have fairly well-developed preferences either for or against research work. Among men desirous of emphasizing the research duties of a faculty position, the "research environment" or "research emphasis" of various jobs under consideration is one of the most important choice criteria.

The ranks of this variable in Table 3 (research emphasis is never higher than fifth in importance) are deceptive; the true significance of "research emphasis" in job decision making is understated. For, although a relatively small number of people

17. Eckert, Stecklein, and Sagen, "College Faculty Members," *AAUP Bulletin*, pp. 520-21.

indicated the importance of "research emphasis," most of the persons who did mention this factor identified it as *the most* significant characteristic in their job choice. Researchers will not only not accept jobs at schools where this research environment does not exist but also will accept the offer from the school that offers the greatest research emphasis. In this sense, for persons who are interested in pursuing research, the factor, "research emphasis," is both a minimum and a key variable.

For example, having received offers from Yale, Princeton, and Michigan, an economist who accepted a job at a high prestige, state school stated that his sole criterion for choice was "time available to do research." Advancement opportunity is dependent upon publication, and publications are dependent upon the time available for writing. Thus, he reasoned, the best job opportunity is that which affords the most time for research and writing. Similarly, a sociologist who had accepted his first job at a prominent state university in the Southeast explained his choice as follows "——— [his school] promised a favorable environment for research . . . freedom to do research. There are opportunities to publish. Active assistance is given. The faculty has had a favorable publication rate in recent years." He too felt that publication was important because it led to mobility and advancement in the profession.

These researchers are seeking a school where research is encouraged and recognized. The availability of research instruments (e.g., computers), of a good library, of secretarial help, and of research assistance makes a job more attractive. The availability of research monies and support in obtaining outside-the-university financing is also sought by research-minded job seekers. They seek a department of active researchers where their colleagues will be stimulating examples and valuable consultants. Reduced teaching loads, specialized graduate level courses, isolated offices, and publishing outlets (a good university press, a monograph series, a professional journal) are also sought. Most important of all is the feeling that one's success or failure will be determined by his research productivity, not his teaching. The universities that offer this environment are almost always consciously committed to research and a research emphasis.

The type of person that feels the greatest need for a research environment is the young, aggressive, self-confident, well-trained professor who is publishing one or two articles a year but who has not yet become well enough known that he can attract outside-the-university sources of financial help in research. He needs the discipline, the stimulation, the facilities the research environment can give him. In our interviewing (see Table 4) we found this individual most often at "high quality" universities, holding the rank of assistant professor. He tended to be young, a Ph.D., educated outside the region. If a university desires to attract the type of man described in this paragraph, it must create the "research environment," for if it does not, the man will seek employment elsewhere.

At the same time, if a university does create a "research environment," other professors will not consider the jobs offered. Scholars that do not cherish research avoid jobs where these opportunities and pressures exist. For them a negative research emphasis is a must, a minimal condition for all jobs that are considered.

Prestige and Reputation of University and Department

Roughly defined, university or department prestige is the ability of a university or a department to command admiration and respect. The qualities that enable some universities to command more admiration and respect than others cannot be exactly identified. Schools achieve prestige for different reasons. Prestige is an evasive, subjective quality that depends as much upon the rater as the rated. The rating process combines elements of rationality with those of emotion and tradition. To name the most important, the ability and subsequent fame of a school's students, the notoriety of the professors and administrators serving a school, the beauty and extent of a school's buildings and grounds, the renown of the school's traditions and course offerings, and the prowess of the school's athletic teams are determinants of prestige. The exact functional relationships and the relative importance of the variables are unknown.

Although subject to only imprecise definition, the relative prestige rating of various universities and departments is a dominant influence upon job choice decisions. According to our survey of Southeastern social scientists there is no stage in the decision-making process where prestige is not important. Only one other variable (location) has more influence upon professorial job choices (Table 3). Nearly one-third of the professors that we interviewed who had the opportunity to consider more than one job offer at the time they accepted their current position stated that the relative prestige ratings of the universities or departments were a major factor in their decision. Answering a different question, of the thirty-seven professors who were considering new jobs at the time they were interviewed, nearly one-half stated that they would not move to a job at a less prestigious institution. And by the fifty-five professors who had considered and rejected job offers from "raiding" schools since accepting their current employment, prestige was stated as a reason for rejecting the competitive offer(s) in 20 per cent of the cases. The following cases are typical:

A young Stanford Ph.D. chose to accept an offer from a high prestige, private school because of its "reputation of being an excellent place to steal people from. It's a good place from which to move. The faculty and the department have a good reputation."

An economist, who had recently moved to a high prestige school, identified the factor that was most important in his selection as "the international reputation of [his school]. It's a better university."

Selecting between offers from Southeastern state universities, an economist said this about his choice: "[His school] is a good university and has a good reputation. [His school] is a member of the B.A. school accrediting association; [the other school] was not at the time."

Similar findings have resulted from the studies of Stecklein and Lathrop, Caplow and McGee, and Anantaraman. Surveying professors who had recently moved to the University of Minnesota, Stecklein and Lathrop report that the University's reputation had a positive influence upon decisions to come to Minnesota more often than any other factor, in 73 per cent of the cases studied.[18] Caplow and McGee, studying the moves from institutions with relatively high prestige ratings, conclude that the attainment of greater personal prestige (which is gained by association with prestigious universities) is the primary motive for upward migration.[19] And Anantaraman, in his study of experienced economists, reports that 96 per cent of his sample were influenced in their choice of academic jobs by the relative prestige of the positions and that, within this 96 per cent, 45 per cent were strongly influenced by prestige.[20] These researchers found prestige to be at least as influential as we did.[21]

Whether it is the most important or only the second most important factor affecting job choice decisions, prestige-seeking does affect in no small way the migratory patterns of professors. Why is prestige so important? What is unique about prestigious institutions?[22]

Although we can do little more than speculate on the answers to these questions, it seems likely that prestige-seeking is simply another manifestation of the motives that cause most persons to choose a career in college teaching in the first place; to wit, the need for recognition, for respect, for the feeling of significance, for the feeling of accomplishment. Teaching affords the oppor-

18. Unfortunately, the authors' discussion of why faculty left Minnesota is not in the same terms. It is impossible to determine the importance of "reputation" in decisions to leave, though the inference is that "reputation" was considerably less important. Stecklein and Lathrop, *Faculty Attraction and Retention*, p. 125, or 74 per cent on p. 15.

19. Caplow and McGee, *The Academic Marketplace*, pp. 148-49.

20. Anantaraman, *Mobility of Professional Economists*, pp. 41 and 54.

21. That professors at small colleges and junior colleges are less imbued with prestige consciousness when deciding among jobs is suggested by the results of the Stecklein-Eckert study of faculty at thirty-two Minnesota colleges. In this study the researchers found that jobs were chosen because of the "excellent reputation of the school, department and/or staff" in only 9 per cent of the cases studied (p. 31).

22. Prestige and institutional prestige, as used here, are different terms. Prestige refers to the ability of a particular individual to command admiration; institutional prestige, the ability of a particular institution.

tunity to express one's thoughts and affect the lives of others. A respected or prestigious teacher is more convincing than one who is not. Not fortune, but fame is one of the most compelling reasons for choosing a teaching career, for few professions offer as great an opportunity to place one's name before the public. For persons who choose an occupation on the basis of the fame they may achieve, it is only natural that they would also choose a particular job within the occupation on the same basis; thus, choose the more prestigious positions. One of the unique features of teaching as a career is that its rewards are in the form of feelings of significance, accomplishment, and importance. Since this is the currency in which teachers are paid, they are simply seeking higher "paying" jobs when they move to more prestigious ones. Unlike in most other professions (with the exception of the ministry), the accepted standard of value is not one's earning capacity but rather one's ability to command the admiration and respect of others.

By teaching at a prestigious institution one's opportunities to enlarge his individual prestige are increased. Despite the understandable pleas of editorial boards to the contrary, if a manuscript is submitted from an institution where the staff is noted for its generally high caliber work (i.e., a prestigious institution) it is more likely to be published than the same manuscript submitted from a less prestigious address. Insofar as additional publications enhance individual prestige, institutional prestige can enhance individual prestige. Insofar as prestige is determined by the company one keeps, the facts are significant that professors teaching at the more prestigious institutions are more likely to have the leaders of the next generation in their classes and are more likely to associate with the better and more respected men in their own field of knowledge. Also, because the skills of one's colleagues at the more prestigious schools are more likely to be helpful in a man's research, they increase his chances of success in research and in turn prestige.

At prestigious institutions one is impressed with an "aura" of having "arrived." Besides its intrinsic value for the ego, the aura can lend confidence to one's own endeavors, both their significance and their accuracy. This too may increase research productivity. In any case, the rewards of the teaching profession (recognition and a feeling of significance) will seem greater.[23]

Before leaving the subject of prestige, let us return to our data for a more detailed look at the types of professors that stress prestige. At the outset of this study the hypothesis was developed that persons who have received their Ph.D.'s from the great graduate schools of the West and Northeast and have published widely are, for reasons of training and interests, more inculcated with prestige consciousness than most. Analysis of our data, however, fails to confirm this hypothesis. The only meaningful, significant difference between the "prestige-conscious" group and our sample as a whole is that an unusually low percentage of the former group is now teaching at the lowest quality schools (as rated by our index), which simply means that those persons who use prestige as a criterion for selecting jobs tend to avoid the less prestigious schools (Table 4).

Evidently our error was to assume that prestige is absolute, that the only locus of prestige is at the very top of the educational hierarchy. Prestige is not absolute but relative. Every university has a reputation, and therefore "prestige" (or lack of it). And, the "prestige" of any two or more schools or departments extending competitive job offers can be compared and ranked. To select a job on the basis of prestige is to choose that job, among those offered, that has the greatest prestige associated with it. It is not necessary to seek, or even to desire to seek, a position at the most prestigious universities and departments.

Type of School

Although other institutional characteristics do not affect job choice decisions as frequently as "research emphasis" and "prestige," in isolated instances some other institutional characteristics

23. For an excellent discussion of why professors esteem prestige and institutional prestige, refer to Logan Wilson, *The Academic Man*, pp. 165-72.

may be essential to the job decision. In want of a better term, a discussion of these "other institutional characteristics" has been grouped under the general heading, "type of school."

Usually due to personal experiences in the past, many professors bear a bevy of prejudices and preferences concerning the type of school by which they would like to be employed. Often these feelings are strong enough to affect the choice of jobs. For example, an economist who had just completed his graduate work at a large Midwestern school and who had, while teaching part-time, seen some of the unpleasant feuding within the department was steadfast against teaching in a large department. Another economist, who had been teaching at a small denominational school for three years and felt the pressures that conservative churches sometimes place upon the faculty at "their" schools, said that he would not seriously consider any new job offer that did not come from a state school. In sharp contrast, we also talked with a sociologist who never considers jobs at state schools. In graduate school, at a large North Atlantic state school, he had witnessed a tangle between the university's administration and the state legislature over the control of funds to run the university. Several other professors, all of them located at the same denominational school which had been in severe financial trouble for the past several years and was showing few signs of improvement, vowed that they would never again choose a job without first making a rather thorough appraisal of the school's financial capacity.

Not all conditions were negative. Institutional growth, for example, was stressed by a significant number of professors. This group, most of them presently teaching at schools that had in recent years enjoyed rapidly improving reputations, stated that they would not accept a job at a school where a dynamic confidence of constant improvement did not prevail. Professors teaching in small denominational schools were prone to require "a religious atmosphere" where they taught. Many of these same professors stressed the importance of close student-faculty relations. For example:

An economist who is able to supplement his income by consulting commented: "I'm willing to stay at [his high prestige, private school] as long as it shows promise of pushing over the brink of greatness. Now we have a new president which is encouraging. I'm willing to stay with [his school] and give it a chance. When the promise of further progress is gone, [his school] will no longer interest me."

Commented a young sociologist, teaching at a denominational college: "The Baptist affiliation made [his school] attractive, for I was an undergraduate at [another Baptist college]. The idea of a growing, improving school was also attractive to me."

A full professor at a small liberal arts college who was a leading scholar in his field explained his choice to return to this less prestigious position at a cut in pay in the following terms: "University life is not for me. One is left with the feeling of anonymity when teaching at a big university; one feels like he's in New York City on 42nd Street at five p.m. The tension of the impersonal, competitive atmosphere is too great. There are pressures from everywhere. Large departments are bound to be fraught with all sorts of tensions and rifts. Professors are a funny, independent breed. They are always operating in an ivory tower, facing inferiority complexes [vis-à-vis their profession] and superiority complexes [vis-à-vis their students] at the same time. Professors are either paranoiac or schizophrenic. Conflict must naturally arise. I couldn't stand the difference in attitude toward learning and life [at the university]."

Colleagues

Teaching colleagues affect the desirability of a job in at least three ways. To some extent fellow members of a discipline who are too distant to make an independent judgment evaluate professors according to the company they keep: those who keep better company are more highly regarded. One or two highly respected professors enhance the reputation of a department (and school). By association, the reputations of all other members of the department are also improved.

In addition to this "artificial" professional advantage of having high caliber colleagues, for the young college teacher his association with a high-powered name in the field often leads to apprenticeship opportunities. Since many of these big names undertake multi-phased research endeavors that are too big for one man to handle, junior faculty members are often delegated phases of the projects. The guidance given by the senior faculty members as the junior faculty member pursues his phase can serve as an invaluable learning experience that will provide a solid foundation for more "independent" research. Likewise, the senior professor gains by his association with competent junior faculty in that the end products of delegation are better products.

A heavy concentration of high caliber senior researchers and teachers is also advantageous, for it allows a sharing of discoveries and problems. Furthermore, it enables the contracting for very large scale research projects that require the direction of several topnotch senior men. The justification for large researching equipment such as computers is facilitated. Really good men go where their colleagues will be stimulating. As Newburn comments, "When the individual concerned is top-level in quality, he is more conditioned [in his selection of alternative teaching positions] by the intellectual setting than by any other single item."[24] The good attracts the good; the bad breeds bad.

It is desirable that one's colleagues be not only good researchers but also good teachers. An individual professor, who teaches a course to upperclassmen, is largely dependent upon the work of his colleagues who have taught the students in earlier years. If his colleagues have taught well, the professor's efforts are more likely to be successful and to yield satisfying results. If, on the other hand, his colleagues have not conveyed properly the elementary concepts, the teaching of an advanced course can be a frustrating and unrewarding task.

Finally, the congeniality of colleagues is often important. In large measure the image of isolated professors pursuing highly individualized projects in cloistered studies is mythological. Professors do talk to each other. And the topic of conversation is as likely to be gossipy or sportsy as intellectual. Not unlike businessmen, college teachers as a rule enjoy a friendly office.

24. Newburn, *Faculty Personnel Policies*, p. 22.

They wish to avoid the unpleasantries of factionalism, backbiting, jealousy, and maneuvering for advantage.[25] At the smaller universities in isolated communities where office friendships must double as social friendships because of the small population of persons in a similar socio-economic-intellectual class, the congeniality of colleagues can be one of the most important elements of job satisfaction.[26]

Serving as a rough index of the determinants of job satisfaction, the answers to our question, "What are the primary advantages of your present job?" by persons who were satisfied with their present jobs indicate that the friendliness and competency of colleagues is more important than any other factor, except location. Persons from smaller departments and schools tended to list the factor even more frequently than others.

Similarly, Mayer, reporting the results of his study of sociologists, states that "colleagues" is the single most important element in job satisfaction.[27] And, reporting the replies of 576 faculty members at four-year colleges, Eckert, Stecklein, and Sagen note that "fine colleagues and administrators" and "intellectually stimulating associations" were both more frequently mentioned as reasons for liking teaching than all except one of the twenty factors listed.[28]

In spite of the close relationships between one's colleagues and job *satisfaction,* differences in would-be colleagues are rarely decisive in job *choice.* That is not to say that one's prospective colleagues never enter into the job choice decision. In our interviews we found several instances where men had been drawn to a particular institution by a close friend or by the professional reputation and writings of an individual within the department.

25. Paul F. Lazarsfeld and Wagner Thielens, Jr., *The Academic Mind* (Glencoe, Illinois: The Free Press of Glencoe, 1958), p. 229.

26. *Ibid.,* p. 25, makes a similar observation, noting that ratings of the importance of on-campus social relations increase as the size of the schools decreases.

27. Kurt B. Mayer, "Salaries and Working Conditions of Sociology Teachers," *American Association of University Professors Bulletin,* Vol. 43, No. 1 (Spring, 1957), pp. 53-54.

28. Eckert, Stecklein, and Sagen, "College Faculty Members," *AAUP Bulletin,* pp. 520-21.

For example, an expert in Russian history was joined by an aspiring admirer. An economist was attracted by one of his undergraduate school professors who had changed schools since the economist's undergraduate days. Accepting lower pay and lower prestige, a sociologist switched jobs so that he could be with a more senior man researching in the same field. And, a historian joined his brother-in-law. In each of the cases observed, a particular would-be colleague (not colleagues in general) was influential in the job choice decision. There were also several instances where intra-departmental bickering had become so violent that men sought other jobs to get away.

Withstanding these exceptions, jobs are rarely selected and rejected on the basis of would-be colleagues. When asked to state the primary reasons for switching jobs, only 9 per cent of our respondents mentioned "would-be" or "had been" colleagues. Only 13 per cent mentioned it as one of the key factors when deciding among alternative job offers, and only one person identified "would-be" colleagues as a minimum job characteristic. In no instance were "would-be" colleagues any higher than fifth in importance among the factors considered in the various phases of decision making (see Table 3).[29]

29. Although the results of the Eckert-Stecklein, *Job Motivations* (p. 32), confirm the unimportance of would-be associates as a decision-making factor when selecting jobs, the responses of the Stecklein-Lathrop sample (p. 125) of newly arrived faculty at the University of Minnesota are apparently contradictory to our conclusions. The University professors mentioned the caliber and congeniality of prospective colleagues as a positive influence upon the decision to come to Minnesota more frequently than any other factor except reputation. The discrepancy in findings can be explained only in part.

The primary difference between the Brown and Eckert samples on the one hand and the Stecklein-Lathrop sample on the other is that the former sample includes professors from different types of colleges while the latter sample includes professors from only one, prestigious university. Of the two competencies in prospective colleagues that may affect job selection, professional competency is more easily judged from afar than sociability. Also, professional competency is easier to measure at a large publication-emphasizing institution like Minnesota, for here if a man is competent, the pressures are such that he will publish. And finally, professors seeking institutions of high prestige like Minnesota are more likely to be concerned with the professional than the social aspect of their prospective colleagues. Placing each of these four assertions together, it is logical to conclude that the faculty moving to Minnesota would, when selecting a job, consider their prospective colleagues more often than the average job selecting professor.

Why are "would-be" colleagues such an unimportant factor in job selections? In the first place, it is virtually impossible to judge either the professional or the social competence of would-be colleagues without actually spending a semester or so observing them. The undercurrents of departmental bickering and rifts between faculty and administration are rarely visible to the casual, two-day observer. Forty per cent of our interviewees stated that they did not know about the congeniality of the department at the time they accepted their current job. Second, even if it were possible to judge competency, would-be colleagues can and do switch jobs. For instance, the economist who followed his undergraduate professor arrived on his new campus to find that the man had moved on to still another university and the sociologist who had sacrificed salary and prestige was with the senior researcher only one year before the latter man switched jobs. The high mobility of college faculty means that selection of jobs on the basis of colleagues is a dangerous practice, even when possible.

University Administration

In most universities there is a formal line of authority extending downward from the Board of Trustees, through the university president and deans, to the department chairman, on to the department members, and finally to the students. The term, university administration, as defined in this study refers to the superstructure above the department members and is meant to include both the administration of the department and the administration of the university as a whole.

The direct effects of university administration upon the migratory patterns of professors are primarily of a negative nature. Jobs are usually not chosen because one administration is believed to be superior to another. Nor is it typical for professors to decide to keep their present jobs because they have found the university administration to their liking. Good university administrations have neither "pulling" power nor "keeping" power.[30] As shown by columns 1, 2, and 4 in Table 3, "administration" was rarely mentioned by our interviewees as either a key or a minimum or a keep factor in their job decisions.

Column 3 of Table 3 tells the real story. Differentials in the desirability of university administration, as they affect migratory patterns, are a pushing rather than a pulling factor. Until professors are not working under "friendly" and competent administrators, they do not appreciate the role that good administrators play in job satisfaction. Only undesirable administrations are noticed. When job switchers were asked, "What were the primary reasons for switching positions?" the answer given more frequently than any other is typified by the statement, "The administration at my former job was totally unacceptable." Twenty-eight per cent listed this factor, usually without listing any other. Undesirable university administrations are obviously driving many professors into the academic labor market. Confirming this observation is the fact that the most frequently mentioned disadvantage of the jobs that our interviewees had left was "administration." A few of the specific cases are cited below:

A young, Berkeley Ph.D. in history had recently moved to a high prestige school in the Southeast from a state university in the Northeast because "the administration was overly strong-minded, . . . reactionary principles were worshipped, . . . the curriculum devised was a purposeless, academic cafeteria line."

Another historian explained his recent move in the following terms: "The administration [at my previous job] was incompetent. In their efforts to increase the size of the school, they admitted unqualified students and kept them around too long."

Still another stated: "[At my previous job], the department chairman was unable to make decisions," "backbiting and back-stabbing were a way of life," "the younger people had to band together to make

30. The extent to which good administrators are able to "talk" a man out of leaving or "talk" a man into coming is not relevant at this point. The current discussion is concentrating upon the extent to which the candidate himself considers the character and quality of university administrations in his job selection, not the extent to which he is affected by university administration.

any headway against the top people." Here "American studies is independent, not in any other department," "the administration is made up of men of integrity for the most part," "the intellectual atmosphere is congenial," they "let me be in my place." He didn't select a third job because "the American studies department was attached to the English department," "the program was an 'orphan child,'" "they try to get one or two key people and then leave little chance for the low men to advance."

A sociologist had left his job at a prominent Middlewestern state university because of the "nasty human relations within the department," "the jealousy by the older, full people," the "constant bickering between faculty and with graduate students."

Reported another sociologist: "I was getting along fine until we changed chairmen. The new chairman and I were constantly at odds. We were constantly feuding. Since he wasn't going to move, I had to."

A publishing economist who had been teaching for seventeen years at a state college decided to seek another job because "the administration was going wild over engineering. . . . The salaries in non-engineering fields were getting more and more out of line with the market. The department of economics was becoming service-oriented to the engineering school. . . . Someone had to contribute proof that the older faculty members in non-engineering fields would not stay forever. The administration was letting things go from bad to worse and I wanted to get out when I was still able."

Indications are that undesirable university administration is by far the most important factor causing professors to leave old jobs. Many times the trouble centers around conflicts between personalities, especially the personalities of professors and their department chairmen. One of our interviewees said that after a run-in with his department chairman over what courses he should teach, it was easier to leave than attempt to mend the rift. Several sociologists had left institutions because they felt their department chairmen were leading the departments toward descriptive sociology whereas they felt empirical or theoretical sociology held more promise, or vice versa.[31]

31. Note in Table 4 that sociologists as a group were more often upset about administration than either economists or historians. This statistic confirmed an impression that the interviewers gained in the interviews.

The inability of a university administration to stand up for the rights and interests of faculty when encountering outside forces (e.g., the church), constant bickering within the ranks of the administration, continuing upheaval in the administration due to rapid turnover, allegedly incompetent administration at the higher levels—each of these aspects was mentioned by one or more of the interviewees as instrumental in his decision to leave his former job.

Another species of complaints centered around the structure of the university. Some professors complained that department chairmen, or their particular department chairman, have too little say in administration. Others objected to the close supervision on their own work by department chairmen. One complaint heard in economics departments that are administered by Deans of Schools of Business Administration rather than Deans of Colleges of Arts and Sciences was that the economics department is service-oriented to the B.A. program, the course offerings in the economics department are too business-oriented, and the economists are second-class citizens to the business professors.

In many ways undesirable administrations push professors into the labor market. It would be wrong, however, to blame all of these exists upon *poor* administration. In some cases, the administration should be commended rather than condemned. In college teaching, the common practice of giving tenure has several strange side-effects. One of these is upon university administrations as seen through the eyes of a tenured professor whom the administrators would prefer not to have around. Since the administrators cannot fire the man, the only way that they can get him to leave is by making life unpleasant for him. If the administrators succeed in their attempts to get the undesired professor to leave and the professor is subsequently interviewed in a study such as this one, the professor will say that he left his previous job because of "undesirable" administrative policies.[32]

32. This may partially explain why, as shown in Table 4, a significantly higher percentage of senior faculty job switchers were upset with their previous administration.

To what extent this was the real motive behind the responses of our interviewees could not be determined.

Future Potential

Two jobs that are essentially identical as of today may well offer very different opportunities for the future. In the first place, one job may be a stepping-stone position whereas the other is not. At one relatively prestigious university in particular we found several professors who had moved to this school because of the reputation it had for having its faculty stolen by even better universities. These men were not concerned about the merits of their present job, but the quality of the jobs that they would be able to obtain because of contacts made while teaching there. In academic labor markets where communications are far from perfect and contacts are important, one's future is in large measure dependent upon one's past. The situation is roughly analogous to professional baseball. If a professor desires to teach at one of the major league institutions, he must carefully locate himself at a place where the major league scouts are most likely to spot him. Being a member of the "right" farm team is important.

Also important is the potential a job offers if the professor does not switch institutions. The rapidity and size of promotions in rank, raises in income, and increases in responsibility can differ widely. It is not uncommon for two schools with very different average and maximum salaries to pay comparable salaries at the "hiring in" rank of assistant professor. For example, according to the AAUP salary survey published in Summer-1962, two Illinois schools, North Central College and the University of Illinois (Champagne-Urbana), were paying almost identical salaries to the average instructor (between $6,600 and $7,500); yet the average pay for full professors at these same institutions differed by about $5,000. At North Central the average salary of a full professor was between $6,700 and $8,200 compared to $11,500-$13,900 at the University of Illinois.[33] For a man who expects to

33. "The Economic Status of the Profession, 1961-62," *American Association of University Professors Bulletin*, Vol. 48, No. 2 (Summer, 1962), pp. 138 and 128.

spend his entire teaching career at one of these institutions and who is interested in his future income, the jobs are obviously not identically attractive.

Promotion prospects also differ among schools. Standard policy is to promote assistant professors to the rank of associate and give tenure after three years of satisfactory service at some schools. At others the time period is five years, and still others, seven. Strict adherence to tables of organization governs promotion policies at still others.

Schools that each year hire-in large cohorts of assistant professors with the intention of letting all except the very best go after several years (the so-called "up or out" promotion policy) offer a quite different future than schools that hire assistant professors only in fields where vacancies are anticipated at the senior level. Regardless of a school's general promotion policy, a particular professor located at a particular school may find that his promotion is blocked by a relatively young senior professor in the same field. If such is the case his chances for advancement in responsibility and rank are small.

Trends differ among institutions. At several universities where we interviewed, the general administrations of the universities were making concerted efforts to upgrade the stature of their departments of sociology. For persons teaching in these departments, the prospect of advancement and growth in prestige appeared especially attractive. In contrast, an economist had left a job at a state school that appeared to be de-emphasizing the social sciences, not because the job was unsatisfactory at the time he left it but because he thought that it would be unsatisfactory in the future.

These differences in job potentials affect the migratory patterns of professors more in decisions of whether or not to *stay at* a particular job than in decisions of whether or not to *go to* a particular job. Unpromising jobs are left; promising jobs are kept; but the apparent promise of different jobs is rarely a key factor in the original selection of a new job. Table 3 shows that estimates of the "opportunities for growth and advancement" offered by competing job offers was mentioned as a significant element in the final selection process by only 7 per cent of the respondents (column 1). The factor was never mentioned as a minimum constraint (column 2).[34]

Yet, even though it rarely influences selection of new jobs, job potential is an important element in job satisfaction. This is reflected by the fact that, in our study, the second most frequently mentioned disadvantage of jobs that have been left and the third most frequently mentioned reason for switching jobs was the "opportunities for growth and advancement." Further confirmation of the importance of job potential to job satisfaction is given by the Stecklein-Lathrop study which reports that the professors who had left Minnesota were more influenced in their decision to leave by the lack of "opportunity for professional growth and advancement" than any of twenty-two other factors.[35]

The importance of potential in job satisfaction and unimportance of the same factor in job selection can be explained as follows. Like the "congeniality of colleagues" and the desirability of "university administrations," the differences in the growth potentials of various jobs are virtually impossible to assess from afar. In fact, we found that at the time their current jobs were accepted, professors knew less about the future potential of their jobs that they were choosing among than about either the university administration or the congeniality of colleagues! Over 50 per cent of the respondents were unaware of their new employers' promotion policies at the time they accepted their jobs. Over 40 per cent did not know what prospects the job they had just accepted held in the way of salary advancements.

If it were possible to overcome this ignorance, the "opportunities for growth and advancement" would undoubtedly be one of the primary means of discriminating among competing job offers. In addition to the evidence cited above, confirming the validity of this suggestive statement are the results of Jerry L. L.

34. These results are confirmed by the two Stecklein studies. See Eckert-Stecklein, *Job Motivations*, p. 32, and Stecklein-Lathrop, *Faculty Attraction and Retention*, Chapter 3 (the latter results are not strictly comparable).
35. Stecklein-Lathrop, *Faculty Attraction and Retention*, p. 53. The findings cited in Chapter 6 are also consoling.

Miller's study of Southeastern graduate students. When the students were asked what characteristics they would like to have in their jobs (as opposed to why they actually chose a particular job) 91 per cent listed the "opportunity for advancement." Professors want jobs which offer advancement possibilities. But the only way that these possibilities can be explored is through job shopping. Window shopping will not do. Estimates made in two-day visits are too speculative to be useful.

Salaries—The A Priori Arguments

At least since the time of Adam Smith, respectable economic theory has held that wage and salary differentials are the primary forces acting upon the distribution of human resources, labor. Workers move from low-paying to high-paying jobs. Therefore, any given employer can increase his labor supply by increasing the pay he offers.

Lately a number of labor economists have come to question the applicability of these theories in labor markets as we know them today. Specifically, these economists are questioning whether or not the pecuniary motivations of workers are strong enough to cause them to switch jobs for relatively small gains in take-home pay. After making an intensive study of New England blue collar workers, Lloyd Reynolds, a pioneer in labor market analysis, suggests that "the processes of wage determination and labor mobility seem to be much less intimately related than one might expect a priori."[36] Workers often become so attached to their localities and employers that they prefer to remain at their present jobs in spite of the economic gains of moving to new jobs.[37] When workers do change jobs, they are apt to accept the first job opportunity that meets their minimum supply price rather than to seek the opportunity that offers the highest earnings.[38] Studies of other blue collar worker labor mar-

36. Reynolds, *The Structure of Labor Markets*, p. 248.
37. *Ibid.*, pp. 76-83.
38. *Ibid.*, pp. 210-12.

kets such as those by Gladys Palmer,[39] Richard Lester,[40] and Heneman-Fox-Yoder[41] have prompted similar observations. Each study infers that the common practice of economic theorists of holding "other things constant," especially those variables that are difficult to quantify, results in a totally impractical theory of mobility. Workers' non-economic desires cannot be meaningfully assumed away.

One of the primary motives for undertaking the current study was to analyze the applicability of economic theories of mobility in the labor market for college professors. Guided by Reynolds' findings in his study of the labor market for blue collar workers and by the general belief that professorial motivations are less pecuniary than the motives of blue collar workers, we hypothesized that the salary differentials offered by various colleges and universities are not the primary determinants of job choice. A priori the validity (or falsity) of the hypothesis is not at all obvious, for there are logical arguments to support both sides.

Consider, first, the argument for the significance of salary differentials.

Professors are human and, like most other men, are constantly faced with nearly infinite shopping lists of desired items and constrained in their purchases by limited financial resources. There is always something more to be bought and never enough money. Since higher salaries mean more purchasing power and greater want satisfaction, professors will move to the schools that offer the highest salaries.

It would seem that the need for professors to pursue the highest paying job obtainable would be even more acute than the need for workers in other occupations. For the tastes of college teachers far outstrip their incomes. According to Duesenberry, one's consumption level is a function of the consumption levels

39. Gladys Palmer, *Labor Mobility in Six Cities* (New York: Social Science Research Council, 1954), pp. 61-62.

40. Richard Lester, "Results and Implications of Some Recent Wage Studies," in R. A. Lester and Joseph Shister, *Insight Into Labor Issues* (New York: The Macmillan Company, 1948), pp. 197-225.

41. Herbert G. Heneman, Harland Fox, Dale Yoder, *Minnesota Manpower Mobilities* (Bulletin 10; Minneapolis: Industrial Relations Center, University of Minnesota, 1950), p. 19.

of close friends and associates: the observation of others consuming stimulates a desire to consume. Unlike many blue collar workers who rarely associate with people with large incomes and correspondingly great appetites for consumer goods, college teachers are often raised in high income families and educated at colleges where at least until recently ability to pay was as great a requirement for admission as ability to learn. After college, because of similar interests and backgrounds, professors are more likely to pick their friends from the country club than the bowling alley set. These friends will often have incomes many times the meager salary paid to college teachers. By association, professors acquire a set of tastes they cannot afford. Even though conspicuous consumption equal to that of businessmen is not expected from professors, this "characteristic discrepancy between income and tastes is bound to give rise to family strains."[42] The outside world will accept poor professors, but the professors and their families will not. They have acquired sets of tastes and desires that exceed their usual incomes. To seek the highest salary possible is the only means to escape this bind and still remain in the teaching profession.

It may be further argued that teaching is little different from other occupations in one respect: high salaries are status symbols. It is true that in a ranking in which many occupations occur, account is taken of the fact that professors are generally underpaid. But when professors are ranked against other professors, no such accounting is necessary, for all are professors and all are underpaid (by the same standard). Within the profession, salary earned can be a quantitative index of status. Those able to move to jobs paying more money would seem foolish to sacrifice status within the profession by not doing so.

Academic salaries are outward manifestations of more than status. Salaries are the most exact and comparable rewards of various teaching jobs. By noting one's own salary over time and by comparing one's own salary with other professors similarly situated, it is possible to determine the attitudes of one's superiors toward the quality and importance of one's work. Far more

42. Wilson, *The Academic Man*, p. 146.

reassuring than words of praise and a pat on the back is the observation that one's department chairman has made the hard decision to allocate an unusually large share of his limited funds for faculty salaries to one's paycheck. Here is a concrete expression of confidence and appreciation that shows that someone in the administration respects and encourages one's work. An analogous argument applies when professors are contemplating a number of different salary-job offers from various schools. Inasmuch as professors value respect and appreciation, high starting salaries and continued increases would seem to draw professors to high paying jobs and deter them from accepting low paying jobs and from remaining at jobs where salary increases are not frequent and significant.

A final reason that salaries might be expected to play a dominant role in the selection of jobs by members of the college teaching profession is that it is possible, with relatively little effort, to make really meaningful comparisons among job offers on the basis of salary. Unlike many of the factors that have been discussed previously (e.g., congeniality and competency of colleagues), salary is quantifiable. To compare jobs, simple subtraction of the one dollars-and-cents offer from another is all that is necessary. There is no need for subjective measure and comparison; complete objectivity is possible.[43] In advance, it is possible to know and to interpret the monetary rewards attached to each job offer. If the behavior of professors is similar to that of the New England blue collar workers studied by Lloyd Reynolds, the knowable and comparable aspects of various job offers will be stressed in the job selection process;[44] therefore, salary.

The case for the proposition that professors choose among job offers according to their salaries is a strong one. But let us

43. The case for the simplicity of salary comparisons may be slightly overstated, though the point is worth making. Difficulties can arise in comparing salary offers; for example, comparing an eleven-month salary and a nine-month salary, comparing a "tri-semester" salary with a "quarter-system salary," and so forth. Even more complications arise when incomes rather than salaries are compared.

44. Reynolds, *The Structure of Labor Markets*, p. 109.

turn to the a priori case against the significance of salary differentials, which is at least as convincing.

First, the very fact that a man has chosen college teaching as a career indicates that financial gain is not one of his prime motivations. Past actions often provide clues to the reasons behind current behavior. Most college teachers have, at some time in the past, made a conscious decision to enter teaching, a career that is famous for its non-economic rewards and infamous for the economic. To quote Logan Wilson, "Those who enter the academic profession are fully aware that they are going into an occupation where possibilities for amassing a fortune are almost non-existent, and their prime motivation is usually not financial gain."[45] Substantiating Wilson's observation is that by Anantaraman about economists: "While salary is the key factor attracting economists to non-academic fields of employment, it is the non-salary features of academic jobs that attract them to academic employment and not salary."[46] Few men seeking financial gain choose careers in teaching, and those who do are quick to desert to another profession, for the disparity of earnings is obvious.

Many studies have been made which contrast the earnings of persons similarly trained in academic versus non-academic jobs. Elbridge Sibley, for example, drawing upon data for the Social Science Research Council, notes that the average annual earnings of social scientists academically employed were roughly 20 per cent below those of social scientists in non-academic positions.[47] Using this statistic as indicative of the differential, if it can be assumed that persons in academic jobs are at least as capable as social scientists employed in industry and government (a valid assumption if ability to earn a Ph.D. is an accurate index of capability in that a disproportionately large number of social scientists outside teaching are without terminal degrees), then it stands to reason that college teachers are consciously choosing to earn 20 per cent less than they might in non-teaching jobs. College

45. Wilson, *The Academic Man*, p. 136.

46. Anantaraman, *Mobility of Professional Economists*, p. 40.

47. Elbridge Sibley, *The Recruitment, Selection, and Training of Social Scientists* ("Bulletin No. 58"; New York: Social Science Research Council, 1948), pp. 10-11.

teachers as a group are persons who are continually displaying their lack of concern for financial gain by their willingness to remain in teaching. It would be inconsistent to expect that, when choosing among teaching jobs, different criteria would be stressed than when choosing among occupations. If professors use the same criteria to choose a particular teaching job that they used to choose the teaching profession, salary and financial gain must play an insignificant role.

Second, unlike most occupations, in college teaching salary is not the measure of power, prestige, and success. This argument is stated well in *The Academic Man* by Logan Wilson: "In common with the clergy and certain other vocations, the academic profession stands somewhat apart in not having its general prestige established primarily in terms of monetary remuneration. There are other important common denominators of achievement and usefulness, so that money becomes important only when these are vague or weakened in significance. Success or distinction in university work is a goal comparable with wealth and power in other occupations." It follows that if the desires for higher salaries are in part motivated by desires for higher prestige, salaries are not as much a factor in job selection decisions in the ministry and college teaching as in other vocations. Other factors are correspondingly more important for college teachers.

A third reason why salaries might, on a priori grounds, be expected to be a relatively unimportant factor in the job selection decision rests upon the sociological hypothesis that individuals' actions are a function of group social norms; that is, people tend to act in accordance with the behavior that others, both inside and outside the group, expect of them. Society sets the pattern to which each individual tends to more or less conform. By this proposition, movie stars are glamorous, bankers are dignified, and so forth.

One of the socially valued norms among college professors is lack of concern for monetary matters. Society expects pro-

48. Wilson, *The Academic Man*, p. 135.

fessors to be concerned about less mundane matters. The "ideal" professor is one who is contemplating the really important questions, not the question, "how much he is being paid for his work?" The "ideal" teacher worries about what he is teaching and what his students are learning, not what he is making. The "ideal" professor is supposedly so absorbed in his profession that salary is not a matter of importance. It is unfashionable, unprofessional to be concerned about salary. In the words of Thorstein Veblen, who had a rare talent for looking into the minds of others, there is a "species of moral obliquity implied in overtly dealing with the matter [of pay]."[49]

Admittedly this stereotype is extreme, yet something like it does exist. If he seeks praise the professor must either hide his thoughts about salary (thereby complicating the task of studies such as this one) or accept the stereotype and live by it. In either case, we would expect salary to be less of a factor in the job selection process than if the social norm permitted overt, monetary-minded behavior.

And fourth, as a practical matter, large salary differentials among comparable institutions are rare. Typically, the salaries attached to the job offers that a particular candidate considers seriously are so nearly identical that they cannot be used as a basis for differentiating. If the original offers are not nearly identical, skillful bargaining can usually make them so. Whether or not salaries would be important in the job selection decision is a moot question for many professors, for they do not have the option of a high salary versus a low salary teaching job. Instead, all of the job offers that interest them have approximately the same salary.

Thus, there is logic to both sides. Sound a priori cases can be structured both for and against the significance of salaries in professorial job selection. These countervailing arguments are little help in resolving the validity of the original hypothesis. Fortunately, the empirical evidence is less ambiguous.

49. Thorstein Veblen, *Higher Learning* (New York: B. W. Huebsch, 1918), pp. 162 ff.

Salaries-Southeastern Study

Our survey of one hundred and three Southeastern social scientists identifies the role of salary in this decision-making process clearly and unambiguously: salary levels are more often a constraining than a determining influence in job choice. Professors refuse even to consider jobs with too low salaries, but once salary minima have been met the choice of jobs is made according to other criteria. This is not to imply that salary has no influence in the final selection of jobs, nor that salary is all-influential as a constraint. What is meant is that salary influences job selection at a relatively early stage in the decision-making process. Up to a certain point (i.e., the minimally acceptable salary) professors are flexible less often on salary than any other job characteristic. Beyond the minimum point, salary is not determinative. Among a group of job offers, all of which have met salary minima, the final selection of a particular job centers upon other factors. Location, reputation and prestige of

Table 5

Importance of Salary in the Job Selection Decision

Question Asked	Rank of Salary Compared to Nine Other Factors Mentioned	Per Cent of Persons Who Answered Who Mentioned Salary
Why did you choose this job rather than one of the others you were offered at the same time?	4	18%
What are the minimum characteristics of any new job that you might consider taking?	1	68%
What were the primary reasons for switching to your present job?	6	13%
What made you decide to stay at your present job rather than accept some of the other offers that have come your way?	5	11%

Source: Table 3

the university and the department, university administration, and the work duties are all more frequent criteria than salary at this stage, though salary is stressed more often than rank, teaching load, colleagues, and research emphasis.

In Table 5 some of the data that led to this conclusion are summarized. Over two-thirds of the interviewees who were seeking new jobs at the time they were interviewed stated the minimal characteristics of the jobs they would accept in terms of salary minima. No other factor was mentioned as frequently. With only one exception, the minima specified were either identical to or higher than "current salary." The reluctance to accept voluntarily a reduction in real salary is reflected in many of the answers to the question, "Have you specified in your own mind the minimal requirements a new job must meet?" cited below:

"at least as much as, possibly more, salary"

"no cut in real income"

"more money" . . . "more salary"

"current earnings matched at a minimal, would like more"

"$2,000 more salary"

"at least the same salary"

"a slightly higher salary"

"salary equal to here"

Unless their new job carried at least an equal salary, most professors could not justify relocation, regardless of the professional advantages that the move might involve.

Yet, salaries are rarely a prime motivation for switching jobs. Only 13 per cent of the interviewees who had switched between academic jobs mentioned salary as a prime consideration in the move. Five other factors were mentioned more frequently. When the question was put more directly, "Was salary a major consideration in the job change?" the "no's" outnumbered the "yes's" by more than two to one. The actions of this group were consistent with its statements. Of the men who had switched between academic jobs, twenty-five of forty[50] or over 60 per cent

50. Actually forty-seven interviewees switched between academic jobs. Unfortunately we were unable to collect sufficient salary information from seven, leaving forty.

had moved without any increase in pay. Ten of the forty were, at the time of the change, actually earning less in their new jobs than they would have been earning if they had remained at their previous position.

Logically, there are two ways in which salaries could stimulate job switching: by causing either movement from jobs with low salaries or movement to jobs with unusually high salaries. Neither movement is evident in our results. Low salaries may drive people out of teaching altogether but rarely to another job within teaching. If low salaries were stimulating exodus, we would expect "low salary" to be mentioned frequently as a disadvantage of previous jobs that were left and present jobs that men desired to leave. But our results indicate that job switchers mentioned "low salary" as a disadvantage of their present jobs (which they desired to keep) as frequently as they mentioned the factor as a disadvantage of their previous jobs (which they left). Analysis also indicates that the group of men desirous of leaving their present jobs listed salary as a disadvantage of their job even less frequently than the group of men desiring to remain at their present job. We must conclude that, although "low salary" is commonly referred to as a disadvantage of teaching jobs, it is a disadvantage that is common to both the jobs not desired and the jobs desired. There is little evidence that indicates mass exiting of professors because of low salaries.

Nor do high salaries attract. When the persons who had more than one job offer to select from at the time they chose their present job were asked "Why did you choose this job offer rather than one of the others?" only 18 per cent answered "salary" or "income." In terms of frequency of mention, salary was fourth ranked behind location, reputation and prestige, and work duties. Answering another question, fifty-seven of the seventy-one professors indicated that they had actually rejected job offers with higher salaries in order to accept their present job. Also reflecting the lack of drawing power of salaries are the responses of department chairmen. When asked if they thought the men who had turned down one of the offers that the chairman had extended would have accepted the offer if it contained a salary that was $500 to $1,000 higher, a majority of the chairmen said "no."

The answers to still other questions indicate the same thing, that salary differentials do not play a determinative role in job decision-making. When professors who had received one or more offers from "raiding" schools while at their current job were asked "Why did you decide to stay here?" only 11 per cent mentioned salary or income as a factor in their decision. Factors such as location, work duties, and reputations of the schools involved were all mentioned more frequently than salary (see Table 5). In another vein, when professors who had already indicated that they were not now looking for other employment were asked "If the salary of everyone on the faculty at your school were to be cut by $1,000 would you start looking for another job?" approximately one-third of the respondents said they would not. These were not men who had spent twenty-five or even five years sinking their roots in the community, for such men were not typical of our sample. These men, who would not move even if their salaries were cut by $1,000, had as a rule been at their current job for less than four years.

Another index of professors' interest in money matters is how much they know about compensation levels (salary plus fringe benefits) at their own school and at other schools. In order to determine depth of knowledge about compensation, two tests were performed. First all interviewees were asked to state the average compensation of a full professor at their school. These guesses were then compared with the actual compensation to determine accuracy.[51] The results of these comparisons are summarized in Table 6. Nearly 40 per cent of the respondents whose answers could be evaluated missed the mark by more than $1,000; twelve professors or 14 per cent missed by more

51. The actual compensations of full professors at the various schools were estimated from AAUP Committee Z data. The assumption was made that a school that was assigned the grade (say) B by the AAUP for the average compensation of full professors was actually paying the average compensation of all schools so classified. This procedure is admittedly imperfect but had to suffice in lieu of the confidentiality of the data required.

Table 6

Knowledge of Compensation Paid to Full Professors

Difference Between Professor's Guess and Actual Average Compensation Earned by Full Professor at Same School	Number of Professors
Less than $500	30
$500-$1,000	21
$1,000-$2,000	21
More than $2,000	12
No Answer*	19
TOTAL	103

* Actual average compensation of full professors could not be estimated for two schools, because neither school allowed the AAUP Committee Z to publish relevant data.

Source: Individual Interviews and "The Economic Status of the Profession, 1961-62," *American Association of University Professors Bulletin*, Vol. 48, No. 2 (Summer, 1962), pp. 120-54.

than $2,000. In the second test the interviewees were asked, "If all full-time faculty members teaching at accredited four-year colleges and universities in the United States were ranked by basic salary (including fringe benefits), in what quartile do you think the average full-time faculty member at your school would fall?" The answers were then compared with the true quartile, the latter statistic obtained from AAUP Committee Z data. The results: roughly half of the respondents, as shown in Table 7, were not able to make even this very general judgment correctly. The tendency was to overestimate. Taken together, these two tests indicate that professors are not well informed on salary matters. Since organizations such as the Office of Education and the American Association of University Professors make salary data readily available, it is probably correct to conclude that the observed ignorance is more the result of disinterest than difficulty in obtaining information. Hence, here is still another indication that professors are not as salary conscious as economist theorists might assume.

The general indifference toward salary matters, beyond the minima points, appears to prevail throughout the profession.

Table 7

Knowledge of Compensation Paid by Own School Relative
to All Other Accredited Four-Year Colleges and Universities

Professor Placed the Average Compensation Paid by His Own Institution	Number of Professors
In Correct Quartile	40
In Too High Quartile	33
In Too Low Quartile	11
No Answer*	19
TOTAL	103

* Actual average compensation of full professors could not be estimated for two schools, because neither school allowed the AAUP Committee Z to publish relevant data.
Source: Individual Interviews and "The Economic Status of the Profession, 1961-62," *American Association of University Professors Bulletin*, Vol. 48, No. 2 (Summer, 1962), pp. 120-54.

There are no apparent centers of indifference and centers of concern. Economists are no more or less salary-conscious than historians or sociologists, and so forth. In order to differentiate the extent to which various sub-groups stressed salary when selecting jobs, the Salary-Stress Index was computed for each professor. Anticipating the computation of this index, we asked individuals nine different questions pertaining to salary. To each of the nine questions one of three answers was given: "Type 1, an answer reflecting concern for monetary matters;[52] Type 2, an answer reflecting lack of concern for monetary matters; and Type 3, a neutral answer or no answer. The Salary Stress Index is

52. The nine answers reflecting concern for monetary matters are: (1) I chose this job rather than one of the others that I was offered at the same time because the salary was higher; (2) I would not have accepted this job unless the salary had been raised in negotiations; (3) If my current salary were to be cut by $1,000, I would start looking for another job, even though I'm not looking now; (4) I am currently looking for another job and one of the disadvantages of my present job is "low or inadequate salary"; (5) I failed to accept another job offered to me because the economic aspects of the other job were not attractive enough; (6) The primary reasons that I switched to my present job include "higher salary"; (7) My salary on my present job is higher than my salary would have been if I had remained at my previous job; (8) Among the minimal requirements for another job that I would consider at this time is "salary"—either higher salary, same salary, or not too much lower salary; and (9) Salary was a major consideration in my change of jobs.

Table 8

Characteristics of Professors Dichotomized According to the Stress Placed Upon Salary in Job Decision-Making

Characteristics	Number of Professors*	
	Salary Stressed[1] (N = 41)	Salary Not Stressed[1] (N = 62)
MARITAL STATUS:		
Married	38	50
Single	3	12
RANK:		
Junior Faculty	23	29
Senior Faculty	18	33
PREVIOUS ASSOCIATION WITH PRESENT JOB:		
Was previously associated with school	3	11
Was not previously associated with school	38	51
EXTENT OF EDUCATION:		
Master's degree only	10	12
Ph.D.	30	50
QUALITY OF SCHOOLS:[2]		
Now teaching at one of the 6 top schools	13	23
Now teaching at one of the 6 lower schools	10	21
RESEARCH PRODUCTIVITY:[3]		
Productive	16	26
Unproductive	25	36
PREVIOUS EXPERIENCE IN TEACHING:		
Without experience	17	25
With experience	24	37
SALARY LEVEL OF CURRENT INSTITUTION:[4]		
Now teaching at one of the 6 highest paying schools	6	10
Now teaching at one of the 6 lowest paying schools	17	25
DISCIPLINE OF SPECIALIZATION:		
Economics	14	21
Sociology	13	20
History	14	21

1. Salary Stressed group includes all professors with a Salary Stress Index greater than .35. Salary Not Stressed group includes all other professors. For a description of the process by which Salary Stress Indexes were computed, see page 235.

2. For a description of the process by which the quality of the 18 institutions sampled was determined, see Appendix D.

3. For a description of the process by which each individual was graded ac-

cording to the quantity and quality of his publications, see Appendix E.
4. Highest and lowest paying refers only to the 18 schools surveyed.
* None of the differences are statistically significant at the 95 per cent level of confidence.
Source: Individual Interviews

the ratio of Type 1 answers to Type 1 plus Type 2 answers. Thus, any individual might have an index between zero (complete lack of concern for monetary matters) and one (extreme concern for monetary matters).

All professors were dichotomized according to their Salary-Stress Indexes. The "Salary-Stress" group includes forty-one professors with indexes greater than .35 and the "Salary-Not-Stressed" group includes sixty-two professors with indexes less than .35. The characteristics of the two groups are contrasted in Table 8. Within the Salary-Stress Group are disportionately large numbers of married, junior faculty members, without Ph.D.'s, who had had no previous associations with the university where they are currently teaching. These findings suggest that salary emphasis is a function of financial need (married need more money than single), the strength of commitment to a particular institution (junior faculty members who have not had previous association with a school are comparatively uncommitted), and stage of education.

But these differences are far less surprising than the general similarity of the two groups. Such important factors as discipline of specialization, research productivity, job experience, quality of institution, and salary level of institution failed to differentiate the groups. Economists were no more interested in salary than historians; first time job hunters, no more than experienced academicians; and persons located at the better and higher paying institutions, no more than others. The indifference toward salary matters cannot be centered upon one particular sub-group of professors; it is general.

Salary—Other Studies

In order to confirm or deny the validity of the conclusion that as a rule salary differentials are not a primary consideration when professors choose among alternative job offers, a conclusion based upon the analysis of interviews with 103 Southeastern social scientists, it is desirable to compare and contrast the findings of previous researchers considering similar hypotheses. Probably the most thorough analysis of motivation in professiorial job choice is that of Stecklein and Lathrop of faculty associated with the University of Minnesota. Most of the findings cited in this many-faceted study point toward the insignificance of salary, and thus confirm the findings of the present study. When asked what factors had influenced their decision to accept offers from the University of Minnesota, new Minnesota faculty members listed eight other factors more frequently than salary.[53] Only 35 per cent of the new Minnesotans stated that salary was a positive influence upon their decision to come to Minnesota and two-fifths (14 per cent) as many indicated that they had accepted the Minnesota offer in spite of a salary disadvantage. Salary was not an important factor in decisions to come to Minnesota.

Nor was salary an important factor in decisions to stay away from Minnesota. Persons who had turned down Minnesota offers listed both "preferred duties of present or alternative position" and "comfortably located and offer not enough better to cause move" more frequently than "salary or rank offer inferior to present or alternative position."[54] Their statements were generally supported by their actions, for in roughly half of the cases, the persons who had turned down Minnesota had accepted positions paying less salary than Minnesota offered.[55]

Nor was salary an important factor in decisions to stay at Minnesota. About one hundred and ten faculty members at the University of Minnesota considered seriously but finally turned down offers to join other faculties. The most frequently mentioned attraction of the jobs that were turned down was "salary." Sixty-three per cent indicated that "improved salary arrangements and better long range salary potential" was a major attraction of the turned down job whereas only 1 per cent listed this as a major

53. Stecklein and Lathrop, *Faculty Attraction and Retention*, p. 125.
54. *Ibid.*, p. 33.
55. *Ibid.*, p. 37.

attraction of their present jobs at Minnesota.[56] For a large majority of these professors, salary was not a big holding factor. In fact, they had decided against leaving Minnesota in spite of the salary advantages of doing so.

Nor was salary listed as the primary reason for leaving Minnesota by those who had accepted employment elsewhere. The strongest inducements to leave Minnesota were "opportunity for professional growth and advancement" and "duties and responsibilities." "Income potential" and "total income at the time of change" were less important than either of these factors.[57] Professors who left Minnesota were not, in general, dissatisfied with either their present or their prospective salary.[58]

The general impact of the Stecklein and Lathrop study is well expressed in the following passage:

Although not mentioned among the top five influences in bringing these new faculty members to the University, the matters of salary and rank deserve a special comment. . . . Most interviewees did consider the matters of salary and rank, viewing them as limiting conditions on positions that they would consider. The majority of the persons contacted reported that they had made a tentative decision about the salary and rank that would be necessary before they would consider any position. After these minimum conditions were met, other factors entered into the decision with added importance.[59]

To paraphrase Stecklein and Lathrop, salary was important as a minimum, but not as a key, factor. This conclusion is in complete accord with ours.

Some of the results of other studies are also corroborative. When Jerry L. L. Miller asked fifty-nine Southeastern graduate students who were in the process of seeking their first jobs after graduate school to indicate what factors they regarded as important in their new jobs, "salary" was listed less frequently than either "time to work in area of own interest" or "opportunity for advancement."[60] John Gustad, after surveying attitudes in

56. *Ibid.*, pp. 63 and 72.
57. *Ibid.*, p. 53.
58. *Ibid.*, p. 51.
59. *Ibid.*, p. 18.
60. Miller, *Exploratory Study*, p. 40.

Southern universities, concludes that administrators "place salary higher on the scale [of reward values] than professors" and that professors value independence, research opportunity, intellectually stimulating colleagues most highly as job characteristics.[61] In their study of 576 faculty members teaching on twenty-three different campuses offering four-year programs, Ruth Eckert and John Stecklein report that "salary" was given as a reason for selecting current positions by only 7.8 per cent of the interviewees: seven other factors were listed more frequently.[62]

It would be incorrect, however, to imply that the results of all previous studies indicate that salaries are without any significance. Neither the previous studies nor the present one comes to such a conclusion. As we have, each of the authors that has been cited in the paragraphs immediately above has placed some qualifications upon the unimportance of salary. For example, Stecklein and Lathrop state, "Salary is discounted as an influence in faculty mobility only if the offers made or received are interpreted as providing no real economic advantage over alternative choices."[63] Miller points out that salary, though mentioned less frequently than two other factors, was mentioned by 82 per cent of his sample as an important characteristic of new jobs.[64] Also, at least one study has come to an opposite conclusion. In *The Academic Marketplace*, Caplow and McGee report that between 48 per cent and 58 per cent of the job changers studied were "said to have been attracted by the offer of a better salary."[65] Although this conclusion is somewhat offset by the fact that only 18 to 21 per cent of the job changers were reported to have been dissatisfied with their salaries at their previous jobs and by the observation that "faculty mobility is not a simple function of salary differentials," there is little doubt that Caplow and McGee would assign a greater importance to salary.[66]

61. John Gustad, "They March to a Different Drummer: Another Look at College Teachers," *The Educational Record*, Vol. 40, No. 3 (July, 1959), pp. 210-11.
62. Eckert and Stecklein, *Job Motivations*, p. 32.
63. Stecklein and Lathrop, *Faculty Attraction and Retention*, p. 99.
64. Miller, *Exploratory Study*, p. 40.
65. Caplow and McGee, *The Academic Marketplace*, p. 55.
66. *Ibid.*, pp. 11 and 99.

In spite of these empirical findings, the general impact of the studies of college and university faculty is that salaries are not an important determinant of job choice. Professors do act in accordance with the stereotype. Whether this de-emphasis upon monetary matters is because professors are truly too concerned with less mundane matters to have time to worry about pay, or because the pre-selection of college faculty militates against persons who are money conscious, or because in professorial circles the primary route to prestige is through research and writing rather than monetary compensation, or because professors lose some of their monetary motivations in an attempt to become more professor-like, other studies, as well as the present study, do show that when professors are selecting jobs there are things more important than salary.

Income Other Than Salary

That salary is not a primary consideration in job choice does not necessarily prove that job choice is not dominated by monetary motivations. Though it is the most important, salary is only one component of the monetary attractiveness of a job. Part of a professor's current monetary compensation comes from sources other than his salary; for example, fringe benefits. As a rule fringe benefits increase the effective incomes of professors from 5 to 10 per cent.[67] Another source of non-salary compensation is remuneration for extra teaching at nights and during the summer. Contract research, consulting, book reviewing, research stipends, and fellowships also provide additional income. By moonlighting, the modal and median member of our sample increased his average annual income by 10 to 20 per cent. Because of these "salary supplements," professorial income tends to exceed salary.

Part of the monetary attractiveness of a job is determined by

67. "The Economic Status of the Profession, 1961-62: Report of the Self-Grading Compensation Survey," *American Association of University Professors Bulletin*, Vol. 48, No. 2 (Summer, 1962), p. 132.

what the income will buy. Because of differences in the costs of living, the same money incomes may not buy the same number of goods. Because of differences in the levels of living, the same money incomes may not seem the same. And part of the monetary attractiveness of jobs is determined by the prospects the jobs offer for income in the future. Consideration of present income alone is not sufficient. The professor who aspires to be an "economic man" must make his job decisions on the basis of differentials in the discounted value of a stream of expected lifetime earnings, not on instantaneous earnings' differentials.[68]

Because of these differences between salary and the broader concept of monetary considerations, it is conceivable that a person who was concerned with monetary matters in general might move to a lower salaried position, or might indicate lack of concern for salary per se. It is, therefore, conceivable that our conclusion that the economic factors are not a major consideration in job choice (above the minima level of salary) on the basis of salary alone is an invalid one. Insofar as possible, let us consider the nature of the qualifications that must be placed upon our conclusion if the concept of monetary matters includes not only salary but also fringe benefits, costs of living, opportunities for outside income, and the present value of future income.

The term fringe benefits is meant to refer to all non-salary compensations for services performed such as employer retirement and insurance payments, reciprocal college tuition agreements, personal use of school facilities and equipment, subsidized faculty housing, free admission to cultural and athletic events, and so forth. According to the scanty evidence at hand, it seems unlikely that differences in fringe benefits affect job choice decisions to a substantial degree. In spite of the fact that differences in fringe benefits can be relatively large,[69] in our interviews not

68. See, e.g., Martin Bronfenbrener, "Potential Monopsony in Labor Markets," *Industrial and Labor Relations Review*, Vol. 9, No. 4 (July, 1956), pp. 586-88.
69. Differences in fringe benefits are not insignificant. Using data from William C. Greenough and Francis P. King, *Retirement and Insurance Plans in American Colleges* (New York: Columbia University Press, 1959) and the American Association of University Professors salary surveys, we made very rough esti-

a single professor mentioned "fringe benefits" as a major factor in his decision to accept a job at his current institution. One-third of the interviewees were not even aware of what fringe benefits were available at the time they accepted their present job. Confirming these observations on the insignificance of fringe benefits are the findings of Stecklein and Lathrop and of Miller. Miller writes: "Few candidates were interested in fringe benefits such as faculty housing, retirement benefits, sabbatical leaves, and life insurance."[70] Stecklein and Lathrop conclude: "The fact remains, however, that a substantial portion of the new staff members were apparently indifferent to the University benefit program."[71] Fringe benefits are not significant for job choice decisions.[72]

Like factors such as congeniality of colleagues and advancement potential, fringe benefits are difficult to evaluate and compare. Without knowing the housing market, for instance, the degree to which housing is subsidized cannot be known. Without being able to anticipate future mobility, it is impossible to determine the economic significance of the fact that the retirement plan is non-vested or that a given school would pay the college tuition for a six-year-old son if the policy is not changed during the next twelve years.

mates of the differences in average (for all faculty) annual employer contributions to retirement plans. The distribution was as follows:

Annual Contribution	No. of Schools
Over $750	2
$500-$750	1
$250-$500	6
Under $250	6
Information Not Available	ε

In general the institutions paying higher salaries are also offering better retirement plans.

70. Miller, *Exploratory Study*, p. 37.

71. Stecklein and Lathrop, *Faculty Attraction and Retention*, p. 25.

72. According to the interviews with department chairmen, there is one general exception to the rule: fringe benefits are a factor that tends to hold long-service faculty in place until their rights become vested. Since faculty that had spent many years at their current institution were specifically excluded from our sample, the depth to which long-service professors are reluctant to sacrifice accumulated rights could not be determined. Also see American Council of Education, *Expanding Resources for College Teaching* ("Reports of Committees and Conferences, Series I, No. 60"; Washington, 1956), p. 106.

As for cost and level of living differences, these are small (all college towns are expensive) and difficult to evaluate and compare. The comparative costs (between the geographic loci of two alternative job offers) of food, housing, recreation, transportation, and so forth are specific to individual tastes and cannot be compared thoroughly until a family has lived in both locations. It is significant to note that none of the professors interviewed mentioned that they had made any attempt to convert the money salaries of various offers into real equivalents.

In contrast to cost and level of living differences, the differentials in opportunities to earn outside income are wide and do affect job selection. The median professor in our sample increased his annual earned income 10 per cent to 20 per cent above basic salary through extra employment, about $1,000.[73] Though some means of earning outside income are not dependent upon teaching at a particular institution (e.g., lecture honoraria, book royalties, magazine writing, extra teaching at another school in another geographic area), opportunities to earn extra money by consult-

73. A crude breakdown on how the professors earned this income is given below:

Method of Earning Outside Income	No. of Professors
Summer Teaching	29
Night Teaching	14
Consulting	27
Other	33
No Outside Income	16

The distribution is as follows:

Outside Earned Income as a Percentage of Nine-Month Teaching Salary	No. of Professors
0%	16
5-10%	18
10-20%	34
20-30%	18
30-40%	5
40-50%	7
50-100%	4
Over 100%	1

As defined here, outside income does not include unearned increments (e.g., income from stocks and bonds), in that these would be the same no matter what particular job the professor was holding.

ing, teaching extra courses at the same school or in the same geographic area, and researching under some type of contractual arrangement do vary by school.[74] The business consultant is typically in a much better position if located in or near a large city. Professors desirous of extension teaching, night teaching, and summer school teaching are likely to find more opportunities at large state schools than at small private ones. Experts in governmental affairs find more outside work in capital cities.[75]

Opportunities for earning outside income affect job choices in the following way. Those persons who have become accustomed to earning such income are reluctant to move to jobs without income opportunities unless the move is at a salary high enough to compensate for the loss. This is simply another reflection of the observation made earlier, in the salary section: professors are reluctant to move to jobs where their annual income would be lower than if they remained in place. They regard not only their previous *salary* but also their previous *income* as a minimum characteristic for new jobs that are to be considered. If the amount of outside income earned is great (such as one man we interviewed who had his own consulting firm in the town where he taught), migration is unlikely. On the other hand, if a professor is earning his outside income by rather conventional means (e.g., summer teaching), there are many schools that can meet his minimum "income" requirements; therefore, the restrictive effects of his current outside income will be less.

Consider finally the effect upon job choice of the "present value of a lifetime income stream" as opposed to "salary." If we were to hypothesize that professors act in ways that are economically rational, then we would hypothesize that professors seek the jobs in which they anticipate the "present value of a lifetime income stream" to be the greatest possible. The rational

74. For a statement regarding the differing university policies in regard to earning outside income, see College and University Personnel Association, pp. 129-30.

75. Mayer, "Salaries and Working Conditions," *AAUP Bulletin*, pp. 45-48, surveyed 268 East Coast members of the sociological society regarding salary and income. According to this survey the median sociology professor earns slightly over 20 per cent more than his nine-month teaching salary through outside jobs. The most frequent source is summer teaching.

man might, therefore, select a job which carried a lower instantaneous salary if he anticipated that the salary at this job would improve enough in the future to offset the original disadvantage or that this job would provide the entree to a future opportunity that would be the most attractive financially.

To what extent the observed indifference toward salary matters is caused by allegiance to the sometimes contrary objective, the maximation of expected lifetime incomes, cannot be answered by the data now available. The effect of estimated life incomes upon job selection is not at all obvious from either this or any of the other previous studies of college professors. Unfortunate as it may seem, this factor has been avoided because of the many methodological problems inherent in the concept. To note the significance of any variable upon behavior, there are two primary procedures: asking the individual why he behaved as he did and analyzing the actual behavior of the individual in light of the motives that might be behind it. In this case neither method is feasible. The concept of "present value of a lifetime income stream" is too nebulous. Though with effort it may be possible to estimate a lifetime of income increments if the professor remains in place at his new job, this is not really an accurate estimate of true lifetime income potential. For he is likely to switch jobs. Since the jobs that will be open to him in the future depend upon which among several jobs he accepts at the present time, the income streams that might be earned in jobs that might become open should be estimated for each of the present alternatives. Because of the inherent difficulties in conveying what is meant by expected income to the interviewees, it might at first seem more feasible to study actual behavior. But this too has its limitations. For the interviewers as well as the interviewees, it is impossible to determine what jobs have higher income potential. Also, there is a strong multicollinearity between high salaried positions and positions carrying high prestige[76] so that if a particular professor's history shows that he has constantly sought higher paying jobs

76. As Adam Smith observed for occupations in general, in college teaching the jobs that are more desirable in non-economic ways generally also carry higher wages.

it is very difficult to determine whether he wanted these coveted positions because of their high salaries or because of their high prestige.

Thus, with reservations concerning the true effect of expected as opposed to instantaneous income, it is our conclusion that not only salary but also monetary factors in general are not of primary importance in professorial job selection decisions. Among jobs that offer a minimally acceptable income (usually the professor's current income), other-than-monetary factors are the primary bases upon which a particular job is selected.

Summary

This chapter has concentrated upon the question, "Why do professors select and reject job offers?" From it emerges a picture of the job selecting professor: a casual but rational decision-maker with a fairly good idea of what features make jobs more, or less, desirable. He knows the job characteristics that are important to him and chooses among competitive job offers accordingly.

Some of these characteristics are so important that he never considers jobs that do not have them, the so-called minimum factors. Academic freedom and independence are demanded in all jobs. Job offers that would require a reduction in salary are unacceptable. If he is inclined toward institutions with a research emphasis and relatively good prestige rating, job offers from small, liberal arts colleges are categorically unacceptable; and vice versa. He is likely to have specified in his own mind an area of the country or type of community in which he will not accept jobs. For the sake of practicality, he rejects without further investigation all jobs that do not meet these minimum criteria.

To the job offers that meet these minimum requirements, he applies a more refined set of evaluative criteria. These are the so-called "key" factors—chosen not only because of their importance but also because they provide a determinable basis for differentiating among substantially similar job offers. Because they are both knowable and variable, these are the factors that allow him to choose the best among the group of acceptable jobs. Location, university prestige, and work duties are the most important key factors. For various reasons, at this final stage of the decision-making process, he is less likely to stress differences in salaries, ranks, teaching loads, university administrations, and future job potentials.

In many ways the professor's motivations defy the assumptions of economic model builders and conform to the stereotype of a man who stresses matters other than money.

VIII

CONCLUSIONS AND IMPLICATIONS

In the foregoing pages we have described the job-seeking and candidate-hunting activities of college professors and administrators in terms of an ordinary labor market, the former being the supplier and the latter the demander of labor services. Resting upon the previous literature and one hundred and fifty-three interviews with social scientists teaching at eighteen of the largest schools in the Southeast, we have attempted to describe and explain the hows and whys of the movement of college professors between jobs. We have attempted to analyze in depth the labor markets for college professors as a stereotype of professional labor markets. Theoretical and policy implications of this analysis and the extent to which the analysis can be generalized to all academic labor markets and to all professional labor markets are the subjects of this chapter. In order to make these statements of implications and limitations more meaningful it may be helpful first to summarize our primary conclusions.

Characteristics of the Demand for Faculty

A labor market has been defined as the locus of the meeting of a demander of labor services and a supplier of labor services. Like blue collar workers who frequent employment offices and white collar workers who read want ads in newspapers and casual laborers who line up in hiring halls, college professors pass through labor markets as they move to new jobs. In these markets department chairmen and deans are the employer agents, the demanders. The deans decide the number to be hired and the maximum amount to be paid to the new men. Department chairmen, who are usually more familiar with available supply and better able to evaluate, are then assigned the task of finding and selecting the right man.

The "right man" is the best available for the money that has been allocated. Department chairmen are realists. When they commence their search for new personnel they rarely saddle themselves with a fixed image of the ideal man, for this man may never be found and even if he should be located he may not be attracted by the fixed resources that have been allocated by the dean. Instead, department chairmen are flexible, regarding teaching experience, the Ph.D., and specific teaching interests. In tight markets inexperienced "near Ph.D.'s" may be hired in lieu of shortages of more qualified personnel. The quality standards set by the department chairmen are loose so that, if the realities of the marketplace demand, a poorer candidate can be hired. But the salary maxima set by the deans remain steadfast. The elastic element in the demand function for professors is neither price nor quantity, but quality. The price to be paid for a new man is essentially set before the department chairman goes shopping. If the price offered is too low, the department chairman simply redefines the unit of labor that he seeks. If the price offered is too high, he does not buy more (two rather than one), but rather he purchases a higher quality service.

As for the types of professors that are in greatest demand, there is general agreement that *effective* teachers, *productive* scholars, *respected* and *renowned* academicians and *pleasant* persons are to be preferred to their opposites. But few candidates have all these qualities, so hirers must decide which are the most important. Here opinions differ, depending upon the particular situation and upon the type of school that is doing the hiring. Colleges which place a heavy stress upon teaching look for subject area competence, verbal ability, leadership qualities, compatibility, and sometimes religious conviction in their candidates. Universities tend to be more concerned with competence as a scholar, publishing potential, and verbal ability. The latter minimize the importance of religious conviction, extracurricular ability and to some extent compatibility.

But judging quality is very difficult. At best it is a time consuming process and at its worst it is a grossly inaccurate one. The task of evaluation is so immense that most departments practice the gather-cut-gather-cut- . . . strategy. Information is gathered on all candidates, a cut is made, harder to get information is gathered on the remaining candidates, another cut is made, and so forth. Most departments are able to reduce their list to five or fewer on the basis of information gathered in casual conversations and from the vitae. But further cutting is arduous. Recommenders are contacted. Although the comments of the referents listed by the candidate on his vita are rarely helpful in that almost all hand-picked recommenders laud their friend to the skies, the referents are contacted on the slight chance that they may point up some previously unknown desirable quality in the candidate or unconsciously reveal a fault. Whenever possible, hiring departments seek their own recommenders, persons who know both the candidate and the hiring department and who were not listed by the candidate. These recommendations are viewed with far greater trust than those that are entirely candidate-oriented. Even with all this help, it is very difficult to decide which man should be invited to campus for an interview and whether or not to offer the job to the invited man. Judging quality is difficult, largely subjective, and sometimes speculative.

But the judgment of quality is not the only problem that besets employers of professorial manpower. Another problem that affects the structure of demand function is the limitation upon resources available for faculty salaries. To schools pressed financially, the distribution of faculty by academic rank is extremely important. Since junior faculty members expect smaller salaries and larger teaching loads, their costs per hour of instruction offered is considerably lower. Large financial economies can be achieved by maintaining a high ratio of assistant professors and instructors to total faculty. In order to maintain a high ratio, it is necessary to do virtually all hiring at the junior faculty ranks and to keep the senior positions open to allow the occasional promotion of a junior man. "Hire at the bottom and promote from within" is one of the standard rules of faculty personnel policy, though there are exceptions.

In order to save money, many colleges virtually preclude the possibility of attracting qualified personnel at senior ranks by allowing associate and full professors' salaries to fall below competitive levels. Because of the costs, inconveniences, and insecurities of relocation, employing colleges are able to pay their established faculty less than they could earn if they were willing to move to another school. The result: a salary structure that is skewed in favor of the more mobile professors who are usually concentrated in the lower ranks.

Limited finances affect the demand function for professors in still another way. One of the real problems that deans must face is the simultaneous equating of both the quality of various departments within the university and intra-university salaries. In some disciplines (e.g., sociology) the general market conditions are tighter than in other disciplines (e.g., history). Taking advantage of the tight conditions, sociologists of a given quality are able to demand higher salaries from their employers than are historians. The dean faces a dilemma. If he allocates the same amount of money to each department to hire a new man at the bottom of their respective departmental hierarches, he will find that the history department is able to get a better man than the sociology department. On the other hand, if he asks the two department chairmen to hire men of comparable quality, he must allocate more money to the sociology department and accept intra-university salary differentials as a fact of life. Either the quality of the departments or the salaries must differ. A majority of the department chairmen that we interviewed advocate allowing the salaries to differ. The actual situation hints of compromise, with historians receiving more than their minimum asking prices.

Finally the character of demand varies by its origin. The need to appoint a new faculty member may arise either from the need to fill a position that has been vacated, i.e., replacement demand, or from the need to expand the faculty, expansion demand. Replacement demand, which accounts for about 80 per cent of appointments, tends to be more urgent, more specific (regarding fields of interest), and less predictable than expansion demand.

Characteristics of the Supply of Faculty

The suppliers in academic labor markets are individual faculty members offering their teaching and research services to the colleges and universities. The supply of college professors can be thought of meaningfully in two different ways: the supply to the market as a whole and the supply to an individual college. At first it would seem that the supply of professors to the market as a whole would be relatively fixed at a point in time, for there are only so many persons with the training that enables them to teach at an advanced level, conventionally the persons with some work beyond the Bachelor's degree. In a strict sense, the supply of potential professors is fixed. But in a practical sense the supply is flexible. The element of flexibility is the pool of persons who have had some graduate school training but who have chosen not to teach at the college level. These persons are employed by industry, by government, and by the primary and secondary schools. To augment total supply, these people can be drawn into teaching, if conditions are made sufficiently attractive.

In the preceding analysis our primary concern has been with the utilization of a given over-all supply of college professors. Accordingly, stress has been placed upon supply to the individual employer rather than supply to the market as a whole. When a college seeks to fill a specific vacancy on its faculty, the relevant supply is less than total supply for two reasons. First, not all persons capable of being college professors are capable of filling the specific position that is open. College teaching jobs are not homogeneous. For example, colleges cannot hire chemists to teach sociology and engineers to teach English. As a rule, graduate students cannot be hired to teach Ph.D. level courses.

The size of the supply to a particular vacancy is largely a function of the particularity of employer demand. If the employer is willing to hire any social scientist, he rules out considerably fewer persons than if he demands only historians between twenty-five and thirty-five years old who have special training in Oriental History and a Ph.D. Yet even the former restrictions rule out physical scientists and humanitarians. The point here is that the employer determines the relevancy of supply through the specification of a minimally acceptable candidate. By deciding upon who *could* fill the particular vacancy, the employer sets a maximum upon relevant supply.

Second, after the employer has established who *could* teach at his school, the candidates decide who *would* teach there under various terms. In the end each candidate decides for himself whether or not he is willing to work for a given employer, and under what terms. The individual employer and candidates together define a supply function that relates the number of acceptable candidates supplied to the attractiveness of the position offered. The employer specifies which candidates are acceptable supply (i.e., which candidates could fill the job) and the candidates specify the minimally acceptable terms. If we were to place the supply function in diagramatic form, "apparent job attractiveness" would be on the y-axis and the "number of candidates acceptable to the employer" on the x-axis. The curve would slope upward to the right, indicating that additional numbers of "acceptable candidates" are willing to work as the apparent attractiveness of the job is increased.

Contrary to the simplifying assumptions of many economists, the determinants of apparent job attractiveness are many and complex. Salary is important; less so are fringe benefits. Candidates rarely make themselves available to employers who offer salaries lower than the ones they are earning at their present jobs. But economic variables are not the sole determinants of job attractiveness. Equally important is location. Professors, an occupational group that is quite mobile geographically, are particular about their environment. Many job offers are chosen and rejected on the basis of differences in climates, cultures, communities, and nearness to recreational facilities and friends and relatives. Professors are also concerned with their work duties. Although the number of hours to be taught is not particularly important, there is a preference for fewer courses and more advanced assignments. Preferences are strong, though varied, concerning the distribution of responsibilities between teaching and research. Since professors seek esteem and respect from their job, they regard appointments at the more prestigious universities as more desirable.

No one variable can be singled out as *the most* important. Preferences are not monolithic. Desirably located schools can attract faculty in spite of low salaries. Similarly, high salaries may be used to induce professors to accept appointments at unknown schools. And candidates may be induced to choose undesirable course assignments if the location and salary are good enough to compensate. The marginal rates of substitution among the factors are relatively high. There are limits, however.

Other important elements in job attractiveness are not readily evaluated without actually serving on the job and, therefore, have less influence upon the quantity of labor supplied. Unsympathetic and incompetent administrators decrease the attractiveness of jobs to the extent that they are the single most important cause of persons leaving jobs. Unfriendly and incompetent colleagues are to be avoided. And jobs without a potential for advancement and growth are less attractive than jobs that show promise in these respects. But these elements of job attractiveness are not readily apparent. They are determinants of job attractiveness and job satisfaction, but not *apparent* job attractiveness. It is the latter variable that is the most relevant to supply decisions.

Evaluating competitive job offers is extremely difficult and time consuming. Although candidates learn about salary, rank, and teaching loads with ease, they are relatively poorly informed on the more subtle aspects of job attractiveness at the time they accept. In spite of their polls of friends and acquaintances, consultation of statistics in the library, and even on-campus interviews with prospective employers, ignorance prevails. Well before the point of full information, the anticipated marginal costs of further investigation exceed the anticipated marginal benefits.

The actual process of deciding whether or not to supply oneself to a particular employer is one of elimination. Most candidates require certain minimum characteristics in their jobs: for example, a position that carries no less prestige than the current position, a salary as good as current salary, and an "acceptable" location. Job offers that are conspicuously lacking in one or more of these minimal features are eliminated without further consideration. A choice among the remaining job opportunities is made on fuller criteria. Each job is compared and contrasted with every other job in a factor by factor analysis. Some factors have to be ignored (e.g., congeniality of colleagues) because of insufficient information. Other factors may be eliminated from consideration because all jobs are about equal in these respects (e.g., rank). In the final analysis, the factors that are important, determinable, and differentiating are the most crucial in the job choice or supply decision. These factors are the location, reputation, and the work duties offered by various employers.

Wise employers recognize that there is a great deal of false activity on the supply side of academic labor markets and that the number of persons who appear interested in their jobs is larger than the number really interested. Approximately one out of every four professors is actively seeking a new job at any given time. Almost all professors are in the market at least to the extent that they like to be informed about job vacancies for which they might qualify. Yet, supply is not all it appears to be. Many professors enter at least the fringes of the labor market with a relatively good job option already in hand (their current job) and little intention of switching. They simply desire to establish their current market value and must simulate a sale to do so. Or they must convince a skeptical employer who is reticent to grant a requested promotion or pay raise that they are both willing and able to go to another position if he does not acquiesce. Or they window shop in hopes of finding an unrealistically fantastic job opportunity. Professors who are in the market for these reasons are not reliable sources of supply.

Only professors who are seeking new jobs for more urgent reasons can be relied upon to consider seriously offers of jobs. Graduate students, who do not have a current job to fall back upon, are the most likely source of supply, though even here a particular school must compete against other schools and in some cases the possibility of the student's returning to graduate studies and completing his degree. Another promising source of supply is professors who either cannot or will not return to their current job. Involuntary separations are relatively rare but they do occur. These persons may have been fired because of personal incompetence, the discontinuation of a special program, or university economy measures. They may have grown dissatisfied with their positions because they were originally deceived and misinformed about the true nature of the job, because they originally miscalculated the job potential, or because they have outgrown the opportunity that originally existed. In any case, these persons are on the market and are potential supply.

Characteristics of the Labor Market

Academic labor markets are complex, indefinite, imperfect, and decentralized. *The* academic labor market is a myth. In practice, the heterogeneity of faculty demand and supply balkanizes the market into many more or less isolated units according to discipline, experience, and to a lesser extent geography. There is a clear dividing line between the markets for historians and sociologists; a less clear one between European and American historians. Experienced college teachers rarely compete for jobs with the emerging graduate students. And only for the very best universities are the markets truly national; the horizons of most demanders and suppliers in the East do not encompass the Far West.

Except at the very best schools the sub-labor markets are rarely well organized. The markets are characterized by many small buyers and many small sellers who are in the market only occasionally. Neither party has taken the responsibility of making an efficient and effective market. Both buyers and sellers are widely scattered and timid about expressing their needs. Neither "positions available" nor "jobs wanted" are adequately advertised. Job-seeking candidates are expected to play the role of the reluctant maiden; direct advertising of one's availability is regarded as "unprofessional." Hiring departments fear that the general announcement of a position available will result in a flood of underqualified applicants that require time-consuming processing. As a result, many job-seeking candidates never learn of the vacancies that would interest them most and many hiring schools out of ignorance are forced to hire less than the best available candidate.

Most of the communication that does take place is channeled through liaisons. When a department seeks a new man it sends out informal feelers in all directions. The department chairman writes the department chairmen at the major graduate schools or, if he knows of them, the most prominent men in the subject area where the new hiree is needed. These letters request referrals, names of persons who could and would consider employment at the hiring school. Similar contacts are made with various friends throughout the country. At the same time, candidates are sending letters expressing their availability to their friends and acquaintances. Hopefully, the person receiving requests for referrals of candidates and the person receiving requests for referrals of jobs will be the same. But there is certainly no guarantee that this will be the case, for the liaisons in the academic labor market are not generally agreed upon. Though over 2,500 formal clearinghouses have grown up to serve the academic labor markets and the needs of college professors, these liaisons are neither generally used nor commonly respected. Communication is still largely dependent upon mutual friends who serve as self-appointed, *ad hoc* liaisons. Chance determines whether or not both demanders and suppliers settle upon the same liaisons, and if the liaisons happen to remember both contacts at the right time.

Although they are by far the most important, informal contacts through obscure liaisons are not the only means of communication. Many candidates, especially emerging graduate students, are swallowing their professional pride and sending their vitae directly to prospective employers, the so-called "mass letters." Others enlist the aid of the "slave market" and the "want ad" pages of professional journals. In some disciplines candidates find jobs through the placement offices at their graduate school. Similarly, the department chairmen who are primarily responsible for hiring occasionally consult the "mass letters," list with the "slave market" and in the want ads of professional journals, and work through placement offices. Commercial employment agencies are still generally taboo.

Yet, methods of communication are still primitive. Both buyers and sellers are expending a great deal of effort with only mediocre results. Only in the better universities is the present system functioning adequately. At this level there are relatively few demanders who are in close touch with the relatively few sources of supply. The informal system serves well and minimizes the effort involved. But the great majority of colleges and universities suffer from the inadequacies of communication in the market.

In general, academic labor markets are characterized by the same balkanization and loose organization that have been observed in the labor markets for blue collar workers. There are, however, several noticeable differences. First, there is very little involuntary mobility in academic labor markets. Largely due to continued expansion in the demand for professorial services and the difficulties of measuring productivity, few employers have found it necessary to fire professors. Most of the movement in academic labor markets is employee-initiated. Second, because of the very few jobs available to a professor within a given commuting area, the geographic mobility of college teachers is considerably higher than that among the typical blue collar worker. Third, the movement of college professors is discontinuous. Very few moves are made during the course of academic terms. Almost all job changes are made either in June, September, or late January. Fourth, professors rarely quit one job before they have already signed for another. And fifth, college professors stress non-economic factors to a greater extent than blue collar workers. Therefore, the economic differentials in employment opportunities are less of an influence upon the direction of mobility.

Implication and Recommendations

Misallocations of labor almost certainly result from the imperfections of academic labor markets, though the extent of misallocation is not immediately apparent. From an economic standpoint college teachers are involved in the production of a capital good, trained high-level manpower. Professors produce a good which in turn produces other goods. They are involved at a relatively early and crucial stage in the production process. Insofar as the misallocation of college teachers decreases the quality and quantity of manpower training, it has a directly detrimental effect upon production.

Economic theory indicates that for a free labor market (e.g., a labor market for college professors) to function optimally: (1) the highest bidder for labor services should be the employer who will employ the given services in the way that will benefit society the most, (2) the persons possessing college teaching skills must be aware of the various advantages offered by jobs with all employers, and (3) the trained college teachers must move toward those opportunities that offer the greatest "net advantage." In academic labor markets it is not clear that any of these ideals is achieved.

Unfortunately, there is no general agreement concerning where professors should be placed in order to maximize their value to society. The optimum distribution of faculty among institutions of higher learning is not known. Some allocations are obviously inferior to others. For example, the relatively few Oriental historians should fill vacancies that demand their scarce skills as specialists (e.g., teaching a graduate level courses in Oriental History) before vacancies that require their less scarce skills (e.g., teaching a freshman survey course in Modern Civilization). But beyond the obvious, the ranking of alternative distributions is extremely tenuous. Consider, for example, the question of the distribution of the most productive men in a given field. Is it desirable for society as a whole to have these men all concentrated in the same institution so that they can exchange ideas and form a high-powered center of learning? Or is it better to have these men scattered throughout different institutions so that many more faculty and students can profit from associating with at least one of them and so that the thinking of the experts does not become undifferentiated? Because the optimum distribution cannot be defined, it is impossible to evaluate existing differentials.

But let us assume that the reward differentials offered by various opportunities do reflect social value. There is still no guarantee that labor will be allocated properly. The mere existence of these differentials is not sufficient evidence that the labor market is moving toward an optimum position. In addition, the differentials must be known; the opportunities must be widely circularized. The correct mobility cannot be expected if the vacancies are unnoticed. The desired wide circularization has been lacking, as is indicated by the fact that the median social scientist interviewed in the current study knew of only one other job opening at the time he accepted his current position. As the centers of graduate education multiply, satisfactory communications become even less likely. The immensity of the present communication problem is best visualized by a 2,000 by 2,000 (the approximate number of colleges and universities) matrix, for each school has the potential both to lose a teacher to or to gain a teacher from any one of the other schools.

Many obstructions to free communication between these institutions exist, both intended and unintended. In addition to the geographic dispersion of both hirers and hirees, the professional standards that speak against overt advertising and the inherent difficulties of evaluating jobs and candidates lend complications. Added to these are the conflicting interests among employers and prospective employees. An optimal information flow from the individual candidate's viewpoint would be one which brought news of all openings to him and to no other candidates and news of his availability and his alone to all employers. The individual employer would benefit most from a system that informed all candidates of his and only his opening and informed no other employers of any candidates available. From this statement it is obvious that it is not always in the best interests of candidate A to let candidate B know of a good job with employer X, or to let X know about B. In most labor markets such conflicts of interest would not have serious consequences, for the primary information flow is through other than the employer and employee. But in academic labor markets these conflicts sometimes inhibit the free flow of information, with employers "hoarding" knowledge and candidates "keeping quiet" about the jobs they find. Complications of communicating are thus increased.

Our studies indicate further that the differentials that now exist among college teaching jobs are in many cases not sufficiently large to stimulate mobility. The attractions of factors that are beyond the direct control of hirers such as the location and prestige of schools often more than offset, in the minds of the candidates, differences in manipulatable factors. This means that a school located in an undesirable Southern town might offer top salaries, attractive workloads, and so forth and yet still have difficulties recruiting desired personnel. In many cases unique appeals of particular schools draw and keep individual professors in spite of the attempts of other schools to compete favorably in every way possible. In spite of its need and its ability and its willingness to structure desirable teaching assignments and pay better than competitive salaries, a low prestige university or a university located in an undesirable climate might not be able to attract certain personnel who place high value on prestige or location. It is conceivable that due to a fortuitous location one school that was not in as great need of Professor A's skills and reflected this by a generally inferior offer might still attract A from another school. Thus, even when differentials are set in accord with differences in social value and these differentials generally are known, professors in some cases still do not respond to them. The resultant allocation of labor is less than optimal.

Solely economic theories explain neither the current distribution nor the direction of mobility in academic labor markets. Professors often consciously choose less than the economically most attractive job alternative. As an abstraction of reality, the theories that assume all "other (than monetary) things equal" are a useful tool in analyzing patterns of mobility and in understanding academic labor markets: as a complete and accurate explanation of behavior, the theories are fallacious. This is not to condemn economic theory, but simply to define its limitations.

From a social viewpoint, if some of these imperfections could be reduced or eliminated, the allocation of professorial manpower would be improved. It would be confusing means and ends to expect professors to alter their preference structure for the sake of model efficiency. Any measures of improvement should assume these preference scales as given. Similarly, until the most desirable distribution of manpower has been established, tampering with existing differentials is of marginal value. It may well be that the conscious determination of differentials in job attractiveness may be the most effective means of achieving a desired distribution of resources, but until we can agree on what distribution is desirable the best strategy is to adhere to those that develop naturally.

The most promising reforms are in the area of better communications, more frequent and more reliable exchanges of information between "candidates available" and "positions available." Because both buyers and sellers are small, scattered, and sporadic participants in academic labor markets, liaisons are essential. Since neither party is interested enough to maintain a market, some third party must do so. As reiterated in the section immediately previous, most of the liaisons now operating in academic labor markets are obscure, not generally known. In order to maximize the probability that both hirer and hiree will find their way to the same liaison, the clearinghouses should, within each relevant labor market, be few in number and generally known. When needing help, both parties should turn to the same place.

The liaison function could be carried out in a number of different ways. The responsibility for creating effective communications in the various academic labor markets could be assigned to professional societies, accrediting agencies, university placement offices, educational foundations, graduate school departments, state and federal governments, or possibly commercial employment agencies. The important thing is that the liaison is highly respected, generally accepted, and frequently used. One plan that deserves further study centers around the professional society. In many disciplines the professional society is a logical center of placement activity, for it has the respect of the profession, the channels of communication, and the feel for the unique aspects of the profession which are not likely to be equaled by other parties.

The plan places the primary burden of initiating communications upon the job-seeking candidates, for it is the candidates whose personal interests are most at stake and the candidates whose unpredictable personal preferences sabotage all attempts to mechanize fully the placement process. Also, the candidates' time is likely to be less valuable to society than the time of a hiring department chairman.

Under this plan all openings and anticipated openings would be published twice a year; for example, January and April. All hirers would be asked or required to list their vacancies with the society. The society would organize and index the vacancies by sub-specialties, experience required, training required, work duties involved (teaching versus research), rank, salary, and prestige of department. The vacancies would then be published in a form similar to V-608 cited on page 115 above. However, schools would be identified. Candidates would consult these job listings and, however they saw fit, contact the desired employers. The contact might be nothing more than the mailing of a vita, or it might involve asking a friend or professional acquaintance to write in one's behalf. The hiring university or college could then act according to its desires. If he were interested, the hirer could write for more details, contact mutual friends, or invite the candidate to campus. If not interested in the candidate or the service, the vita received could be thrown away.

The primary advantage of this system or one similar to it over the present informal communications methods is that every candidate is at least able to make his availability known to every employer that interests him. In a sense, it is equality of rights. The candidate is exposed to a much broader spectrum of opportunities; the employer, to a broader spectrum of candidates.

There are of course problems. First, there is the financing. In most disciplines such a system would require a full-time person, mailing expense, and publication costs. In the physical sciences and some of the social sciences a large portion of this expense could probably be offset by asking profit-making recruiters to pay for listing of their vacancies. But the main listers, the universities, could not be both required to list and then charged for the service. Other means of financing might involve the use of society dues, a fee charged to the candidates using the information contained in the publication of vacancies, or reliance upon the United States Employment Service.

The other primary problem is usage of the service once it is established. Experience indicates that both employers and employees are reluctant to use formal placement services. Employers are reluctant to list and, therefore, candidates rarely read the lists of jobs now publicized on a limited basis in some professional journals. The solution may be compulsory listing of vacancies on the part of the hiring institutions. The force of compulsion might be the refusal on the part of the professional society to allow men from non-co-operating departments to publish in its journal and present papers at its meetings. It is true that this penalty would not hurt many of the lesser schools where the faculty is not interested in publishing and presenting, but these schools need such a service so badly that they would present no problem. In the past it has been the better schools that have resisted the move toward formalization of placement procedures. This penalty would be especially onerous to these very schools. If all schools were required to list vacancies, the prestige now associated with the disuse of formal agencies would disappear. If all jobs were listed and appropriately and extensively indexed, the readership among candidates of these opportunities would certainly rise.

Although there are many yet unsolved technical problems in the particular plan, which demand considerably more thought and study, our analysis of the academic labor markets in the Southeast suggests that some such liaison is necessary, desirable, and feasible. This liaison should not and would not, however, completely supplement the informal communications system as it now exists. When the services being sold are as intangible as the teaching and research services of college professors, the informal liaisons are needed as evaluators of jobs and candidates, even if the initial lines of contact are more structured. When available and feasible, informal job communications are actually preferable to the more formal. The point is that there must be an acceptable alternative means of finding out about jobs and candidates where the informal procedures are not operating effectively.

Concluding Observations

Not all candidates and hiring institutions need to suffer equally from the imperfections that now exist in academic labor markets. Though society as a whole must suffer from the misallocations, for any single institution and any single candidate it is possible to capitalize upon these imperfections to one's own advantage. In a well-functioning labor market all candidates are made aware of all jobs. Full information hurts institutions that are offering inferior jobs because knowledgeable candidates will usually not come to these schools. Such institutions fare better in an imperfectly competitive market where some candidates learn only of their jobs. Similarly, in an imperfect market where many of the very good candidates do not learn about some of the good jobs, the mediocre candidate has a better chance to get them.

In the market as it exists today there are several things that an employer can do to turn the imperfections to his advantage:

1. Advertise vacancies as widely as possible so that he will maximize the number of applicants.

2. Remember that a responsible and effective department chairman must develop and maintain professional friends and acquaintances. As long as the primary communications channels are through such liaisons it behooves every hirer to know as many potential liaisons as possible.

3. Where feasible, make recruiting trips to some of the nearby graduate schools and talk with prospective candidates. The business recruiters have found this method effective. The few department chairmen that had done something like this stated that they found it quite helpful and intend to continue the practice.

4. Avoid the fee-charging employment agencies.

5. Cut heavily from the accumulated list of candidates on the basis of "paper" knowledge and preliminary information in order to keep the task of investigating and evaluating the candidates within manageable proportions. Although mistakes will be made in such cuts they are likely to be less serious than the mistakes of omission that result from collecting too few names.

6. When the best candidate is found, do not expect that money alone will cause him to accept the job. Invite him to campus and apply sales pressure. Stress the non-economic desirability of locality, community, responsibility for advanced courses, and the like and minimize the importance of factors where other schools can make higher bids.

Similarly, the job-seeking candidate may:

1. Concentrate upon developing friends and acquaintances that might serve as liaisons.

2. Make extensive efforts to inform all friends and acquaintances and some people in hiring positions of his availability. The direct mailing of vitae to hiring departments does not hurt his chances. In disciplines where the U.S.E.S. has set up a convention slave market, he should use it. In disciplines where there is a general excess supply of candidates, he should intensify efforts, for

the employer is likely to find an acceptable candidate with little effort and not look beyond.

3. Encourage his graduate school to send out a list and description of candidates available for employment, if this applies.

4. Investigate only the most promising jobs in detail; otherwise, none of the jobs will be known well.

5. Have important, respected, known people write recommendations. Recommendations are far more helpful if the receiver knows the sender.

These techniques will benefit those who are smart enough to use them as long as imperfections remain in academic labor markets.

Limitations

It is important to emphasize that our observations and analyses of the Southeastern segments of three disciplinary labor markets may not accurately reflect either the behavior in the same markets in other regions or the behavior in other markets within the same region. The generalization that all labor markets are similar to the ones studied cannot be justified. Our results must be viewed for what they are: a detailed statement of the structure of particular labor markets. The extent to which the characteristics of the markets studied do in fact resemble those of academic labor markets in general cannot be determined until the other markets are studied.

The conclusions reached apply only to the group interviewed. In many ways this is a special group. In order to be in our sample a professor had to be willing to participate and presently teaching either sociology, economics, or history, in the Southeast, at a school with at least 1,200 students, at a school where he was a relative newcomer.

Because of the greater stress upon teaching vis-à-vis research, the lower pay and prestige, the greater acceptance of less formal education, the more frequent financial problems, the differences in the work duties performed, and so forth, the labor markets through which professors finally locating jobs at smaller, less well known schools may be very different. Southeastern labor markets may be somewhat unique because the Southeast must import college teachers trained in other regions, because the undergraduate enrollments are growing less rapidly and graduate enrollments more rapidly in the Southeast than in the nation as a whole, because there is a general feeling that the Southeast is culturally underdeveloped, because the students trained in the public high schools of the region are not as well prepared as similarly situated students in other regions. Social scientists, who are constantly analyzing human behavior of all types, may be more conscious of markets and market structures than professors in the humanities and the physical sciences. The different roles of non-university connected employers in the physical sciences and in the humanities also limit the generality of our conclusions.

The persons interviewed had almost all passed through their respective academic labor market during a period of high excess demand. Studies of blue collar labor markets indicate that behavior in markets characterized by excess demand is quite different than markets characterized by excess supply; we would expect the same to be true of academic labor markets. Similarly, our sample included a disproportionately large number of the relatively more mobile professors who undoubtedly have a different attitude toward the labor market than relatively stable college teachers.

In short, generalization to other markets is dangerous.

APPENDIXES

APPENDIX A: INTERVIEW GUIDE TO THE INTERVIEWS WITH NEW FACULTY

The interviews were divided into five parts: background questions, the present job, the movement between jobs, the previous job, and possible future jobs.

I. Background Questions.

1. WHEN WERE YOU BORN?

2. ARE YOU MARRIED?

Male, married	86
Male, single	13
Female, married	2
Female, single	2

3. WHAT IS YOUR CURRENT RANK?
AT WHAT RANK WERE YOU HIRED?

	Current	Hired
Full professor	15	8
Associate professor	36	20
Assistant professor	45	58
Instructor	7	15
Other	0	2

4. PLEASE TRACE CHRONOLOGICALLY YOUR EDUCATION.

Location of education:	High School	College	Last Graduate School
Same state	6	9	4
Southeast but not same state	25	29	29

Southwest or Far West	15	17	14
Great Lakes and Plains	26	25	34
North Atlantic and Northeast	23	16	19
Foreign	6	6	3
No answer	2	1	0

Highest degree obtained:

Bachelor	0
Master's	22
Ph.D.	80
No answer	1

Years away from Ph.D.:

Less than 3 years	30
4-6 years	17
7-10 years	18
Over 10 years	15
No Ph.D.	23

5. WHAT ARE YOUR MAJOR FIELDS OF INTEREST?

6. WHAT ARTICLES AND BOOKS HAVE YOU WRITTEN? (See Appendix E.)

7. LIST CHRONOLOGICALLY THE PROFESSIONAL JOBS THAT YOU HAVE HELD IN THE PAST. (Do not include jobs held while attending graduate school full time.)

Job immediately previous was:

In business	7
With government	8
Teaching at the same type school	23
Teaching at a different type school	20
Other	3
No previous job	42

Job immediately previous was in:

Same state	3
Southeast but not same state	21
Southwest	5
Middle West or Plains	14
Far West	5
Northeast or Middle Atlantic	11
Foreign	1
No previous job	42
No answer	1

II. Present Job.

8. HAD YOU EVER BEEN ASSOCIATED WITH THIS UNIVERSITY BEFORE BECOMING A MEMBER OF THE FACULTY?

Yes	14
No	89

8A. If associated ask, HOW?

Undergraduate alumnus	4
Graduate alumnus	4
Previously on faculty	3
Relatives matriculated	2
Other	3

9. ON THE AVERAGE HOW MANY HOURS DO YOU TEACH PER TERM?

Less than 4	1
4-6	6
7-9	38
10-12	46
More than 12	12

10. DO YOU HAVE ANY OTHER MAJOR COLLEGE RESPONSIBILITIES? If yes ask, WHAT?

11. WHAT ARE THE MAIN ATTRACTIONS OF YOUR PRESENT POSITION?

Salary	17
Rank	1
Courses taught	37
Teaching load	16
Future potential	13
Reputation and type of school	19
Colleagues	40
Location	63
Research emphasis	17
Administration	30
Other	24

12. WHAT ARE THE PRIMARY DRAWBACKS?

13. WHAT FRINGE BENEFITS DO YOU RECEIVE AS A FACULTY MEMBER?

Mentioned freely:

Life insurance	63
Retirement plan	63
Medical insurance	71
Recreation facilities	13
Chance to earn extra income	14
Travel allowances to meetings	8
Location in college community	29

14. IN WHAT WAYS DO YOU SUPPLEMENT YOUR BASIC SALARY? (See page 244.)

14A. If supplemented ask, BY WHAT PERCENTAGE DO THESE SUPPLEMENTS INCREASE YOUR INCOME ABOVE YOUR BASIC SALARY? (See page 244.)

15. WOULD YOU LIKE TO HAVE MORE OPPORTUNITIES TO SUPPLEMENT YOUR INCOME?

Yes	42
No	61

15A. If yes ask, WHAT TYPES OF OPPORTUNITIES WOULD YOU LIKE TO HAVE MOST?

16. IF YOUR SALARY WERE CHANGED PROPORTIONALLY, WOULD YOU LIKE TO INCREASE OR DECREASE YOUR TEACHING LOAD?

Keep load the same	77
Increase load	14
Decrease load	9
No answer	3

17. IF ALL FULL-TIME FACULTY MEMBERS IN THE U.S. WERE RANKED BY BASIC SALARY, WHERE DO YOU THINK THE AVERAGE FULL-TIME FACULTY MEMBER AT YOUR SCHOOL WOULD FALL? IN TOP ONE-FOURTH? IN TOP HALF? IN BOTTOM HALF? IN BOTTOM ONE-FOURTH? (See page 234.)

18. HOW MUCH DO YOU THINK THE AVERAGE FULL PROFESSOR EARNS AT YOUR SCHOOL? (Include fringe benefits but not outside or summer income in your estimate.) (See page 235.)

III. Movement Between Jobs.

19. HOW DID YOU FIRST LEARN ABOUT THE JOB YOU NOW HOLD?

From:

Graduate school thesis adviser	11
Graduate school	24
Friend at a professional meeting	12
Friend by letter or phone	36
Journal want ads	2
University placement service	4
Private fee-charging placement service	1
Mass letter	7
Other	6

20. WERE YOU "LOOKING AROUND" FOR A JOB AT THE TIME?

Yes	69
No	33
No answer	1

20A. If looking ask, WHAT HAD YOU DONE TO FIND A JOB?

Informed graduate school of my availability	39
Informed friends	43
Attended conventions	25
Contacted unknown departments via mass letters	10
Other	1

20B. If not looking ask, HAD YOU EVEN THOUGHT OF CHANGING JOBS BEFORE YOU WERE APPROACHED?

| Yes | 23 |
| No | 10 |

21. AFTER FIRST HEARING ABOUT THIS JOB, WHAT DID YOU DO TO LEARN MORE ABOUT IT?

Nothing	9
Polled friends	38
Visited campus	53
Discussed with major professors	19
Checked catalogue and other statistics	33
Other	20
No answer	1

22. WHICH AVENUE OF INVESTIGATION WAS MOST HELPFUL?

None outstanding	7
Polling friends	18
Visiting campus	44
Discussing with professor	7
Checking catalogue	1
Other	9
No answer	17

23. DID YOU VISIT THE CAMPUS?

Yes	53
No	50

23A. If visited ask, DESCRIBE THE VISIT.

24. WHAT DID YOU KNOW ABOUT THE JOB AT THE TIME YOU ACCEPTED?

Salary	99
Fringe benefits	69
Salary advancement	51
Rank	97
Promotion possibilities	64
Hours taught	94
Courses taught	79
Quality of students	65
Extent of library	74
Availability of research monies	57
Secretarial services	48
Office facilities	72
Departmental relationships	61
Committee responsibilities	46

25. WHAT DID YOU NOT KNOW, OTHER THAN THE THINGS MENTIONED ABOVE?

26. DID YOU REALIZE THAT YOU WERE ACCEPTING THE JOB UNAWARE OF THE THINGS YOU DID NOT KNOW?

Yes	61
No	36
No answer	6

27. DO YOU NOW FEEL THAT ANY SUBJECTS WERE "DISCREETLY NOT MENTIONED" PREVIOUS TO THE TIME YOU ACCEPTED THE JOB?

Yes	24
No	77
No answer	2

28. WOULD YOUR DECISION TO COME TO YOUR PRESENT POSITION HAVE BEEN DIFFERENT IF YOU HAD KNOWN MORE ABOUT THE POSITION?

Yes	13
No	88
No answer	2

29. DID YOU KNOW AT THE TIME YOU ACCEPTED THE JOB IF OTHER CANDIDATES WERE BEING SERIOUSLY CONSIDERED FOR THE SAME JOB?

Yes, others were	51
Yes, no others	11
Did not know	40
No answer	1

30. AFTER THE OFFER WAS EXTENDED, HOW SOON DID YOU ACCEPT?

Immediately	27
Few days	15
One week	14
Two weeks	20
Three or four weeks	8
Over four weeks	16
No answer	3

31. WAS THE ORIGINAL OFFER THE SAME AS THE FINAL OFFER?

Yes	63
No	39
No answer	1

31A. If not same ask, WHAT CHANGES WERE MADE?

Salary	31
Moving allowance	3
Other economic changes	2
Rank	2
Other non-economic changes	7
No answer	1

31B. If not same ask, WOULD YOU HAVE ACCEPTED THE OFFER IF THESE CHANGES HAD NOT BEEN MADE?

Yes	13
No	18
Don't know	8

32. DID YOUR PREVIOUS EMPLOYER KNOW THAT YOU WERE CONSIDERING ANOTHER JOB?

Yes	63
No	5
No answer	35

32A. If yes ask, WHAT DID HE DO?

Salary raise greater than otherwise	13
Other economic changes	6
Non-economic changes (e.g., rank raise)	3
No changes	41

33. DID YOUR PREVIOUS EMPLOYER OFFER TO INCREASE SALARY?

33A. If yes ask: DO YOU THINK YOU WOULD HAVE BEEN OFFERED THIS SALARY INCREASE IF YOU HADN'T THREATENED TO LEAVE?

34. DID YOU KNOW ABOUT ANY OTHER OPENINGS AT THE TIME YOU DECIDED TO ACCEPT?

Yes	88
No	15

35. DID YOU INVESTIGATE ALL OF THESE OPENINGS?

Yes	48
No	40

35A. If no ask, WHY NOT ALL?

Salary of other offers too low	4
Low prestige of other offers	10
Location of other offers	6
Attractiveness of this job	8
Accepted prior to development of other offers	14
Other	2

36. WERE ANY OF THESE OPENINGS CONCRETE OFFERS?

Yes	56
No	27
No answer or not relevant	20

36A. If yes ask, HOW MANY CONCRETE OFFERS DID YOU HAVE?

One other offer	23
Two other offers	14
Three other offers	9
More than three other offers	10

36B. WERE YOU ABLE TO CONSIDER THESE OFFERS SIMULTANEOUSLY?

Yes	59
No	4
No answer or not relevant	40

36C. WHY DID YOU CHOOSE THIS JOB RATHER THAN ONE OF THE OTHERS? (See page 186.)

37. ABOUT HOW MANY DAYS OF PRODUCTIVE TIME DID YOU LOSE BY INTERVIEWING, MOVING, ETC.?

1-3 days	9	22-28 days	6
4-7 days	24	1-2 months	9
8-14 days	26	Over 2 months	5
15-21 days	13		

IV. Previous Job.

38. WHAT WERE THE MAIN ATTRACTIONS OF YOUR PREVIOUS JOB?

39. WHAT WERE THE PRIMARY DRAWBACKS?

	Attraction	Drawback
Courses taught	11	13
Teaching load	8	12
Research opportunities	12	3
Colleagues	13	12
University administrators	2	30
Geographic locations	24	11
Salary	17	10
Potential of department or individual	7	14
Other	11	10

40. WHAT WAS THE PRIMARY REASON FOR SWITCHING POSITIONS? (See page 186.)

41. WHAT MADE YOU CHANGE JOBS AT THE TIME YOU DID, RATHER THAN A YEAR EARLIER OR LATER?

42. WHAT WAS YOUR RANK AT YOUR PREVIOUS JOB?

42A. WHAT WOULD YOUR RANK HAVE BEEN IF YOU HAD STAYED THE NEXT YEAR?

Same rank	23
Promotion in rank	20
No previous job or previous job not in teaching	60

43. HOW DID YOUR STARTING SALARY AT YOUR PRESENT JOB DIFFER FROM WHAT YOUR SALARY WOULD HAVE BEEN IF YOU HAD STAYED ON AT YOUR PREVIOUS JOB?

Approximately the same	10
New job was 1-10 per cent higher	4
New job was 11-20 per cent higher	3
New job was 21-40 per cent higher	3
New job 1-10 per cent lower	7
New job over 10 per cent lower	0
No answer	76

44. HOW DID YOUR CHANGE AFFECT HOW MUCH "OTHER INCOME" YOU EARNED?

No change in other income	24
Substantial increase	11
Small increase	16
Substantial decrease	4
Small decrease	2
No answer	47

45. WOULD YOU SAY THAT SALARY WAS A MAJOR CONSIDERATION IN THE JOB CHANGE?

    Yes   14
    No   29

V. Current Availability.

46. ARE YOU CURRENTLY "LOOKING" FOR ANOTHER POSITION?

    Yes   22
    No   78
    No answer   3

46A. If no ask, IF THE SALARY OF EVERYONE ON THE FACULTY HERE AT YOUR PRESENT JOB WERE CUT BY $1,000 WOULD YOU START LOOKING?

    Yes   50
    No   23
    No answer   5

46B. If yes ask, HOW ARE YOU LOOKING?

Informed graduate school	4
Informed friends	12
Listed with college placement office	0
Listed with private placement agency	0
Advertised in journals	0
Attended meetings	8
Other	0
No answer	35

46C. If yes ask, WHAT TYPE OF JOB ARE YOU LOOKING FOR?

46D. If yes ask, HAVE YOU SPECIFIED IN YOUR OWN MIND WHAT MINIMAL REQUIREMENTS THIS JOB MUST MEET? If yes ask, WHAT ARE THEY? (See page 186.)

47. HAS ANYONE CONTACTED YOU ABOUT A POSITION SOMEWHERE ELSE SINCE YOU'VE BEEN AT YOUR PRESENT JOB?

    Yes   76
    No   27

47A. If yes ask, HOW MANY TIMES HAVE YOU BEEN CONTACTED?

Less than once a year	21
About once a year	33
Several times a year	20
Many times a year	0
No answer	2

47B. If yes ask, HOW WERE YOU CONTACTED?

47C. If yes ask, HOW SPECIFIC WERE THESE CONTACTS?

47D. If yes ask, WHAT MADE YOU DECIDE TO STAY HERE?

Salary	6
Rank	0
Courses taught	15
Teaching load	3
Future potential	5
Reputation and type of school	11
Colleagues	1
Location	16
Research emphasis	4
Administration	2
Other	5

48. WOULD YOU ENCOURAGE YOUR FRIENDS AND PROFESSIONAL AC-QUAINTANCES TO TELL YOU OF OPPORTUNITIES ELSEWHERE?

Yes	101
No	2

49. HOW FAMILIAR ARE YOU WITH THE PAY SCALES AND WORKING CON-DITIONS AT OTHER UNIVERSITIES?

49A. If familiar ask, HOW DID YOU FIND OUT?

AAUP and other published reports	51
Previous teaching and studenting	13
Friends at other schools	62
Results of job hunting	8
Listings in journals and at slave markets	12
No answer	19

50. HAVE YOU EVER SERIOUSLY CONSIDERED A JOB OUTSIDE TEACHING?

Yes	58
No	45

50A. If yes ask, WHAT TYPE?

In business	16
With government	22
Other	20
No answer	0

50B. If yes ask, WHY DID YOU NOT ACCEPT OTHER WORK?

Too little money	4
Dislike other work	9
Considered merely because of availability	5
Temporary setbacks caused me to look	5
No answer	35

51. IF YOU LEARNED THAT YOUR APPOINTMENT WAS NOT GOING TO BE RENEWED NEXT YEAR HOW WOULD YOU GO ABOUT FINDING AN-OTHER JOB?

APPENDIX B: INTERVIEW GUIDE TO THE INTERVIEWS WITH DEPARTMENT CHAIRMEN

The interviews were divided into three parts: background questions, questions about a specific recent appointment, and questions concerning general policy.

I. Background Questions.

1. HOW MANY YEARS HAVE YOU (THE CHAIRMAN) BEEN ON THE FACULTY AT THIS SCHOOL?

2. HOW MANY YEARS HAVE YOU BEEN DEPARTMENT CHAIRMAN?

	On Faculty	Chairman
Less than 3 years	2	23
4-10 years	12	13
More than 10 years	35	12
No answer	1	2

3. LIST 4 RECENT APPOINTEES TO THE FULL-TIME STAFF OF THE DEPARTMENT. FOR EACH INDICATE WHERE HE CAME FROM, WHAT HIS SPECIALTY IS, AND AT WHICH RANK HE WAS HIRED.

Immediately prior to their present jobs the men hired lived in:

Same state	4
Southeast but not same state	19
Southwest or Far West	7
Great Lakes or Plains	16
Middle Atlantic or Northeast	2
Foreign	2

Men hired received their highest degrees from schools located in:

Same state	1
Southeast but not same state	16
Southwest or Far West	6
Great Lakes or Plains	10
Middle Atlantic or Northeast	2
Foreign	2

Men hired were most recently:

Studying in graduate school	18
Teaching at another college	26
Working with government	1
Working with business	0
Unemployed	0
Other	1

Men were hired at the rank of:

Full professor	4
Associate professor	10
Assistant professor	28
Instructor	5
Other	3

II. (The interviewer is to choose one of the 4 recent appointees listed by the department chairman and pursue the following questions in regard to this man.)

4. HOW DID IT COME ABOUT THAT YOU HAD AN OPENING FOR THIS MAN?

Previous man retired	6
Previous man left voluntarily	17
Previous man left involuntarily	2
Net addition to the departmental staff	25

4A. If retirement ask, ARE RETIREMENT RULES HERE FLEXIBLE? If flexible ask, WHY DID THE PREVIOUS MAN RETIRE IN THAT PARTICULAR YEAR?

4B. If voluntary separation ask, WHY DID THE PREVIOUS MAN LEAVE? HOW MUCH NOTICE DID HE GIVE? WHAT ATTEMPT, IF ANY, DID YOU MAKE TO KEEP HIM?

4C. If involuntary separation ask, WHY DID YOU FIRE THE PREVIOUS MAN? HOW MUCH NOTICE DID YOU GIVE HIM? HOW LONG BEFORE NOTICE WAS GIVEN HAD YOU FELT THAT HIS WORK WAS NOT SATISFACTORY?

4D. If net addition to the staff ask, HOW DID THIS COME ABOUT?

5. HOW DID YOU GO ABOUT LOCATING THE NAMES OF PERSONS WHO MIGHT FILL THE VACANCY?

Members of the staff wrote friends for suggestions	39
Department chairman wrote graduate schools for suggestions	23
Staff solicited names at professional gatherings	6
Department chairman pursued mass letters	11
Other	2

6. IN THE END ABOUT HOW MANY NAMES OF PERSONS EVEN REMOTELY CONSIDERED FOR THE OPENING DID YOU ACCUMULATE?

One	7	Six	7
Two	1	Seven	3
Three	4	Eight	1
Four	2	Nine or more	20
Five	2	No answer	3

7. HOW MANY CANDIDATES DID YOU ATTEMPT TO LEARN MORE ABOUT?

One	10	Six	6
Two	6	Seven	1
Three	9	Eight	0
Four	9	Nine or more	5
Five	1		

8. WHAT DID YOU DO TO FIND OUT MORE ABOUT THESE CANDIDATES, AND WHICH TECHNIQUE WAS THE MOST USEFUL? (See page 141.)

9. WHAT SCHOOLS WERE THESE CANDIDATES FROM?

Same state	6
Southeast but not same state	29
Southwest	8

Middle West and Plains	34
Far West	16
Middle Atlantic and Northeast	24
Foreign	3

10. HOW MANY CANDIDATES DID YOU BRING TO THE CAMPUS FOR IN-TERVIEWING?

None	8	Three	4
One	26	Four	1
Two	9	More than four	0
		No answer	2

11. WAS THE MAN YOU HIRED INTERVIEWED ON CAMPUS?

Yes	38
No	10
No answer	2

12. DID YOU CONTACT ANY PERSONS WHOM YOU BELIEVED TO BE COM-PLETELY SATISFIED IN THEIR PRESENT POSITION AND INVESTIGATE THE POSSIBILITY OF MOVING THEM?

Yes	19
No	26
Not in this case	5

13. IDEALLY BUT REALISTICALLY, DESCRIBE THE MAN YOU WOULD HAVE LIKED TO HAVE FOUND TO FILL THE VACANT POSITION.

14. WHICH OF THE CHARACTERISTICS MENTIONED WERE ABSOLUTELY ES-SENTIAL TO GET THE JOB?

Man must have specific teaching specialty or specialties	31
Man must have Ph.D. at the time hired	14
Man must have some teaching experience	9
Other	19

15. DID THE MAN YOU HIRED MEET YOUR IDEAL?

Yes	24
No	24
No answer	2

15A. If no ask, WHY DID YOU NOT CONTINUE YOUR SEARCH UNTIL FIND-ING THE IDEAL MAN?

We had exhausted the market	9
It was getting late in the year	1
We couldn't attract the ideal man	5
The man hired was acceptable	1
The man hired was about to accept another offer	1
Other	7

16. IF A CANDIDATE WITH THE MINIMAL QUALIFICATIONS HAD NOT BEEN AVAILABLE WHAT WOULD YOU HAVE DONE?

Delayed retirement or denied leave of absence	2
Hired full-time staff member for one year only	15

Overloaded present faculty and left vacancy open   21
Hired several part-time instructors   4
Other and no answer   8

17. HAD YOU USED ANY OF THESE STOPGAP MEASURES PRIOR TO THE TIME THE MAN WE ARE TALKING ABOUT WAS HIRED?
Yes   17
No   31
No answer   2

18. WHAT SORTS OF THINGS DID YOU KNOW ABOUT THE MAN HIRED AT THE TIME THE DECISION WAS MADE TO HIRE?

19. WHAT SORTS OF THINGS DID YOU NOT KNOW?

20. DID YOU KNOW WHETHER HE WAS LEAVING HIS FORMER JOB VOLUNTARILY OR UNDER PRESSURE? WHICH WAS IT?
Knew, voluntarily   28
Knew, under pressure   0
Did not know   4
No answer or not relevant   18

21. DID YOU KNOW IF YOURS WAS THE ONLY JOB THAT HE WAS CONSIDERING AT THE TIME?
Yes, ours was the only one   14
Yes, ours was one among several   20
No, we did not know   15
No answer   1

22. ON WHAT BASIS WAS THE MAN HIRED CHOSEN INSTEAD OF OTHER CANDIDATES FOR THE JOB? WHAT QUALITIES MADE THE MAN HIRED STAND OUT FROM THE OTHER CANDIDATES?
Good recommendations from his friends   13
Good recommendations from mutual friends   9
Good training   14
Good impression during interview   10
Most extensive prestige and publications   7
Geographic origin other than present staff   1
Other   9
No answer   6

23. WHO WAS IN ON THE DECISION TO MAKE THE OFFER?

24. WHAT GUIDELINES WERE USED TO DETERMINE THE SALARY OFFERED?
Salaries of present staff members   13
Salary of man hired at previous job   3
Salaries paid by comparable schools   5
Most we could get from the university-wide
    administrators   18
Salary of man who left   1
What we had to pay to get the man   11
Other   1

25. DID YOU KNOW HOW MUCH THE MAN HIRED WAS EARNING IN HIS PREVIOUS POSITION?

    Yes   19
    No   12
    Not relevant or no answer   19

26. DID YOU KNOW THE SALARY FIGURES INVOLVED IN ANY OTHER OF-FERS THAT THE MAN HIRED WAS CONSIDERING AT THE TIME?

    Yes   13
    No   15
    No answer or not relevant   22

27. DO YOU THINK YOU COULD HAVE OFFERED THE MAN HIRED A SIG-NIFICANTLY LOWER SALARY AND STILL HAVE GOTTEN HIM?

    Yes   18
    No   17
    Don't know or no answer   15

28. DID YOU INCLUDE ANY NON-SALARY ITEMS IN THE OFFER WHICH ARE NOT USUALLY INCLUDED? (e.g., course load below normal, moving expenses, promise of promotion or tenure, university housing.)

    Yes   12
    No   38

28A. If yes ask, WHY WERE THESE NON-SALARY ITEMS OFFERED INSTEAD OF A HIGHER SALARY?

    Source of funds different   3
    An additional inducement extended in bargaining   5
    Other   4

29. WHEN (relative to interview if any) and HOW (e.g., phone, letter, person) WAS A FIRM OFFER EXTENDED?

    During interview   7
    Several days after interview   11
    More than a week but less than a month after interview   15
    More than a month after interview   4
    Before interview   2
    No answer or no interview   11

30. HOW SOON WAS A REPLY EXPECTED?

    Within one week   8
    One to two weeks later   20
    Two or four weeks later   8
    Over one month later   1
    No time limit specified   3
    No answer or others   10

31. WAS THE ORIGINAL OFFER THE SAME AS THE FINAL OFFER?

    Yes   36
    No   9
    No answer   5

31A. If same ask, WOULD YOU HAVE BEEN WILLING TO MAKE ADJUST-MENTS IF THE MAN HIRED HAD BEEN HESITANT?

Yes   12
No   24
If yes ask, WHAT TYPE OF ADJUSTMENTS?

31B. If not same ask, HOW DID THE FINAL OFFER DIFFER?

31C. If not same ask, WHY?

32. TO HOW MANY OTHER PERSONS WHO HAD TURNED YOU DOWN HAD YOU PREVIOUSLY OFFERED THE JOB?

None   32
One   9
Two   5
Three   1
No answer   3

32A. WHY DID THEY TURN YOU DOWN?

Our job offered too little prestige   1
Salary and other aspects of their present job improved   4
Higher salary elsewhere   3
Didn't want to live in the South   1
Other   6
No answer   8

33. DO YOU THINK THEY WOULD HAVE COME IF YOU HAD OFFERED A SIGNIFICANTLY HIGHER SALARY?

Yes   6
No   7
No answer or doesn't apply   37

PART III. General Policy Questions.

34. WHAT FEATURES ABOUT TEACHING AT YOUR SCHOOL IN YOUR DE-PARTMENT DO YOU STRESS WHEN RECRUITING NEW FACULTY?

35. WHAT PERCENTAGE OF YOUR STAFF DO YOU THINK WOULD LEAVE FOR ANOTHER TEACHING JOB THAT OFFERED $2,000 PER YEAR MORE PAY?

Less than 25 per cent   16
26-50 per cent   10
51-75 per cent   7
More than 75 per cent   7
No answer   10

36. IN YOUR OPINION WHAT KEEPS YOUR STAFF HERE?

Professional ties   28
Community ties   27
Cost of moving   6

Loss of outside income opportunities   2
Nearness of retirement   15
Other   9

37. HOW RELUCTANT ARE YOU TO HIRE MEN AWAY FROM SCHOOLS THAT MAKE AN EFFORT TO KEEP THEM?

Not at all   34
Quite   2
Only reluctant when it's a close friend or neighbor   7
No answer   7

38. DO YOU HAVE ANY "GENTLEMEN'S AGREEMENTS" WITH NEARBY SCHOOLS NOT TO MAKE OFFERS TO EACH OTHERS' FACULTIES?

Yes   13
No   37

39. WHAT POLICIES DO YOU HAVE THAT DISCOURAGE THE HIRING OF PARTICULAR GROUPS OF OTHERWISE QUALIFIED PERSONNEL?

39A. AT WHAT RANK DO YOU DO MOST OF YOUR HIRING?

Full professor   2
Associate professor   8
Assistant professor and instructor   40

40. WHY DO YOU HIRE MOSTLY AT THE ASSISTANT PROFESSOR AND INSTRUCTOR LEVEL?

Hire mostly at another rank   10
Costs less   11
Only rank at which we can compete favorably   15
Like to promote from within   21
Other   3

41. ASSUMING THAT THE UNIVERSITIES ARE OF COMPARABLE QUALITY, WOULD YOU PREFER TO HIRE A MAN WHO HAD TAUGHT (SAY) 6 YEARS AT ONE UNIVERSITY OR 2 YEARS AT EACH OF THREE UNIVERSITIES?

6 years at one   26
2 years at three   0
No preference per se   4
No answer   19

42. DOES YOUR SCHOOL ESTABLISH A FIXED MINIMUM OR MAXIMUM SALARY FOR EACH RANK?

Yes   27
No   23

42A. If yes ask, ARE THESE EVER BROKEN?
If yes ask, FOR WHOM ARE THEY BROKEN?

43. IS A CONSCIOUS EFFORT MADE TO KEEP YOUR PAY SCALE IN ACCORD WITH SALARIES AT OTHER SPECIFIC UNIVERSITIES?

Yes   23
No   24
No answer   3

43A. If yes ask, WHICH SCHOOLS ARE USED AS STANDARDS OF COM- PARISON?

Nearby schools   14
Schools of the same size   6
Schools of the same type (e.g., private liberal arts)   14
Other   4
No answer   3

44. ARE YOU CONSISTENTLY COMPETING WITH ANY SCHOOL OR GROUP OF SCHOOLS FOR FACULTY?

Yes   10
No   37
No answer   3

44A. If yes ask, WHICH ONES?

45. DO YOU FEEL THAT IT IS MORE IMPORTANT TO HAVE EQUITY OF RATES OF PAY BETWEEN DEPARTMENTS WITHIN UNIVERSITIES (E.G., SOCIOLOGISTS AND ECONOMISTS) OR BETWEEN UNIVERSITIES WITHIN DEPARTMENTS (E.G., FLORIDA AND NORTH CAROLINA)?

Comparable rates within university   14
Comparable rates within doctrine   32
No answer   4

46. HAVE INCREASES IN THE GENERAL SALARY LEVEL AT YOUR SCHOOL APPEARED TO SIMPLIFY RECRUITMENT?

Yes   36
No   3
Other   11

47. HOW MUCH EXPANSION IN ENROLLMENT IN UNDERGRADUATE CLASSES WOULD BE NECESSARY BEFORE YOU WOULD EXPAND THE SIZE OF THE DEPARTMENT FACULTY BY ONE? HOW MUCH EXPANSION WOULD BE NECESSARY BEFORE TWO NEW MEN WOULD BE HIRED?

48. IF ENROLLMENT REMAINED THE SAME, HOW LITTLE WOULD A "QUALI- FIED MAN" HAVE TO BE WILLING TO ACCEPT IF HE WANTED A JOB HERE NEXT YEAR? (ASSUME THAT NO ONE CURRENTLY TEACHING LEFT.)

49. ABOUT WHAT PERCENTAGES OF THE MEN WHO LEFT THE DEPART- MENT IN THE LAST 5 YEARS HAVE DONE SO EITHER BECAUSE YOU PURPOSEFULLY ENCOURAGED THEM NOT TO STAY OR YOU OUT-AND- OUT ASKED THEM TO LEAVE?

Percentage who left voluntarily:

100 per cent   25
50-99 per cent   7

Under 50 per cent   1
No answer   17

50. HOW MUCH NOTICE DO YOU GIVE THE PEOPLE YOU DECIDE NOT TO REHIRE?

51. WHY DID THE PEOPLE LEAVE VOLUNTARILY?

52. HAVE YOU RECENTLY SUCCESSFULLY RETAINED SOMEONE WHO WAS "THINKING OF" LEAVING?

Yes   26
No   17
No answer   7

53. WHAT DID YOU DO TO KEEP HIM?

Salary increase   12
Rank increase   5
Reduced or changed workload   2
Made non-monetary promises about the future   11

APPENDIX C: THE IGNORANCE INDEX

The Ignorance Index was designed to measure how much individuals know about their new jobs at the time they accept them. The numerator of the index is equal to the number of "correct" answers to the following six questions:

1) At the time you accepted this job did you know about the following items: salary? academic rank? hours of classroom teaching? courses to be taught? extent of library facilities? office facilities? fringe benefits? quality of students? promotion possibilities? congeniality of staff? availability of research monies? salary advancement? availability of secretarial services? committee duties? (*If The Candidate Answered "No" On Five Or More Of The Items Listed, One Point Was Added To The Numerator.*)

2) If not, did you realize that you were accepting the job unaware of these matters? (*If Answer Was "No," One Point Was Added To The Numerator.*)

3) Did you visit the campus? (*If Answer Was "No," One Point Was Added To The Numerator.*)

4) Do you now feel that any subjects were discreetly not mentioned previous to the time you accepted the job? (*If Answer Was "Yes," One Point Was Added To The Numerator.*)

5) Would your decision to come here have been different if you had known more about the position? (*If Answer Was "Yes," One Point Was Added To The Numerator.*)

6) Did you know at the time you accepted the job if other candidates were being seriously considered. (*If Answer Was "No," One Point Was Added To The Numerator.*)

The maximum numerator is, therefore, six. A numerator of six indicates extreme ignorance. The denominator equals the total number of questions answered, usually six.

APPENDIX D: THE QUALITY INDEX

An hypothesis was that the market behavior of professors currently located at relatively prestigious schools would be substantially different from that of other professors because of basic differences in the market structures and in the personalities of the two professorial groups. The more prestigious schools are usually in closer communication with the major graduate centers where new college teachers are trained and, therefore, could be expected to have fewer supply shortages. The more prestigious schools stress research and provide the reduced teaching loads, libraries, research equipment, and the atmosphere to aid professors in meeting their demands; whereas the less prestigious schools stress teaching and counseling. At the more prestigious universities professors live in an atmosphere of publish or perish which is worlds apart from the friendly, easy-going way of life at small colleges. Professors from renowned universities are accorded more recognition and respect by fellow members of their professions. Insofar as one group of professors thrives upon professional recognition and competition whereas the other does not, it would be expected that groups of professors currently located in low pressure atmospheres would differ significantly from those located in high pressure settings.

In order to test this hypothesis, the Quality Index was developed as a measure of institutional prestige. Prestige itself is difficult to measure without arduously surveying a broad sample of qualified judges. In the absence of such a survey, a composite measure of some of the more quantifiable determinants of prestige was developed. Specifically, each school was ranked (one to eighteen) on each of the following factors:

1) Number of Ph.D.'s awarded (school awarding most Ph.D.'s ranked first).
2) Number of volumes in the library.
3) Number of library volumes per student.
4) Percentage of full-time faculty with Ph.D. degree.
5) Budget per student (total current income per student).
6) Tuition (ranked separately for state and non-state schools).

For each school a mean rank was determined. According to its mean rank or Quality Index a school was placed in the top one-third of the schools (mean ranks of 2.5, 2.5, 2.5, 4.3, 6.2, 7.0), the middle one-third (mean ranks of 8.0, 9.8, 10.5, 10.7, 11.3, 11.8), and bottom one-third (mean ranks of 12.0, 12.3, 12.5, 12.8, 13.5, 16.7).

APPENDIX E: THE PRODUCTIVITY INDEX

For a number of reasons it was hypothesized that professors with a research and publication orientation approach the labor market differently than professors who stress teaching. Since most professors can choose which aspect of the college teacher's workload to stress, we might expect that the factors that cause one group of professors to choose teaching rather than research (or vice versa) might also influence labor market behavior. Moreover, professors become known in their professions by publishing, not teaching. Insofar as being better known might affect market strategy, we would expect the market behavior of the two groups to differ. Finally, within most disciplines, the publisher is esteemed more highly. The laudable reputations of excellent teachers rarely project beyond the confines of the teacher's own campus, whereas praiseworthy writings are carried throughout the world in professional journals and in books. Insofar as respectability affects the confidence of the supplier and the behavior of the demander, we would expect the labor market behavior of publishers and non-publishers to differ.

In order to test the hypothesized difference in market behavior, our interviewees were dichotomized into two groups of "productive" and "unproductive" according to their scores on the Productivity Index.

In computing each individual's Productivity Index, one point was awarded for each of the following accomplishments:

1) Written a Ph.D. dissertation.
2) Published one or two papers in professional journals (presentations at professional meetings and chapters contributed to books were regarded equivalent to a published paper).
3) Published three or more papers in professional journals, and
4) Published one or more books.

An individual's productivity index could vary from zero to four; higher scores reflect greater productivity. Professors with scores of three and four were deemed "productive" whereas professors scoring zero, one, or two were classified as "unproductive."

No judgments are intended by the choice of names for the groups. The "unproductive" classification means only that a man has not published a great deal. The non-publisher may not be lazy. Rather he may be a man in the beginning stages of his career, or a man that has decided to devote all of his time to classroom teaching, or a man that is active in the administration. These "unproductive" professors may very well be more valued members of the faculty than certain "productive" professors.

For the development of a measure quite similar to this productivity index, we are indebted to Lazarsfeld and Thielens, *The Academic Mind,* p. 408.

INDEX

A

Academic labor market, delineated, 257; imperfections, 257-58; contrasted to other markets, 259-60; misallocations of labor, 260-63

Acquaintances. See Friends

Adams, Leonard P., 126n

Administration as factor in job choice. See University administration as factor in job choice

Advertising, self-advertising self-defeating, 110, 117-18

Allocation of labor, significance of, 5-7; in academic labor markets, 260-63

American Association of Collegiate Schools of Business, 44n, 200

American Association of University Professors, 63, 116, 154, 200, 233-34, 241n

American Council on Education, 10n, 243n

American Sociological Association, 115

Anantaraman, Venkatraman, 61n, 74n, 126n, 208n, 227n

Availability, methods used to advertise by candidates, 91-94; methods used to advertise by employers, 94-102

B

Behrend, Hilde, 72n

Berelson, Bernard, 132n

Blind letters, use by candidates, 93; use by employers, 100-1; jobs found through, 102, 105; mentioned, 95n, 108

Blockage problem, 37, 99

Bronfenbrener, Martin, 242n

Browne, Kenneth, 117n

Business, as a source of professors, 73-75

C

Campus interviews. See On-campus interviews

Candidate hunting, theory of, 109-10; extent by region, 130-31; extent by discipline, 131; extent by size of department, 131; extent by prestige, 131-32; suggestions for, 267

Candidate hunting methods, pursued, 94-102; pursued successfully, 102-5

Candidates, making availability known, 91-94; selection of, 151-53

Candidates evaluate jobs. See Job choice criteria

Caplow, Theodore, 54n, 55n, 97n, 111, 117n, 119n, 122, 128n, 152n, 163n, 208n, 240n

Cartel in economics, 101

Centralized clearinghouse, 134, 263-66

Centralized placement, the case for, 124-25

Coercive comparisons, 156, 158

Colleagues as factor in job choice, sta-